WHY ME?

JOHN C. KIM

WITH PAUL E. KIM

WHY ME?

Published by JAMA Publishing
4201 Wilshire Blvd., Suite 445
Los Angeles, CA 90010

JAMA Publishing is the publishing ministry of Jesus Awakening Movement for America/All Nations (JAMA), a prayer and spiritual awakening movement calling on Christians to repent and pray that God, in His sovereignty, would send revival and renewal to America and the world. For more information on JAMA and its ministries, go to www.jamaglobal.com or call (323) 933-4055.

First printing, October 2013

Printed in the United States of America

ISBN: 978-0-9845432-6-7

To Sarah Sung, my beloved wife, my best friend,
the love of my life, my cheerleader.

There is no one as loving and dedicated as you.

CONTENTS

INTRODUCTION

This book is a true story of a young man who bitterly left the poverty-stricken and war-recovering countryside of South Korea to ambitiously pursue the "American Dream" in California. That dream seemingly came crashing down when he was diagnosed with a terminal liver disease. All hopes for him and his family were apparently dashed. But by the mercy of God came not only healing and transformation, but in place of the idolatrous "American Dream" came a greater call to Alaska and a vision for America and the nations.

This book is my story. Let me rephrase. This book is a story about God's forgiveness, love, and blessing upon my life. None of the pages that follow can be explained apart from His work, His wisdom, and His favor. As Brennan Manning once put it, "all is grace." The book is divided into three parts – "God's Love," which focuses on my personal transformation and the hardships of Korea and the early years in America, "God's Blessings," which centers on the fruits of my personal transformation, especially in the family context, and "God's Call," which chronicles God's use of my personal transformation for the younger generations, Alaska, America and the world.

This book is a story about our extraordinary God transforming someone who was poor, forced to skip 10 meals, raised by a widowed mother, arrived with his wife on the Pacific shores of America with a couple hundred dollars and three bags, and spoke broken English. This is the same God that is at work in you. In that regard, I hope and pray that this book will encourage and empower you to dream bigger things for God and pursue greater things for His Kingdom. *Why not?*

Soli Deo Gloria,
JCK

September 19, 2013
Monterey, California

PART 1
GOD'S LOVE

Chapter 1
THE DEATH SENTENCE

It was the summer of 1976. Sunny, Southern California. I was an assistant professor at picturesque Pepperdine University and had been since 1973, teaching American Government and public policy. Just a couple of months ago, the students had selected me as the "Most Outstanding Faculty of the Year," less than four years after I had first set foot on campus, and less than nine years after I had first set foot on American soil. My wife and two kids were doing well. Could it get any better? I felt the wind at my back. I felt that I had finally arrived.

Or so I thought. As I was preparing my lecture notes for the upcoming fall trimester, I started losing my appetite. The smell of Korean food – food that I loved and grew up consuming – became intolerable. Soon, water was difficult to swallow as my stomach literally felt like a taut, blown-up balloon. Severe fatigue haunted me. And sleep further escaped me as the tightness caused by my bloated belly made breathing extremely hard.

I went to see my doctor, Dr. Donald Wakelin, whose initial diagnosis was gallstones. He told me to go to Glendale Community Hospital for some testing, including an upper gastrointestinal X-ray. Based on the test results, I was scheduled to have a cholecystectomy (surgical removal of the gallstones) on September 27. In the morning before the surgery, for reasons unknown to me, Dr. Wakelin ordered additional testing, including more blood tests and a liver scan. Later that morning, Dr. Wakelin came into my hospital room and said, "Choon [which was my Korean name], we cannot operate on you because we found that your liver appears to be in bad shape based on the tests from this morning. If we operate on you, we may not be able to stop the bleeding during the operation, and you could die." Shocked and deeply dismayed, and annoyed that I would be further delayed in getting back to work, my wife and I were sent to the fourth floor of the hospital for a liver biopsy. I was discharged the following day and told to return after the biopsy results came back.

On October 1, 1977, my wife and I returned to the hospital, where I was taken to the emergency room to see Dr. Wakelin. My wife took a seat in the waiting area. He introduced me to two liver specialists, one of whom started examining me. The other asked if I've ever had a serious illness before. We discussed that I had contracted infectious mononucleosis in February 1970 (while I was working on my graduate degrees), for which I was treated by Dr. Wakelin.

"All the test results indicate that your liver has inflamed to almost double its size and has completely deteriorated with cirrhosis," the specialist then said. "Your liver has lost most of its ability to function, and I don't think it's possible to recover it."

"Can my liver be operated on?"

"No, I don't think we are able to operate on you due to the severity of the cirrhosis. We think you have less than a year to live, maybe nine months."

"You mean I am going to die within a year? Is that what you're saying?!"

Lightning had struck. Complete and utter devastation. The words "less than a year" and "nine months" did not seem real to me. *It could not be real. That couldn't be the diagnosis. Thirty-seven years young and already deemed medically terminated, with no hope for any treatment? This cannot be! What about my wife?!* So paralyzed and floored by this "death sentence," I asked Dr. Wakelin if he could tell her the news. He walked out of the room and headed to the waiting area. Moments later, I heard my wife cry out, "No! No! No!" My heart was broken. Shredded to pieces.

Despair enveloped me. Numbed, I asked if there was anything that could be done: a cure, a transplant, anything. Nothing.

Nothing could be done. They simply suggested that I take some Vitamin C and rest. In other words, my treatment was to rest until I died. My wife was distraught. On our way home from the hospital, I could not say a word to her. I couldn't even face her. After all that she had done for me, and had left behind for me, to get me where I was. She had dedicated her life to me. She had sacrificed her educational aspirations to support me. To care for me. To do everything for me so I could singularly focus on my studies. So that I could earn my master's and doctoral degrees and establish myself as a respected professor. So that we could finally live an enjoyable life in America, the land of opportunity and freedom. Without her, I would not have been the first Korean (or Asian) American in U.S. history to earn a Ph.D. in political science (American Government concentration). And now her husband was dying.

My wife and I had been on our way toward the American Dream. In January 1973, after an extremely competitive process, I had been invited to teach courses in American Government and public policy as a full-time faculty member at Pepperdine, even though I had not yet completed my doctoral dissertation. Three years later, in May 1976, I had received the teacher-of-the-year award, a total surprise considering that there were other more experienced professors who had served Pepperdine a lot longer than me. The summer of 1976 had been our best summer in America – an unbelievable time spent with my wife, Sung, and our daughter, Sharon, who was eight, and our son, Paul, who was two. It was the first time I had thought, *We have finally seen the end of our hardships since immigrating to America. We have finally settled down in this country. Now, we'll be able to live well. No more cultural-adjustment difficulties. No more financial stress. All the hard work and sacrifice are beginning to pay off.* And then disaster – I was going to die of liver disease. *Why me?*

As we arrived at our apartment, I was overwhelmed with sadness for Sung. Her dreams were shattered. I felt so helpless. So powerless. What could be going through her mind? I couldn't imagine. As we opened the door, I went straight to the couch to lie down. I was exhausted. Sharon was watching a show on TV where the main character happened to be dying of liver cancer. This was all too surreal. And cruel. *I guess that's how it'll end for me too.* Later that evening, I told my senior pastor the news and asked if he could mobilize the leadership and the congregation to pray for me. He said he would.

My condition grew worse. The smell of food – especially my all-time favorites: bulgogi (sliced sirloin), kalbi (barbeque short ribs), and kim-chee (fermented Chinese cabbage) – made my stomach heave. I soon went from being 165 pounds to 127 pounds. At the same time, my stomach stretched out like that of a pregnant woman. It was as if my stomach was filled with a water balloon. As my liver continued to deteriorate, it began to lose its ability to cleanse the toxins in my blood. These toxins would then spread to my skin, making it tremendously itchy. There was frequent bleeding when I scratched. The nights were especially difficult. Not only could I not sleep because of the physical manifestations of the liver disease, but also from the unbearable anguish in my heart from hearing my wife cry out in prayer in the next room throughout the night or seeing my children sleep so peacefully without a clue as to the fate of their daddy. *Why me? Why does it have to be me? Dear God, what have I done that's so wrong that I deserve to die as a young man?* I became enraged. I became angry. Angry at God.

My wife called Edward and Dorothy Hall. The Halls were more than friends; they were like our American parents. No one had helped us more than they had since we had come to America. They symbolized everything that was good about this nation. Mr. Hall had fought in World War II. They poured out their love and kindness on us. They took us in. They taught us what faith in action looked like. The way they lived their lives, centered in Christ, deeply impacted my wife and me (and to this day greatly influences us). We gave our son Paul the middle name of Edward when he was born.

The Halls immediately came to see me after speaking with my wife. Mr. Hall brought a booklet with him about a natural diet program which helped cure critical illnesses, including cancer. Mr. Hall also mentioned a clinic in Santa Monica that was known to treat terminal patients using organic and holistic treatments. That night I read the booklet. A lot of it made sense to me. So the next morning we made an appointment with Dr. Brad Harter at the Santa Monica clinic. Dr. Harter reviewed my records and examined me. He then ordered more blood work and urine tests. Several days later, we discussed the results. "Dr. Kim, you have absolutely no energy. Not even one percent. It's a miracle that you are still alive. You must have incredible mental strength. And willpower. But you are at the stage of 'no return' for your liver. The liver is beyond recovery. I have never seen anyone who has had your condition and recovered. It will take nothing short of a miracle to cure you. Nonetheless, let's do our best! Let's put our faith in God." Dr. Harter then said a prayer for us. After we all said, "Amen," my heart was uplifted. I could tell that my wife was encouraged as well. He gave her all the dietary instructions I was to follow and she immediately went to work. Though I still had a lot of trouble swallowing anything, I summoned all of my strength and tried my best to follow Dr. Harter's diet program. But my condition did not improve. My stomach could not handle the amount of food I had to consume each day.

I continued to deteriorate. I was dying. I was left with no other choice but to go to God.

Chapter 2
BIG BEAR MOUNTAIN

Wrestling with Myself and God

I resolved to go to Big Bear Mountain, located three hours northeast of Los Angeles, to do business with God. My wife and a friend of ours drove me to a small cabin we rented at the mountain. After praying for me, my wife, with tears in her eyes, and our friend dropped me off, leaving me with some water and juice, which was all my body could handle. I needed to be with God. Alone. I wanted to know why I had to die at such a young age. I wanted to know why my two young children would have to grow up without their father. I wanted to know why my wife would become a widow. I wanted to know if I could ever be cured – if I could ever get another chance to live. I wanted these answers from God. And I was determined – as Jacob was at Jabbok– not to come down from the mountain until He answered. It was June 18, 1977.

But I couldn't pray once I settled into the cabin – I was filled with too much worry and despair. *How is my family going to live without me? Who will take care of my wife? My children? What will happen to them? What about my insurance and benefits? What about my university benefits? What about my mother in Korea?* In my anguish and anxiety, I cried out to God. *Lord, my wife and I left everything to come to America! We were able to overcome tremendous odds and I became a professor. We have tried to faithfully serve you, Lord, at our church as deacons. By your grace and love, we finally were able to settle down in America. You brought us to this country and we've come so far – why must I then die of this miserable disease at this young age?* I wept profusely.

Each day in the cabin I was getting worse. I had no strength in me.

No energy. No voice. My outbursts to the Lord were like whispers. I couldn't really drink the water or juice so I used a straw to wet my tongue. My body was itchy all over. My breathing was labored. The pain from my liver and abdomen was excruciating. Lying down did not make things any better, because my stomach was swollen like that of a woman in the last weeks of her pregnancy. I could never feel comfortable – lying on my back put too much pressure on my spine; shifting to either side, my swollen belly fell to the floor with a thud. I was totally restless. And in a lot of pain.

But I was compelled at that time to read the book of Psalms and went into deep meditation on God's word. Reading the ups and downs of King David's life began to stir my heart and my soul. As David was going through the valley of the shadow of death, he cried out to the Lord in pain and repentance; and yet, at the same time, he also praised God with songs of thanksgiving, of rejoicing, of exaltation. Although I had read through the Psalms numerous times before, these verses had never moved me as profoundly as they did this time. They were causing me to reflect on my own life – now that I was in my own valley of the shadow of death. They were, through the Holy Spirit, deeply convicting. Deeply nourishing.

The Toxins in My Soul

It was June 24, 1977. I had been on Big Bear Mountain for six days. I felt weaker than ever. Sustained only by a little water and juice, I was now suffering from severe headaches. And immense pressure in my chest. I had to get out for some fresh air. I grabbed a blanket and went out through the cabin's back door, and immediately felt the chilly evening air. It surely did not feel like the beginning of summer at this altitude. I saw a fallen tree about a hundred feet away and mustered all of my strength to reach it, crawling on my knees some of the way. Once I reached the tree, I knelt down and covered my body with the blanket. I then wrapped my arms around the tree and pleaded to God with everything that was within me, everything that was in my heart and mind, and I begged for mercy. I was desperate. *Dear God, please have pity on me! Please grant me your mercy and favor! You blessed us with my degrees and with my teaching position. You blessed us with the gift of children. You blessed us by transitioning us to this new country. You blessed us in allowing us to serve at our local church. Your grace has enabled us to accomplish all of this. I'm recognized as a Christian by many in the community. So if I die at this time in my life, not only will all the knowledge that I have gained from my studies, and all the gifts, talents and abilities that you have nurtured in me, be wasted, but also your name won't be glorified. Please give me one more chance to live! Dear God, I want to live so much!* I continued to cry out to God in this fashion for quite some time. But these were not the kinds of prayers that God wanted to hear from me. These were desperate pleas that came from fleshly reasoning. These were selfish petitions. They did not seek God's heart or His will, but my own survival.

Exhausted, I stopped praying. As soon as I finished, God uttered these words through my own mouth with a loud voice: "Don't you know that you are dying because of the toxins in your soul rather than the toxins in your blood, which are physically killing you?!" I was shocked. Frightened. The fact that the Almighty God opened my mouth and spoke these words to me (by using my own voice!) in such a clear and unmistakable fashion – and doing so, not in my native Korean tongue, but in English, as I had just been praying to Him in English. This made me tremble. It was indescribably humbling. All the years that I had been serving God as a deacon. All those Bible studies. All those sermons I had heard and verses that I had read. All the songs and hymns that I had sung since the 10th grade. All the things that I had confessed. All the things that I had professed. All for what? Death looked me straight in the eye and I still couldn't pray in a way that pleased Him, with a contrite heart, in acknowledgement of His sovereignty, holiness, and grace. Oh, how I lacked such understanding of Him! Oh, how I still was so selfish, how I still clung to myself and my accomplishments, and not really to Him. So God, in His mercy, intervened and spoke pointedly to me that I was dying because of the toxins in my soul. Because of my sins.

God then began to show me many of the sins that I committed in my life. Every single one of these sins – one by one by one – flashed before my eyes like mini-episodes on a television screen. Every image, every frame, every snapshot was excruciatingly detailed. Every sin was toxic.

A "Whitewashed Tomb"

Up until that point in my life, I was a very proud man. I lived as if I was better than others – morally, ethically, intellectually, and spiritually. I never considered myself to be a man of great sin. An occasional sinner (yes), not perfect (okay), but I thought I lived a relatively clean and morally-upright life. As a young adult in Seoul, Korea, I served as the president of my university's Christian Student Movement and the Korean Christian Student Movement. I was also one of the leaders of the Moral Re-Armament (MRA)[1] movement, fighting against social injustice in Korea. I served my local church in Seoul as a Sunday school teacher, choir member, leader of the young adult fellowship and was the youngest deacon (becoming one at 24). And after moving to America, my life consisted of nothing other than work and school (and the library), my church, and my family. I was faithful to my wife, dedicated to my daughter and son, passionate as a professor, committed to my students, and diligent as a deacon. I felt I was, overall, a good man.

I also thought that, internally, I was spiritually mature and that my faith was strong. I thought I had experienced renewal and transformation at the numerous "revival" meetings and church conferences that I had attended. I thought I was forgiven of, and free from, my sins after repeatedly confessing them at these events. I often proclaimed how much I loved God and worshipped Him. I thought I did the best that anyone could ever do in living a life of sincerity, faithfulness, and integrity. And I thought I was doing it all for God and my family. Again, I felt I was, overall, a good man.

However, when my sins were exposed before my own eyes as I was clutching that fallen tree, I felt as if I were a "whitewashed tomb" (Matt. 23:27). On the outside, so pristine and unblemished, and yet on the inside, nothing but decay, filth, and death. When God showed me sin after sin after sin, I broke down in deep sorrow and tremendous grief. I was not a good man. Far from it. I was a depraved sinner deserving of death. I started to understand what the Apostle Paul meant when he confessed that he was the chief of all sinners; I too began to acknowledge before God that I was the worst of all sinners.

God revealed to me that I was filled with pride, bitterness, hatred, envy and jealousy, covetousness, insecurity, inferiority (and superiority) complexes, greed, ruthless ambition, and selfishness. Constantly dissatisfied, I was easily angered. I hardly ever admitted that I was wrong and repeatedly fingered the blame on others. I was always right. I lived my life according to the ways in which I wanted to live. I was not centered at all on Christ, but on my wants and ambitions. My ego tainted my relationships with Him, my wife and children, my co-workers and colleagues, friends and fellow congregants. Yes, I served diligently at church and my cup appeared to be clean on the outside, but on the inside I was rotten. Spiritually, I found myself to be far more repugnant than the corpses (and their awful stench) that I used to handle in hospital rooms as an orderly. God was showing me that He indeed opposes the proud (James 4:6). God was showing me my true colors. God was showing me my hypocrisy. I was totally broken.

Later, on a pad of paper, I wrote down every single sin that God had revealed to me on Big Bear Mountain so that I could repent to God and seek forgiveness and reconciliation from others for those sins. I wrote down 52 pages.

In addition to revealing my true, sinful character, God reminded me of how the history of where I came from had laid the groundwork of the sins that were particular to me: the failures, injustices, and discriminations of my past, and the cultural root of my ambitions and personal desires – what's known in Korean as "han."

Chapter 3

MY MOTHERLAND

Korea: A Long History of Suffering

Before I explain what "han" is, it probably makes sense for me to briefly summarize the (mostly modern) history of Korea, my birth country. Knowing full well that I will not do justice in covering the long and rich history of Korea in just a chapter, I at least want to share some important aspects of Korea's history and culture – of which I was a product – and how I was able to leave my motherland to go to America.

Korea is a beautiful country and has often been called "The Land of Morning Calm." Its history, however, is filled with centuries of heart-wrenching stories where her very survival as a nation, and as a distinct culture, was constantly at stake. It could be said that (up until very recently) Korea's history is nothing other than a series of painful defeats and devastating humiliations. Surrounded by aggressive neighboring powers, Korea has been invaded over 700 times[2] by the Chinese, the Manchus, the Mongols, the Khitans, the Jurchens, the Russians, and the Japanese (including the last Japanese colonial annexation of Korea from 1910 through 1945).

More than 4,000 years of Korea's existence has been marked by oppression, persecution, invasions, wars, conflicts, and a constant struggle to keep not only Korea's territorial integrity, but her unique cultural and traditional identity. I dare say that Koreans have probably suffered more than any other race or ethnicity in history. Countless times, attempts have been made to eradicate every aspect of Korea. And yet, the Korean peoples' impeccable resilience, tenacity, perseverance, willpower, sacrifice, courage, and national pride have enabled their (and their homeland's) survival through generation after generation.[3]

The Gospel Comes to Korea

Korea has also been referred to (by the West) as the "The Hermit Kingdom" and remained in relative isolation until the late 19th century. In 1882, the U.S.-Chosun[4] Chemulpo Treaty of Amity and Commerce finally opened Korea to America. This was followed by similar Korean treaties with other Western nations.[5] This paved the way for Christianity. Professor Young-Sik Kim writes: "The Chemulpo Treaty guaranteed safety of foreign missionaries and soon the Korean Peninsula was flooded with American Methodist and Presbyterian evangelists eager to spread the Gospel among the Korean populace."[6]

Early in 1884, the Presbyterian church appointed Dr. Horace N. Allen as its first missionary to Korea and the first medical officer at the U.S. Foreign Affairs Mission in Seoul. He also became the personal physician and confidant of Korea's King Kojong. According to Professor Kim, King Kojong readily granted Dr. Allen's petition for the establishment of a Western-medicine hospital and on April 10, 1885, the first Western medical hospital in Korea, Kwanghyewon (Global House of Benefits), opened its doors, staffed with American doctors. Dr. Allen was also instrumental in founding the Severance Medical Hospital and University, with generous contributions from an American philanthropist, Louis Henry Severance. The Severance Hospital and University were then merged into Yonsei University, a major private university in Korea today. Dr. Allen later became the U.S. ambassador to Chosun in 1901. Around the same time:

> The Methodist Church appointed Dr. and Mrs. W. B. Scranton, his mother Mrs. Mary Scranton and the Rev. and Mrs. Henry Appenzeller as the first missionaries to Korea, who with A. B. Hall, founded churches as well as the first school for handicapped Koreans. . . . In June 1885, Mary F. Scranton, the mother of Dr.

W.B. Scranton, came to Korea at the age of 52 and established the Ewha Girls School and later, the Ewha University. She died in Korea in 1909. Today, the Ewha University is one of the largest women's colleges in Asia and the most prestigious in Korea.[7]

In 1888, Lillias Horton came to Korea as a medical missionary and became the first American woman doctor in Korea. She married Horace Underwood in 1889, who had come to Korea in 1885 as the first Presbyterian minister. The Underwoods spent 30 years as missionaries in Korea. Along with translating hymns and scriptures into Korean, Mr. Underwood founded the Chosen Christian College in Seoul and established the first official Korean Presbyterian Church in 1887. As Professor Kim further explains:

> By the time Japan annexed Korea in 1910, American missionaries had established about 800 schools for 41,000 students. The missionary schools, from kindergarten to college, were well staffed and financed. In contrast, the Chosen public schools had less than 20,000 students. Some of the American schools became well known for their quality education and some missionaries in China sent their children to Korea for education. For example, Rev. Billy Graham's wife, Ruth Bell, attended the Pyongyang Foreign School in North Korea.[8]

When these missionaries arrived in Korea from America, the Korean people were already under tremendous fear of foreign invasion, especially from the rivalry between China and Japan for hegemony over the Korean peninsula and, to a similar extent, the rivalry between Japan and Russia. The Korean government's inability to handle its own factional internal divisions (some of which resulted in assassinations) left the Korean people helpless in responding to the provocations of its powerful neighbors and their willingness to invade Korea. There was nowhere the people could turn to and ask for help – all four sides of the Korean peninsula (north, south, east, and west) were dead ends. There was no place but to look up for help (Ps. 121:1-2). It was during this critical juncture of Korean history that the Gospel of Jesus Christ was introduced. As told to me by the late Dr. Won Sul Lee, a noted historian and Christian leader in Korea (and my former professor and mentor), "among the revolutionary turning points of Korean history, no turning point was more significant than the introduction of Christianity" because the "Gospel has been the most potent history-making force in the world."[9]

When the missionaries introduced the Gospel to Korea, the Koreans were immediately drawn to Jesus Christ, who they felt not only understood suffering, turmoil, and oppression, but who would provide lasting comfort in the midst of pain and misery. In their weakness, the Koreans turned to Christ for strength. In their despair, the Koreans turned to Christ as their hope. Many received Him as their Lord and Savior. Christ's atoning work on the cross, His death-defeating resurrection, and His eternal Kingdom – where tears of sorrow would be replaced with tears of joy – which await those who believe in Him were the best news for a people that had long experienced only heartache.

Not only were Koreans drawn to the person of Christ, they were drawn to the Americans who brought His message of hope and redemption. According to Professor Kim, King Kojong believed that of all the foreign powers that had a presence in his country, the United States was the only one that he could trust as having no "hidden agenda."[10] As such, he hired many Americans – most of whom were Christian missionaries – to serve as advisors and officials in his court. They effectively and compassionately introduced Korea to modern education, medicine, public health, technology, public administration and democratic ideas. Today, there is a cemetery outside of Seoul where over one hundred

Americans are buried.[11] These Americans died in Korea not as soldiers, but as missionaries, medical doctors, and educators during a period of tremendous upheaval in Korea's history, beginning in the late 19th century. According to Professor Kim, these men and women truly loved and sacrificed their lives for Korea and the Korean people, and "willed to be buried in their adopted country."[12]

The Pyongyang Revival

Soon after the birth of Christianity in Korea, God intervened in the Korean church in a most miraculous way. During a weeklong Bible study conference in Pyongyang in January 1907, some 800 men, who gathered from all around the country, suddenly experienced an extraordinary outpouring of the Holy Spirit. William Newton Blair, a missionary who attended the gathering, relayed: "As I entered the room [there was] a sense of God's nearness, impossible of description. . . ."[13] The whole audience began to pray and they were taken over by the Holy Spirit and transformed. God came to them in Pyongyang that night: "Man after man would rise, confess his sin, break down and weep. . . . My last glimpse of the audience is photographed indelibly upon my memory. Some threw themselves full length on the floor; hundreds stood with arms outstretched towards heaven. Every man forgot every other. Each was face to face with God."[14] A genuine, God-sent revival took place.

And the overflow of the Holy Spirit did not stop with the conference in Pyongyang. When these men returned to their homes and churches, they took the fire of the Holy Spirit with them. "Everywhere the story was told the same Spirit flamed forth and spread till practically every church, not only in North Korea, but throughout the entire peninsula had received its share of blessing."[15] The transformation was such that "all through the city [of Pyongyang] men were going from house to house, confessing to individuals they had injured, returning stolen property and money, not only to Christians, but to non-Christians as well. The whole city was stirred."[16]

It's important to note that in the four months leading up to the "Pyongyang Revival" (September 1906 - January 1907), some twenty missionaries (mostly Americans) in that city began to pray fervently every day at noon (later, at 4:00 p.m.) for Korea's revival while repenting of their owns sins and the sins of Korea. They repented of their own pride and comfort in the ministries they ran in Korea. Some historians claim that without these daily prayers of repentance and revival, there may not have been a revival in Korea.[17]

The historic "Pyongyang Revival" in 1907 became the engine that sustained the Korean Christians' new-found faith in God and prepared them for the hardships that were to come: the Japanese annexation of the Korean peninsula (1910), Japanese colonial rule (1910-1945), the division of Korea (1945-49), the Korean War (1950-1953), and the aftermath of that conflict.

The Japanese Occupation

After Japan defeated the Russians in the Russo-Japanese war (1904-05), Russia recognized Japan's interest in the Korean peninsula, and Korea was forced to become a protectorate of the Japanese by the Eulsa Treaty:

> In 1905, Japan took over Chosun's [Korea's] foreign affairs and all foreign missions in Seoul were ordered closed and all Chosun [Korean] diplomats in foreign nations were recalled. Edwin V. Morgan was the last American ambassador to Chosun. He had the dubious honor of closing down the U.S. mission in Seoul on December 8, 1905.[18]

Less than five years later, in 1910, under a threat of force and intimidation, Korea was coerced into signing the annexation treaty with Japan. Korea was officially annexed.

Conditions under Japanese colonial rule were brutal and inhuman. According to Dr. Lee, the plight of Koreans under Japanese rule was comparable to the oppression that the Israelites had suffered in Egypt under the Pharaohs. Deprived of all their rights as human beings, the Koreans were reduced to the status of slaves. The Japanese government ruled with an iron fist over the Koreans; no voice of opposition could be permitted.

It was especially hard for Korean Christians, who were persecuted by the Japanese colonial rulers. Due to the Korean Christians' unwillingness to worship the Japanese gods of Shintoism, persecution of Christians during Japanese colonial rule was unprecedented. Countless Christians were harassed, persecuted and jailed, and only those who relented into outwardly following Shintoism were freed, while those who were determined to worship none other than God Almighty paid a dear price. Many were tortured or burned to death.[19] The Korean Christians were also particularly targeted because of their role in the Korean independence movement and their association with the rise of Korean nationalism.[20] The March First Movement (of 1919) against Japanese colonial rule was organized by 33 Korean leaders, 16 of whom were Christians. This movement was sparked by the ideals espoused by President Woodrow Wilson in his Fourteen Points at the conclusion of World War I, particularly the principle of national self-determination, where each nation should be allowed to choose its own form of government. Millions demonstrated throughout the country, expressing their desire to restore the sovereignty of Korea. Although this was a peaceful demonstration, the Japanese colonial rulers did not respond in kind. Many churches were burned down and hundreds of Christians perished, while thousands, including women, were imprisoned, beaten, and tortured.[21]

Conditions worsened when the Japanese demanded that the Koreans provide more material goods to support Japan's war efforts in Asia. After already taking more than half of their grains and income in the form of taxation, they asked the Koreans for "free, voluntary contributions" to win the war. The munitions industry needed anything made of metal, so even the poor were forced to give up their spoons, brass bowls, silver chopsticks and the nails in their walls. Materials, buildings and facilities belonging to Koreans were confiscated at will by the Japanese government and many male and female workers were sent to war camps.[22] Colonial assimilation (the "Japanization" of Korea) was in full force when, starting in 1940, the Japanese government ordered Koreans to abandon their monosyllabic surnames and adopt multisyllabic Japanese names, and police were mobilized to enforce this order.[23] As a result, Koreans lost their traditional family names. I lost my Korean name (Kim) and was forced to take a Japanese one. The use of the Japanese language was also "strictly enforced, while the Korean language was thoroughly suppressed."[24]

On August 15, 1945, approximately 25 million Koreans[25] were finally freed from Japan's yoke as the imperialists surrendered to the Allied Powers to effectively end World War II. Some of the American missionaries and educators (or their offspring) who were expelled by the Japanese in 1941 after Pearl Harbor, returned to Korea to pick up where they had left off.[26] But no sooner were Koreans celebrating their country's liberation than they had to face the harsh reality of their country being divided by the Allied Powers along the 38th parallel, with the North occupied by the Red Army of the Soviet Union and the South by the U.S. Armed Forces. Bitterly disappointed, Korea wondered how the Allied Powers – who fought with them against colonial imperialism – could agree to such a thing. Feeling utterly betrayed, the Koreans could not believe that after chasing out one master, Japan, they ushered in two others, the USSR and the USA.

The life of the non-communist elements in the North became increasingly difficult. Many leaders and intellectuals left their homes and loved ones to take refuge in the South. Many Christian families, to escape persecution, also fled to the South (one of those families was my wife's). As the communist-dominated People's Committee tightened its grip in the North, the 38th parallel hardened into an iron curtain. Although the U.S.-USSR Joint Commission meetings were tasked to reach an agreement on Korea's future, with countless meetings held with Korean leaders, the Cold War was in full swing, and there was no hope for a resolution. It was evident that the only alternative was to establish a separate government in the South, since the Soviet Command had already established a puppet regime in the North under the leadership of Kim Il-Sung.

On May 10, 1948, a historic national election was held (only in the South; the North did not participate) under the auspices of the United Nations. Over 95% of registered voters cast their ballots to elect 200 members to the Constitutional National Assembly.[27] The Korean Constitution was then enacted, and the Assembly elected Syngman Rhee as the first president of the Republic of Korea. The new government was formally installed on August 15, 1948, exactly three years after Korea's liberation from Japan.

The Korean War

On June 25, 1950, less than two years after the establishment of the Constitutional Assembly and the inauguration of President Rhee, the North Korean army invaded the South. It was a fateful Sunday morning. I witnessed the North's all-out attack in terrifying fear. I witnessed the destruction of war. I trembled. I was 10 years old.

But under the heroic leadership of General Douglas MacArthur, the U.S. Armed Forces joined the United Nations forces in repelling the Soviet and North Korean armies and recovering the Southern portion of the Korean peninsula. Through a cease fire agreement between North Korea and the United Nations in July 1953, the armed hostilities ceased, but the devastating impact it had on Koreans remained. The severed country was flattened, nothing but ruins and rubble. All told, it is estimated that 2,000,000 Koreans[28] died in the war, with millions more wounded. Orphans numbered in the tens of thousands. And millions of refugees from the North poured into the South to find safety, shelter, and food. More than 54,000 U.S. soldiers lost their lives and hundreds of thousands more were wounded.[29]

I have heard that more than 10 million family members and relatives were also separated as a result of the war. Today, very few of these severed families, even with the help of the American Red Cross, other non-governmental organizations, and the South Korean government, have any idea what has happened to their parents, children, spouses, siblings, and other relatives for almost 60 years. The North has never been willing to address this indescribable tragedy, outside of a handful of token reunions among selected families. These meetings are short-lived, lasting at most a couple of days with families forced to separate again. While so close in proximity, only divided by the 38th parallel's "Korean Demilitarized Zone," these separated family members are, in every imaginable way, completely shut off from each other without any opportunity to communicate (no visits, no letters, no calls, no email). North Korea's brutal dictatorship does not allow its people to make any contact with relatives in the South and in other parts of the world. Sadly, Korea is the only divided country in the world today. And tragically, North Korea is probably the most isolated.

It is no surprise then that throughout Korea's long tumultuous history, a unique component of its people's character developed

– what's known as "han." I certainly was no exception. According to Dr. Shalom Kim, "in Korean, 'han' denotes the most profound pain and suffering in the experience of misery and trouble in life. 'Han' ('jeong han' – emotional suffering, and 'won han' – deep-rooted hatred and bitterness) includes all the aspects of the English word 'suffering,' but suffering does not convey the full picture of 'han'. 'Han' is an expression which conveys suffering on multiple levels – personal, communal, family, cultural, trans-temporal, multigenerational, and at the same time, universal."[30]

Born in 1939, during the height of Japan's oppressive colonial rule, and growing up during the Korean War, and encountering difficult trials as a boy and young man in Seoul, I was deeply rooted in "han." As I will get into more later, "han" tainted everything that I did and was the catalyst for me to leave Korea and immigrate to America.

Korean Emigration

The opening of the "Hermit Kingdom" also opened the door for Koreans to immigrate to foreign countries. The history of Korean immigration really began in 1902 when Charles R. Bishop of the Hawaiian Sugar Planters' Association visited Korea and requested that the government send Koreans to Hawaii as laborers. Having had practically no history of immigration, most people were afraid to venture into a Western country. Historical records show that American missionaries played a role encouraging Korean Christians to respond to the challenge by telling them that life on Hawaii's sugar plantations would not be as bad as they thought. As a result, the first group of emigrants, made up of 102 people, sailed from Inchon to Hawaii on December 22, 1902 and arrived in January 1903. Of the people who came over, 47 were known as Christians, mostly Methodists.[31]

By 1944, as World War II was still ongoing in the Pacific, there were (a) 2.1 million Koreans in Japan, mobilized for hard labor or comforters for Japanese soldiers, (b) 1.6 million in Manchuria, (c) 100,000 in Mainland China, (d) 200,000 in the Soviet Union, and (e) 30,000 in the United States. Altogether, there were about four million overseas Koreans in 1945 when World War II ended. After the conclusion of the War, about 2.2 million of them returned to their homeland. During and after the Korean War (1950-1953), Korean women who married American GIs followed their husbands to the United States and subsequently invited their relatives from Korea to join them.

In 1965, when the New Johnson Act (a.k.a. Rodino Bill) was promulgated, there was a mad rush of Asian immigrants into the United States. Before the end of the 1960s, 34,500 Koreans came to settle in America.[32] My wife and I were two of them. During the 1960s and 1970s, a large number of Koreans also immigrated to countries in Latin America (such as Brazil, Argentina, Bolivia, Uruguay, and Paraguay) as well as Germany, seeking a better life. Up until the 1960s, Korea was one of the poorest countries in the world. When I was a college student in 1961, I remember Korea's per capita GDP being only $91 U.S. dollars.[33] Those who had seen no hope to improve their lives in Korea grabbed any chance offered to them to migrate to other countries. Even college graduates and white collar workers were happy to go to Germany and some parts of Europe to be blue-collar miners.

During the 1970s and 1980s, the opening of the Middle East and Southeast Asia for construction projects for Korean companies enticed many young Koreans to work as overseas laborers. Many remained in those countries after their contracts expired. Since the Summer Olympics Games were held in Seoul in 1988 and the FIFA World Cup in 2002, business opportunities opened for Koreans to move to many countries in the world. As of 2010, the number of ethnic Koreans in America (or Americans with Korean heritage) is approximately 1.7 million.[34]

The Korean people's motives for moving to other countries varied. But one constant among these immigrants was the desire to give their children a better education, and the dream of living well. That is the dream that I had.

Chapter 4

THE EARLY YEARS IN AMERICA

Three Bags and $200

When I was a college student studying politics and international relations in the early 1960s in Seoul, one of my professors quoted in class this statement made by then-Prime Minister Lee Kwan Yoo of Singapore attesting to the power of America: "When America sneezes, the whole world gets pneumonia." Prime Minister Lee was also quoted as saying, "When two huge elephants are fighting each other on grass, the grass gets crushed; and when they made love to each other, the grass gets equally crushed." This was in reference to the Cold War between the U.S. and the Soviet Union, and no matter whether the two superpowers were on good terms or bad, all the nations of the world would be directly affected. As I was listening to this in class, it motivated me to go to America to study its government and learn why the U.S. was so powerful.

While Sung and I were dating, she also expressed a desire to study in America. She received a B.A. with honors in English Literature from Ewha Women's University, and was working as an assistant editor for the Korea Journal, an English publication issued by the Korean headquarters of the United Nations Educational, Scientific and Cultural Organization (UNESCO). When she found out that I wanted to study American Government in the U.S., she was very excited. She wanted to come with me.

Sung and I dated for one and a half years and were married on March 11, 1967, in Seoul. While we were preparing to go to America (and our honeymoon in Japan), Sung's mother passed away from lung cancer. She was 59. The whole family, especially Sung's father, was deeply grieved over this loss. Sung's mother was incredibly kind to me after we got to know each other, and I had hoped that someday she would come to America and spend time with us.

On June 15, 1967, we left for America, carrying with us only $200 (Koreans traveling overseas were only allowed by the government to take $100 per person due to a shortage of foreign currency reserves) and three pieces of luggage. We left Korea with hope for a better life by attaining advanced degrees, but we were filled with tremendous anxiety, especially Sung. She still grieved over her mother's death. She was leaving her entire family for an unknown future in an unknown land with an unknown culture. She knew that this journey was going to be hard. She knew that there were no guarantees. Yet she had incredible faith in God – and trust in me. It was a risk that she willingly took with much prayer. There were many tears shed by our families at Seoul International Airport.

On our way to America we stopped by Tokyo, Japan to spend a few weeks with our friends and mentors, Masahide and Chako Shibusawa, whom I first met in working to bring reconciliation between Korea and Japan with the Moral Re-Armament movement. When Mr. Shibusawa came to Korea in late 1966, and had learned that we were engaged, he invited us to come to stay with him and his wife for our honeymoon. The Shibusawas are one of the most respected and admired families in all of Japan. Mr. Shibusawa's grandfather (Eichi) was a key architect in restoring the empire of Emperor Meiji from Shogunate (Meiji Restoration), and his father was the Minister of Finance right after World War II. Masahide, my friend, was known as one of the "wise men" who had advised six Japanese prime ministers for over five decades. We ended up staying five and a half months in Japan under their care. It was an unforgettable honeymoon with first-class treatment by the Shibusawas. They were incredibly generous.

Before we left Tokyo for Los Angeles, we were surprised to find out that my wife had become pregnant. While this was great news to us, we were overcome with worry as to how we – poor graduate students-to-be – would be able to financially care for this baby.

Right from the start, and even before we arrived in America, things were already not going as planned. Yes, we wanted children. But not this soon. But we trusted in God's sovereignty, gave thanks to Him for this blessing, and resolved to do our best in raising this baby in America.

With our tearful farewell to the Shibusawas at Tokyo Haneda Airport, we boarded a plane departing for America. During the long flight crossing the Pacific, thoughts raced through my head. *How are we going to fit in in this strange country? How are we going to afford to live? To raise a baby? How am I going to be able to study in a language that's foreign to me? What if I fail? What if the studies are too hard? Who's going to help us? Is there any hope for us?* We landed at Los Angeles International Airport on November 28, 1967. No one welcomed us at the airport. It was a stark reminder that we were really on this journey alone. But I was resolved more than ever to do whatever it took to fulfill my dream of earning my master's and doctoral degrees in American Government and becoming a professor.

We had finally arrived in America, the land of the free. The land of opportunity.

Wigs and Morgues

Although I was admitted to the graduate schools of UCLA, Stanford, Columbia, and the University of Southern California (USC), my wife and I decided to go to USC for a number of reasons, primarily because Sung found a second aunt in Glendale (outside of Los Angeles), who could help us during the pregnancy. With Sung's aunt's help, we were able to temporarily move into a tiny studio in Glendale. For the first two and a half years we lived in Glendale, we didn't have a car. I think that's a record for the longest time a Korean family has lived in the Los Angeles area without a car.

I would begin my studies at USC in the fall semester of 1968, so that gave me about eight months to earn some money for my family. I had to find work quickly, especially with a baby on the way. One evening, we were invited over to Sung's friend's home for dinner. We had previously stayed with them for about a week before Sung had found her aunt in Glendale. The friend's husband showed us a bag filled with a dozen wigs and told me that I should sell them to the African-Americans who lived in the South Central area of Los Angeles. He said that there was a lot of money to be made in wigs as they were very popular in the black community. He mentioned that a number of other Koreans were becoming rich from this business. I knew he was sincerely looking out for us, so I felt some obligation to hear him out and listen to his advice. Whether I wanted to or not.

The next morning, I reluctantly grabbed the bag of wigs and took a long bus ride to South Central L.A. After getting off, I stood at the street corner watching many cars and people pass in front of me. There were many potential customers. But as I was about to open the bag of wigs, I paused and collected my thoughts. *Why did we come to America? What was my purpose in coming here? To make money? To get rich? To run a business? Didn't I come here to study? To earn my master's and doctoral degrees? Wasn't that the original plan?* After coming to my senses, I closed the bag, got on the next bus, and returned to my wife's friend's home. I told her husband that I could not go through with it. Disappointed, he said, "I guess you are not hungry enough yet. Your studies can't make your stomach full." He went on and on. About how irresponsible I was. About how ignorant I was. About how this was easy money. I just sat there, swallowed my pride, and took the berating. After my wife and I left his home, I was more determined than ever. I made a promise to myself. *I came to America to earn my graduate degrees – live or die, that is the road I will take.*

Fortunately, with Sung's aunt's help, I was able to find a job as a janitor at Glendale Community Hospital, which was close to where we lived. The job paid $3.25 an hour. I did my best in cleaning the operating rooms, the hallways, as well as the patient rooms. My supervisor praised my work – whatever I did, I always gave it my best.

Since I worked during the night shift for the first few months, I was the only man who could assist the nurses in transferring patients who had died during the night from their rooms to the refrigerated morgue on the fourth floor. One night, the head nurse of the night shift called for me while I was cleaning the kitchen. A nurse on the second floor needed assistance in transporting a deceased patient to the morgue. When I got to the patient room, a chill ran through my body as I saw the nurse prepare the dead body for transport. I could only just stand there. Watching. Motionless. I didn't know what to do. This was the first time I had been asked to do anything like this. "Choon," the nurse asked, "why don't you lift his head and shoulders, and I'll take the legs and we'll move him to the gurney." *I couldn't possibly lift up the head and shoulders!* Terrified, I gently pleaded with the nurse, "I'll lift up the legs and you do the head, okay?" She chuckled and we switched sides.

We took the body to the hospital morgue's cold storage unit. The cold air that escaped when I opened the door gave me another chill throughout my body. I was not feeling well. Upon placing the body in a large steel drawer, the nurse checked an ID tag on the ankle and pushed the drawer in. And that was it. That was the end of life. I realized that you cannot take anything, not even a single penny, when you die. Whatever the amount of wealth you have amassed throughout your life, whatever you achieve, or whatever position you've held, the harsh, cold reality is that when you die, you cannot take any of it with you. Whether famous or ordinary, old or young, rich or poor, educated or uneducated, whether black, brown, white, red, or yellow, everyone dies. Death is the one true equalizer. For a few minutes in that cold storage unit,

God was trying to teach me a great and profound lesson. *What is the purpose of our lives on this earth?* But I wasn't really listening.

After hearing the steel drawer slam shut, I wanted to get out of the morgue. As soon as possible. As I hastily pushed the empty gurney out the door, the nurse laughed, "Are you scared, Choon?"

"First time dealing with a dead body."

"Once you get used to it, it's a piece of cake."

She was right. I did get used to it. During my night shifts, I transported, transferred, and stored a number of deceased patients. I wasn't sure why but it seemed that patients tended to die during the night.

After learning what I was doing at work, including the long hours and the night shifts, my wife couldn't stand seeing me laboring so hard with such menial tasks for such little pay. Crying, she begged me, "Let's go back to Korea. It's too hard for you. It's too hard for us."

"Sung, let's persevere through this for a few more years, and I promise you, we'll be fine."

Sharon

On April 28, 1968, by God's grace, our daughter Sharon was born at Glendale Community Hospital, the place where I worked as a janitor. She was the most beautiful little thing I had ever seen. Because we were barely scraping by, immediately after Sharon was born Sung started work at the accounting office of Glendale Community Hospital. Sung's heart ached knowing she couldn't care for her newborn daughter and be there for her on a daily basis. Of all the things we were going through at this time, this was the hardest for her. She cried every time she dropped Sharon off at a nearby babysitter's home on her walk to work. Since we did not have a car at that time, and to reduce our commute times, we moved from our small studio to a one-bedroom apartment across the street from the hospital.

While growing up in Glendale, Sharon was so loved by our neighbors and friends. During those trying times, she brought great joy, comfort, and hope to me and Sung. She was a gift in the midst of hardship.

From a Janitor to an Orderly

The doctors and nurses at the hospital showed a great deal of interest in my advancement within the hospital. They trained me to be a practical nurse and an orderly for the surgery department. I soon left my janitorial position and started work in the operating rooms as an orderly. My new shift was from 6:30 a.m. to 1:30 p.m. I no longer had to work the night shift from 11:00 p.m. to 6:00 a.m. Hallelujah!

I loved working in the surgery department. The mornings were extremely busy. I was the first person to arrive at the hospital to prepare the operating rooms, making sure that everything was in working order. I cleaned the lights, set up all the equipment, and checked the instruments (which were sterilized during the night). This all had to be done 30 minutes prior to the doctors' surgery prep. After everything was set up, a nurse and I went up to the third floor to pick up the patients for surgery.

Surgeries involved amazing team work. I was impressed by how hard the doctors and nurses worked. At times, I would wipe the sweat off the doctors' and nurses' brows and faces. Unless there were emergencies, most surgeries were finished by eleven o'clock in the morning. After a day's work, the surgical nurses and I would clean the operating rooms and prepare for the next day's surgeries. The nurses then gave me specific orders to be done for the following morning's set up.

I loved the operating room environment. I loved the teamwork. I loved the camaraderie. And most importantly, it was the best place for me to practice listening and speaking English. Nurses talk. A lot. On any and every possible subject. During breaks. After work. During work. And all of them, including the head nurse, were so incredibly kind to me by going out of their way to teach me how to listen and speak English properly by including me in their conversations. Whenever we finished our work early, we spent the rest of our time talking until it was time to go home. Finding that a woman's pronunciation, in general, was much clearer and easier to understand than a man's, I was well trained in conversational English during my time in the surgery department. I thanked God for that invaluable opportunity.

After seeing my dedication to my work at the hospital, some of the doctors advised me to go to medical school and told me that they might arrange a scholarship for me. I politely declined. I told them that the reason I came to the U.S. was to study American Government. They were intrigued and impressed by my plans. They told me if I ever changed my mind, to let them know. I was flattered.

Prior to starting my studies at USC, my supervisor said, "Choon, I know you're starting school soon, but we still need you here. So I want you to work in the operating room at least part time, including Saturday mornings. You've been very reliable. You work very hard. I need you here."

"Yes, of course, ma'am. I will do my best. Thank you so much." I was filled with thanksgiving. I could still make money while studying at USC.

And those studies couldn't come soon enough.

Chapter 5
USC

William Lammers, My Mentor

When I decided to study political science, with a concentration in American Government, I couldn't find a professor at USC who was interested in helping me. I decided to start at the top and ask Dr. William Lammers, chairman of the Political Science Department and a renowned scholar in U.S. presidential politics and public policy. Filled with trepidation, I went to his office. Thankfully, he was there. Thankfully, he couldn't have been nicer. In my broken English, I nervously introduced myself and my proposed course of study and asked him if he would be my faculty adviser. He said that as far as he knew, there were no international students in America who had earned, or were on their way to earn, political science graduate degrees with a concentration in American Government. He didn't think I would be the exception, expressing that it would be nearly impossible to earn master's and doctoral degrees in that field without having any background in the subject. He then tried to politely convince me, ever so delicately, to focus my studies on comparative government, international relations, or political theory. Undeterred, I explained to him the statements made by Singaporean Prime Minister Lee and why I came to America. That my dream was to study American Government. And I pleaded with him to help me in realizing that dream. He paused for a few moments and recommended that I think it over and come back to see him during his office hours the following week.

I couldn't wait that long. The next day, I waited for him near his office, hoping to catch him when he returned from one of his classes. He was surprised to see me so soon. "Mr. Kim, aren't you supposed to come back next week?" I followed him into his office and asked for a few minutes of his time.

"Dr. Lammers, I know you are very busy, but I could not

wait another week. I could not sleep last night. I really want American Government to be my concentration. If it's true that no international student has ever earned a Ph.D. in that concentration, then I would like to be the first one. If I fail to get good grades in my prerequisite and American Government courses at the end of the academic year, I will change my concentration. But if you give me a chance and accept me as your disciple and train me as much as you can, I am certain I'll overcome the obstacles. I will do my best. Please help me, Dr. Lammers."

A wide grin spread across his face. He then looked me straight in the eyes for what seemed like an eternity. "Mr. Kim, are you determined to take on this daunting challenge?"

"Yes, Dr. Lammers! I am more determined than ever. The only reason why I came to America is to learn about America and study American Government. I am willing to take this challenge if you can train and mentor me."

His grin now wider, he extended his right hand and I shook it appreciatively. Immense relief poured over me. I was overjoyed. I was to see him every other Friday morning from 8:00 a.m. to 10:00 a.m. in his office.

My first semester at USC finally began in September 1968. I couldn't have been more excited – and scared. Because I had never studied American Government before, I was required to take a number of prerequisite courses, such as American History, the U.S. Constitution, American Society and Culture, Economics, American Democracy: Theory and Practice, American Party Politics and Elections, Executive and Legislative Processes, and the Judicial Process. I had to complete these courses before I could even begin any of my graduate coursework. *This is going to be quite the journey. And I am in completely unfamiliar territory in an unfamiliar land.*

Studying, Studying, and More Studying

I poured everything into my studies. I gave it my all. I wanted to show the world that I could do this. I wanted to show my family that I could do this. I wanted to show everyone back in Korea that I could do this. That I could accomplish a dream that, according to Dr. Lammers, no other international student had yet accomplished.

Because of our newborn baby Sharon, it was difficult for me to concentrate at night in our small apartment. I made a special request to the night supervisor of the hospital for access to the doctors' library in the evenings so I could study. I spent many hours there. I probably spent more time there than at our apartment. When doctors came to the library for some research or to review X-rays and found that I was studying American Government, they would engage me in discussions, mostly on current issues regarding public policies. This gave me a chance to ask them a lot of questions about America – its society, culture, politics, and economy. The doctors were very knowledgeable. They were well-versed in the workings of their country and gave me great practical insight in how governmental policies were actually affecting their day-to-day lives. I was learning from them things that I would not have been able to read from a textbook. These conversations were invaluable. And I like to say they learned a little from me as well and my observations as an outsider. When doctors would make their evening rounds, some of them would come to the library just for the sake of engaging me in these political, social, economic, and cultural dialogues. Some of these dialogues made their way into my papers.

My weekly schedule did not leave much time for sleep. For four days a week, I would spend the entire night studying at the hospital library, and at around 5:45 a.m. on Monday, Wednesday, and Saturday mornings, I would go home, wash up, eat a quick breakfast before heading back to the hospital to prep the operating room for surgery by 6:30 a.m. On Mondays and Wednesdays, as soon as my hospital shift ended at 1:30 p.m., I would rush home to grab my course materials and bag, walk (or run) 10 blocks to catch the 2:00 bus, transfer to two more buses, arrive at USC, and then run to my first class. After classes were finished, I usually headed to the library where I was able to review my notes and reflect on what I had learned that day. On Tuesdays and Thursdays, after having several hours of sleep (from studying the night before), I would spend the entire day at the school library.

Every other Friday morning, I spent two hours with Dr. Lammers to discuss the assignments he had given me. These reading assignments were in addition to my regular coursework. They were torturous. It was hard keeping up. It was hard keeping the promise I made to Dr. Lammers. It was hard to keep going like this. *There just isn't enough time during the day. There just isn't.* One Friday morning, Dr. Lammers asked, "Choon, how many articles did you review before breakfast this morning?"

"Dr. Lammers, I got up, washed up, and ate my breakfast as fast as I could, and came to meet you on time. What could I have possibly done before breakfast?"

With a big smile, he responded in jest, "What did you do during the entire night before breakfast?"

Although Dr. Lammers was kidding (somewhat), I got the message. From that point on, I stayed up many nights, pouring out everything into my coursework and Dr. Lammers's assignments. Because of the language barrier and the lack of prior coursework in American Government, I always felt that I was playing from behind. To compensate, I would substantially cut my sleeping hours. I averaged only four hours of sleep during my time at USC. One morning, my wife came into our small study (we had moved into a two-bedroom apartment at this time), "Yeobo [Korean for 'honey'], you have been sitting on that chair for more than 78 hours straight. You have not slept for more than three days and three nights. Are you going to kill yourself?!" Until she spoke, I had not realized I had been working on a paper for that long without taking a break, without taking a nap. That's how focused I was on studying. That's how obsessed I was.

Bob Blackstone, My Classmate

In addition to keeping up with the course load and Dr. Lammers's assignments, I had received some slights and ridicule by my American classmates when they learned about my pursuit of a doctoral degree in American Government. *What was this foreigner doing studying that?* But by God's grace, I met a wonderful Christian brother, Bob Blackstone, who happened to be on the same graduate track as me. He was an answer to my prayers. I invited him to lunch on campus one day and asked if he could review and edit my papers. He said he'd be glad to. I was ecstatic. I also asked him to organize a small study group every Friday afternoon to review the past week's lessons and prepare for the following week's assignments and discussion topics.

These get-togethers made my Friday nights even longer. The four of us met four to six hours every Friday afternoon. Sometimes our meetings would go longer. We were really a team, with Bob as our leader. We worked extremely hard together. We shared notes (they told me I was the best note-taker) and prepared our assignments and discussion topics together. We made the commitment to do our very best to help each other so that we would be on top of everything that was covered in class. And we were. About a year after we started meeting, the four of us began to dominate the classroom discussions. One of my classmates said to me at lunch, "Choon, you talk too much in the class discussions and debates!"

"Do you remember the early days when I was trying to participate in class with my broken English? You guys never gave me a chance to finish my thoughts, and cut me off and took over the discussions. That made me so mad. I was so frustrated. This is my revenge!" We both laughed.

Earning the Doctorate

With Dr. Lammers's personal mentoring, Bob Blackstone's generous help, our study group meetings, and my wife doing everything possible to help me (including typing my papers and review notes), I was able to complete all my prerequisites and graduate courses with very high marks in 1973. I even took additional courses that were not required (mostly during the summer) in public administration (federal, state, and local), public decision making, business management and leadership, statistics, social and behavioral psychology, and business economics. Because my concentration was American Government and public policy, I wanted to cover all aspects of U.S. public policymaking – political, social, economic, management, leadership, international, multi- and cross-cultural, and psychological. I wanted to learn everything about America. I also was awarded teaching and research assistantships, so I didn't have to pay USC's expensive tuition anymore. The stipend from the assistantships and my wife's salary from the hospital enabled us to finally purchase a car in 1970, two-and-a-half years after we arrived in Los Angeles. It was a Pinto, the cheapest car ever made by Ford.

With the completion of the coursework, up next were the qualifying exam (given once a year) and the doctoral dissertation as the final requirements for a Doctor of Philosophy in Political Science (American Government). To prepare for the exam, I asked the department assistant for the questions to the last ten exams. In reviewing and analyzing those questions, I developed about 20 integrated and comprehensive questions. I then answered those questions, writing about 200 pages per question, for a total of

4,000 handwritten pages. This took months. I eventually shared those pages with my study group and they were flabbergasted. They asked me to pare down the answers to about 20 pages per question for their own review and preparation. With this in hand, I was confident that the four of us would do very well.

The qualifying exam was six hours per day for three days. *Eighteen hours for a written test!* But the questions on the exam were not that unfamiliar as I had already analyzed 10 years' worth of exams. Just as I predicted, my study group did exceptionally well. And I received the best evaluations and highest scores from my professors. In fact, the department had my exam on display for a year as the model exam. Dr. Lammers was very proud.

Dr. Lammers and I then met to discuss my doctoral dissertation. During my graduate studies, I had developed a particular passion on issues concerning the U.S.'s energy policies, stemming, in part, from OPEC's (Organization of Petroleum Exporting Countries) oil embargo against the U.S., Japan and the Western European nations. The embargo was caused by the Yom-Kippur War in October 1973 between Israel and a coalition of Arab countries that resulted in the Arabs' defeat. The embargo had a devastating impact on the industrialized nations of the world, causing the 1973 energy crisis. The timing could not have been more perfect for a dissertation on U.S. energy policy. Dr. Lammers and I agreed that I would immediately research why the U.S. had failed to develop a national energy policy, U.S. energy resource development and its environmental impacts, the international petroleum trade, and green energy. After a long and painstaking process of research and field work, around the end of 1974, I completed my doctoral dissertation on "U.S. Energy Resources Development and Community Environmental Impacts." I received a Doctor of Philosophy in Political Science (American Government) in the spring of 1975. I finally got my Ph.D.

Pepperdine University

Before completion of my dissertation, I was encouraged by a friend to apply for an assistant professor position at Pepperdine University that would begin in the spring of 1973 (I had already taught two classes at Pepperdine in 1972). I applied, but I did not think I had much of a chance. There was too much competition. And the selection committee had raised the issue of whether or not a foreign-born faculty member would be able to teach American Government and U.S. public policy. I was able to enlist seven professors to strongly endorse my candidacy for the position, including Dr. Lammers who wrote:

> "To Whom It May Concern,
> Hire Mr. Kim, he is the best!
> William Lammers, Ph.D."

Dr. Lammers was a true gentleman and scholar. He was always very kind and warm. He was an intellectual giant and a wonderful lecturer. I later learned that he was a deacon at a local Presbyterian church, which made perfect sense, considering how generous his Christ-like heart was for me. For almost six years, he mentored, trained, and molded me. Even to this day, I have always tried to emulate him as a professor, as a scholar, and as a mentor to others. When I later moved to Alaska, my wife and I invited him and his wife to spend a week with us. But unfortunately due to his father-in-law's illness, he wasn't able to come. I was deeply saddened when I later learned he had died of cancer. I recently visited his wife and told her how much her husband had impacted my life, professionally and personally. Tears still come to my eyes when I think of him and all that he did for me.

By the grace of God, Pepperdine offered me the assistant professor position, starting in January 1973. Just as I poured out everything into my studies, I poured out everything into my teaching and my students' learning. I fell in love with teaching. It was confirmation from God that this is where he wanted me to be. In the classroom. Teaching students. Teaching them about American Government, including the U.S. presidency, the legislative process, party politics and the election process, public policy making, the judiciary, the administrative process, and organizational theory and behavior. In February 1970, we were scraping by with only one dollar in the bank. Now, I was teaching full-time at Pepperdine University and in 1976, the students had elected me the best teacher of the year.

I would not have been able to achieve any of this without my wife. The whole time I was away in the classroom, at the hospital, in the library, in Dr. Lammers's office, and meeting with my study group, I was away from my wife and daughter. My wife took care of everything and spent many, many hours typing my review notes and paper after paper after paper (I was a terrible at the typewriter). She was the real backbone of the family. The glue. And because we needed the money to raise Sharon and support our family, she willingly sacrificed her own dream in coming to America – her graduate degrees – to work full-time at a hospital so I could fulfill my dream. I've never met any woman who was as dedicated to her family as she was during this time (and even now). It was never easy for her. On the one hand, she never had any time to herself; on the other, she was either literally or figuratively all alone in a foreign land. But I was so prideful and so driven and consumed by my personal ambitions, I never showed my appreciation to her. I rarely thanked her for all that she did.

And it had to take God on Big Bear Mountain for me to realize any of this.

Chapter 6

ARROGANCE AND INFERIORITY

Two Sides of the Same Coin

I struggled with inferiority. Ever since my father died when I was six. Growing up, I was very poor. This inferiority complex took further root when, after putting everything into getting admitted to Seoul National University (the best university in Korea), I was rejected – twice. I was deemed a failure. By everyone who knew me.

It only got worse when I started at USC, being the only international student in the classroom; in fact, the only non-Caucasian. Intimidated, I felt very inferior to my classmates who had no foreign accents and were extremely articulate. Some would impatiently and mercilessly interrupt me before I could finish explaining my thoughts, leaving me embarrassingly silent – and seething with anger and frustration. *Why couldn't I have been white and born, raised, and educated in America, like my classmates?* I felt so out of place. I wanted to fit in but it was such a struggle.

Things seem to be getting better after becoming a full-time professor at Pepperdine. But after gaining national attention for my academic work on energy and the environment, and garnering praise from both my colleagues and the students, my inferiority complex seamlessly morphed into arrogance. Pride and arrogance dominate the lives of many secular scholars, academics, and intellectuals. I was no different. Professors, by and large (and I certainly would know), love to boast. They tend to believe they have achieved success not through give-and-take, forging relationships, or compromise (like many in business or even politics), but on their own persevering abilities and talents in the classroom, in the library, and on the typewriter/computer.

I believe that is why it is so hard for scholars to admit that they are sinful and need someone outside of themselves to save them. If they think they don't need to be saved, that nothing is wrong with them, that they achieved everything on their own, then they have no use for Jesus Christ.

My so-called "Christian life" was now a pendulum swinging back-and-forth between inferiority (not to be mistaken with godly humility) and superiority (not godly courage and boldness). On Big Bear Mountain, the Holy Spirit convicted me to repent of my dual personality, which was not only killing my soul, but had hurt my wife and children, church members and pastors, colleagues and friends. It had damaged and poisoned every relationship that I had. This mindset (inferiority and superiority), which controlled my behavior (from deep depression, anger, and bitterness to extreme elation), and hardened my soul, swung on this axis of selfishness. I was the center of my life, not God. When I didn't get what *I* wanted, I felt inferior. When things weren't going *my* way, I felt bitter. When I got what *I* wanted, I felt superior. When things were going *my* way, I felt proud.

This was a duality that God wanted me to crush. My life was at stake. So I cried out to God to cleanse me of these awful sins.

As I was tearfully repenting to God, especially of my arrogance and inferiority-driven bitterness, God revealed to me that the root of my particular sins were the layers of "hans" in my life. Everything that I had sought to achieve – all my desires and ambitions and motivations – was selfishly to rid myself of any "han" that I had accumulated in my life. I was so consumed by this – and lacked the peace of God which transcends all understanding (Phil. 4:7) – that I thought that the only way to achieve true peace was to do all that I could to obliterate them through accomplishments and accolades. This is why I was so fiercely driven, so fiercely competitive, so fiercely ambitious.

But the achievements were never enough. As the satisfaction of one layer of "han" being eliminated quickly wore off, there was another one that needed to be dealt with. And another. And then another. Like the endless peeling away of an onion. It never stopped. There was never true rest. Or peace. Only constant complaining and groaning. Dissatisfaction. Bitterness. I was down. Unhappy. Depressed. And now dying. All because I was a prisoner of me and my "hans."

The "Han" of Hardship and Failure

It was hard growing up in Korea. Being fatherless made it even harder. Poverty was widespread. The land lay in ruins after the war. Joy was rare in households, mine included. There was no laughter at my home. There was no happiness. My mother, widowed at the age of 34, worked day and night to provide for us – leaving for the fields or the town's swap meet before dawn and returning late at night. She chose not to remarry, and instead poured out her life to take care of me and my older sister. She did everything for us with the hope that her only son would go to Seoul National University, study well, land a good job, and provide financial security for the family. This was the hope she clung to as she toiled for her children.

I was an excellent student at Jeonju High School and I, along with my teachers and peers, was confident that I would pass Seoul National's entrance exam. But I failed. Not once, but twice. My teachers were in disbelief. *How could he fail? Twice?* I brought shame to my family and was the talk of the town. My uncles and aunts and others in our village brutally humiliated me. *After all your mom did for you, after all her sacrifices, you couldn't even do this for her?* I couldn't face my mother. I couldn't look in the mirror. Guilt, shame, sorrow, and disappointment washed over me. I was completely broken. The future seemed so bleak. So dark. *I am a complete failure.*

I attempted suicide. Three times. I even failed at that too.

I eventually received a scholarship to attend Kyung Hee University in Seoul. In March 1960, I left home and boarded a train bound for Seoul with 380 won in my pocket (about 35 cents), which could only buy me two bowls of noodles. I missed the welcoming ceremony for my freshman class.

Generously, one of my friends housed me in his rented, single room on the hilltop of Ahyeon-dong's slum area in Seoul, Korea. Since I couldn't afford the bus fare to go to school, I had to walk down from the hilltop to Seodaemoon, through downtown Kwanghwamoon, Jongro, to Dongdaemoon, Sinsul Rotary, Chungryangri Rotary, Junnong, Chongryangri Rotary, past Jaekidong, and Hwikyungdong, and then onto the main gates of Kyung Hee University. The trek from the west side of Seoul to the capital's east end took more than two hours. Many times I starved while taking those long walks to school, and when I saw the buses and cars passing me by, I was filled with deep anger. I wanted every one of them to be engulfed with flames and burned to the ground. *Why couldn't I have a little money to ride a bus? Why is this society so unfair and unjust?* The "han" of inferiority and failure-driven bitterness in my heart continued to grow.

Once, I was forced to go without 10 straight meals. After four days without eating, I became so hungry that I considered stealing some food or money. In my desperation, one day after class I went to see a friend of mine who was boarding at a house near Kyung Kee High School. I walked hurriedly for an hour in hopes to share his meal, but I arrived after dinner was over. I was crushed. All he could give me was a little snack and 100 won (about 10 cents). He had no other funds as he had yet to receive his allowance from his parents and was delinquent on his boarding fees. One-hundred won wasn't even enough to buy a bowl of noodles. Walking back to Ahyeon-dong, I saw a little makeshift tent selling grilled sweet potatoes, chestnuts and other dried foods. I didn't have enough to buy those items, but a row of packaged biscuit crackers (used for the military) caught my eye. Exactly 100 won for a bag. I ate those crackers as fast as I could. As soon as I arrived back at my friend's place, I drank a lot of water. Later that night, because the biscuits contained a lot of yeast, I felt so bloated that I could hardly breathe.

In early May, several of my high school friends learned about my financial and commuting situation and asked me to room with them at a place much closer to Kyung Hee University. They also offered to feed me. I will never forget their kindness, even though they themselves had little to go on. Their landlord later asked me to tutor his kids. Soon I was making enough money to pay for food and the occasional bus ride.

I did very well at Kyung Hee University. I was the recipient of the prestigious Sam Il Scholarship (founded by Jung Lim Lee) through a nationwide selection process, and the University Scholarship, which included a stipend that was more than sufficient to cover my expenses. I would never be able to repay what the Sam Il Scholarship Foundation, and especially the founder and president of Kyung Hee University, Dr. Young Shik Cho, did for me. Dr. Cho was a powerful international peacemaker, passionate public entrepreneur, and the most generous man I have ever known. He was also a teacher and mentor and became a life-long friend. At my commencement in 1963, Dr. Cho awarded me (out of 2,800 graduating seniors) the President's Award for my academic accomplishments. For the moment, I felt profound satisfaction. I felt a "han" (of academic inferiority and failure) peel away.

But that didn't last very long. Kyung Hee University was a great school (and I am prouder than ever of having attended there), but it wasn't considered top-tier at the time. So it was extremely difficult to find a decent job after graduation. This was another bitter pill that I had to swallow. Despite all the scholarships and awards from Kyung Hee, I was still considered a failure simply because I didn't go to Seoul National. I hated that. I hated living in a society consumed with college rankings, with little regard for a person's character, work ethic, and wisdom. I hated being deemed a failure. I hated Korea. *I will prove you all wrong.*

The "Han" of My Upbringing

During my junior year in college, I dated a woman who was also a student at Kyung Hee. She majored in piano. She was beautiful. I was in love. I wanted to marry her.

Her mother wanted to meet me so she took me to her home. After some small talk, her mother asked questions about my background. After some back-and-forth, she said this to me, "You are the only son in your family. You were raised by a widow. You are poor. You are from a poor province (Cholla Do). You are not going to the best university. I simply cannot allow you to date my daughter. As of today, you are to stop dating her." I was stunned. And utterly humiliated. *How could she say that to a young man whom she never met before! She doesn't even know me! And her daughter goes to the same school I do!*

But according to Korean culture, she knew enough. None of what she said wasn't true. That was my background. That's who I was, at least on paper. These were handicaps in the eyes of this culture that I couldn't run away from. That I couldn't hide from. That I couldn't argue with. I had failed in meeting this society's standards of "marriage material." I had failed – again. Tempted to desperately beg her mother to allow me to continue dating her daughter, I instead held my tongue, accepted her decision, and left. *You just wait and see.*

The mother's words caused a great deal of pain in my inner being.

It's not just that I lost a girl that I wanted to marry, but the reason why I lost her. It made me even more bitter. This humiliating experience stayed with me for a very long time. And only added another layer of "han" to my heart.

By the grace of God, I eventually met my wife, Sung. The best thing that ever happened to my life. But my "hans" didn't go away.

Chapter 7

SUNG MAI LEE

Meeting My Wife

Two years after leaving the home of my then-girlfriend, I prayed to God about my future wife. I prayed to God that He would give me a born-again Christian woman with the same theology (reformed), the same value system, excellent communication skills, and a woman who loved to laugh. While I didn't care if she came from a wealthy family, I did ask God for someone who came from a large family with lots of siblings because I never had that – for me it was just my mom and my sister.

My Christian friend at UNESCO arranged for me to meet his co-worker, Sung Mai Lee, at a café (known in Korea as a "tea house"). By His sovereign grace, God introduced a woman to me who met all the qualities that I was praying about – and "immeasurably" more than I could've ever "asked or imagined!" (Eph. 3:20). When we first met, I immediately fell in love with her big and beautiful smile. *This could be it!* We began dating and grew to like each other a lot. Our relationship got to the point where I wanted her to meet my mother. Although Sung knew I wasn't rich (she had paid for most of our dates and I hardly made any money at the time as one of the leaders of the MRA), she didn't realize how poor I was until she came over to meet my mom. She later confessed to me that she was taken aback by our poverty.

My mom liked Sung very much and our relationship became more serious – it soon became my turn to meet Sung's family. I knew her family was different than mine, but Sung never went into details. The whole idea of meeting them made me extremely nervous. I couldn't stop thinking of the last time I had to do this – and how humiliating that was.

When we arrived at the gates of her house, I noticed the car of a high-level government official parked in front.

"Whose car is that?" I asked. She said it belonged to her older brother. The house was enormous. The grounds were incredible. Immaculate. I started sweating. *This is not going to go well.*

"Don't worry, you will do just fine." *Easy for her to say.*

As we were walking towards the house, Sung's father, Dr. Young Wook Lee, came out to greet us. Here we go. He immediately threw his arm around my shoulder and smiled, "Deacon Kim, welcome to my home." He then introduced his wife and Sung's seven siblings (and a few of their spouses who were there) to me. This was all too intimidating. I really was not feeling well. *This is what I get for asking God that my future wife come from a big family!*

Her father then ushered me to his study and we sat down to talk. Just the two of us. The warmth from his face was so embracing, so encouraging. He made me feel so at ease. I was in the presence of a godly man. Remarkably, he never asked about my accomplishments or what I was doing or anything about my background (I did tell him everything upfront nonetheless). He seemed most interested in hearing about my faith. I told him that right after the Korean War, when I was 14 years old, a church was built in the center of our district. It was the first time I had ever seen a church. My mother was a Buddhist at the time.

Teenage gangs were prevalent in the countryside after the war, populated by youth whose lands lay in ruin and who had no hope in the future. Fights between regions and villages were the norm. This was our escape. This was our release. This was the way it was. Curious about this newly constructed church, I mobilized my friends and fellow gang members to throw stones at the church and on its tin roof and ring the church bell during the times people would gather for "service" and singing. Disruption was our goal. And we were pretty good at it.

In the spring of 1955, my eldest uncle called me into his room and told me that his daughter, my older cousin, was going to marry the pastor who started the new church. The shenanigans would have to stop I was told. In lieu of the rock-throwing and church bell-ringing, I was ordered to attend every Sunday service. No exceptions. I had no choice but to obey. My uncle was the leader of the district, the eldest of the family and since I had no father, he was the closest thing I had to one.

This "religion" that was being force fed to me was of no interest. I regularly attended, but I regularly tuned out. During the summer, after my cousin and the pastor were married, the pastor asked me to help him with the children's vacation Bible classes. He needed someone to be his administrative assistant: check the attendance, pass out the papers, record the test scores, tally the grades for prizes and rewards, and other tasks. I said I'd help.

Sitting in the back during the classes, I listened to my new cousin-in-law tell the children stories about Noah, Abraham, Joseph, Moses, Joshua, David and Jonathan, Daniel, and Jesus Christ. I was fascinated by these stories. He talked about sin and the cross, repentance and forgiveness, salvation and eternity, death and resurrection, and works and grace in a way that kids could grasp. I was intrigued. I had never heard anything like this. I asked if he could lend me a Bible.

I started reading through the Bible, but it was difficult to understand so I asked him to teach me. So for once or twice a week for six months, he taught me the Scriptures and how to read it. At the end of those six months, he gave me a test. I passed. He then asked if I wanted to confess that I was a sinner, repent of my sins, and receive Jesus Christ as my Lord and Savior and publicly profess my faith. I said yes. In December 1955, at the age of 16, I was baptized in front of the same congregation that I used to constantly torment with my friends.

I continued to share with Sung's father that in college, my friends and I served at a new Presbyterian church (Hwikyung) near Kyung Hee University. I also served as President of the Korean Student Christian Movement on my campus and eventually as one of the national leaders of the movement in 1962. I was then appointed by Hwikyung Church's ruling elders as a deacon in January 1964, at the age of 24. This appeared to please Sung's father immensely: "Really? At such a young age? You must have strong faith in God. As far as I am concerned, faith in Him is the most important thing. If you are a man of faith, God will take care of everything for you." *This is not going so bad after all. Maybe he likes me.*

Towards the end of our time, I said, "Dr. Lee, although I have nothing to show you now, and nothing to give your daughter but my love, if you bless our marriage, and let us go to America to further our studies, I will do my best in taking good care of her with all my love, from the bottom of my heart, for the rest of my life." He had a big smile on his face. As was customary, I then knelt down and bowed to him with my head to the floor and thanked him. The meeting could not have gone better because he could not have been a kinder man. He hugged me and escorted me out of his study as the rest of the family was waiting for us. After bowing to Sung's mother and saying goodbye to the rest of the family, Sung and I left to a nearby café. *Phew. It was over!*

Sung's Escape from the North

While we were drinking coffee, waiting anxiously for the verdict of whether Sung's father would bless our marriage, I asked her to tell me more details about her family.

She said that they came down from the North in 1945 right after the August 15 liberation of Korea from the Japanese annexation. The Northern region of the Korean peninsula (now the Democratic People's Republic of Korea (DPRK) or North Korea) was immediately occupied by Soviet troops, under the agreement of the Great Powers. The Communist regime in the North was hostile to Christianity and began harassing and persecuting Christians.

Sung's family had a long Christian heritage – it was one of the first Christian families in the North's Hwang Hae Do region and Sung's father was a third-generation elder. Sung also grew up pretty affluent. Her father was one of the pioneering Western-medicine doctors in Korea and had a successful medical practice. Her mother was educated at the Teachers College of Seoul National University, and was a schoolteacher before she married Sung's father. She too came from a long line of Christians. Sung's family was an obvious target for persecution – they were Christians and they were prosperous (also owning a large grain field with a number of hired workers). One morning, Soviet troops arrived unannounced at her father's hospital, seized it, and, because of its size, made it into one of their regional headquarters. They also occupied a part of her house (which was adjacent to the hospital). In a manner of minutes, everything that her family owned had come under Soviet control. This was unspeakably unnerving to the family. It was both surreal and scary to Sung who, just a child at the time, would see Soviet troops in and around her home.

Sung's father began planning the family's escape. There was no other choice in his mind. He found the owner of a large fishing boat who, for a substantial fee, was willing to secretly take the family across the border and into the South on the Yellow Sea. Then, on the morning of the planned escape, Sung's father asked a Soviet commander for permission for his family to take a day trip to visit his and his wife's parents and extended family. Because this commander and his troops were particularly fond of and trusted Sung's father (he took great medical care of them), the commander gave his approval. That was the last day Sung saw her house. And all her belongings. To prevent any suspicion from the

Soviets, she and her family took nothing with them when they left their home – not even a bag of extra clothes or food. They left everything behind, except the clothes on their backs.

They first went to see Sung's grandparents where her father told them about the plan to escape. The next morning, after tearfully saying goodbye to them, they visited some other relatives as they made their way to the departure point. It was a fairly long journey to the small dock where the fishing boat was waiting for them. Night had already come. Everyone hurried onto the boat and went below deck. No one was to come out until the border had been crossed. And no one was to make any sound during the entire escape. It had to appear like nothing other than a simple fishing boat doing rounds on the Yellow Sea. In the dead of night, the boat disembarked. And in a few days, by God's grace, the border was crossed and the family arrived in Incheon, 40 miles from Seoul. The voyage was difficult and physically exhausting, but thankfully no one was hurt. Sung's father's plan was executed perfectly.

As the boat approached Incheon Harbor, the entire family came out onto the deck for the first time. There was celebration. There was hugging. Laughter. Prayers of thanksgiving. And tears. Although Sung was only four and half years old at the time, the entire scene is forever etched into her memory. She remembered what it smelled like when she saw Incheon Harbor. "It smelled like freedom," she told me.

Her father began practicing medicine in Yong San, Seoul, and was again very successful. Soon he was able to build a hospital clinic. But just as the family was finally feeling settled into their new surroundings, the Korean War broke out in 1950 and the family fled to the deep South (Busan), where they stayed until the hostilities ceased in 1953. As war refugees for three years, under constant fear of persecution by the Communists and their sympathizers, the family, by God's grace, did not suffer a single casualty. Upon their return to Seoul, all that was left of their father's hospital clinic and their adjacent home was a large, bombed-out hole. Again, the family had to start all over. Despite all this turmoil, Sung was able to attend one of the best girls' middle schools and high schools in the country (both Ewha), where she was an alto for the choir which won two consecutive national championships. She then went to Ewha Women's University, majored in English Literature and graduated as a four-year honor student. After graduation, she was hired, following a nationwide competition, by the Korean arm of UNESCO.

I asked about her siblings. She said that her oldest brother was one of the few survivors among the Marine Corps lieutenants during the Korean War, and was now a top ranking government official. A brother-in-law was a renowned surgeon and another brother-in-law was the president of a large corporation. All her siblings attended Ewha, Seoul, or Yonsei Universities. And all of them were delivered by their own father at his hospital! She added that her father continued to work at the hospital next to their home in Donam Dong, Seoul.

She told me that she loved coming home every day after work to spend time with her family. She never saw her mother and father fight, much less argue. They were a model couple to her. The best parents. She was especially close to her father; probably the closest out of all the kids. She said that her father was way ahead of his time in that he was very westernized, very affectionate, very open, and very funny. It was her father who encouraged her to attend Ewha (rather than Seoul National) and major in English and head to America for an advanced degree. "Now I met you," said Sung, "and we are both dreaming to go to America. How prophetic my father was."

The Family's Verdict

It was an incredibly moving story. But I could not help but feel more anxious (and pessimistic) about the future of our relationship – *why in the world would a family like that approve of someone like me? How could her father say yes to us?* After dropping Sung off, I returned home. Still no answer. I hardly slept that night. I asked my mom to pray for me and Sung.

The next day, Sung and I were to meet for lunch at a restaurant near UNESCO. When she walked in the restaurant, she had a huge smile on her beautiful face. It was the smile I fell in love with when I first met her. "My father approved." *Yes!* I wanted to scream, but had to control myself since we were in a public setting. It was the most exciting moment of my life. She told me that her father had rounded up the entire family after we left for the café and asked Sung's mother and all of Sung's siblings for their opinion. Everyone voiced their disapproval. Everyone. All legitimately wondered how I would be able to care for Sung. Understandably, her mother was very concerned seeing that I had nothing materially or financially to offer and, on top of that, I was taking her daughter away to America. After everyone had a chance to speak, it was Sung's father turn. He told them that he wholeheartedly approved of the relationship and our future marriage: "In all respects, he does not seem qualified to marry my daughter. Except one. That is his strong faith. I am confident that this faith will make him a great person and build a wonderful family. I have already seen his potential. He is a very sincere and faithful man. Sung will have a happy life."

But she didn't have a happy life for the first ten years of our marriage. Because of me.

Chapter 8

TRUE REPENTANCE

With Awakening Comes Repentance

During my time with God on Big Bear Mountain, I was also severely rebuked by the Holy Spirit for being so beholden to the face-saving culture of Korea. That culture, rooted in Confucianism, is dominant in the Northeastern region of Asia (especially Korea, Japan, and China), and can be destructive. One can waste so much of their life wondering what others think. I was no different. I spent a lot of time and energy on things that I did not care for, all to save face. I was in cultural bondage. And it was draining. And wasteful. And sinful. (I'm in no way suggesting that we should not be respectful, ethical, and peaceful in our relationships with others – we must be – but we must live our lives for Christ, not for anyone else). Instead of being attuned to what would please my heavenly Father, I was more sensitive to how others viewed me. This was caring too much about the outside of the cup, and not what was on the inside. This was another sin that I had to repent of.

I was also convicted of my bitterness towards those who had caused me pain – including those in the early years of my life in Korea. When I left Korea with Sung, I resolved never to return. And never to forgive. That society deeply wounded me because of my so-called handicaps and shortcomings (fatherless, poor, no Seoul National University), and I vowed to do everything it took to prove everyone wrong. Little did I realize – until Big Bear Mountain – that my passionate determination to do so, which I had justified as righting the wrongs in my life, only ended up hurting others, and now, was killing my soul.

The hurts, slights, humiliations, and "hans" in my heart were so embedded, so entrenched, so ingrained, so intertwined, and so cancerous, that forgiveness was a foreign concept to me. Yes, I heard sermons on forgiveness. Yes, I did Bible studies on forgiveness. Yes, as a Christian, I knew I was called to forgive. But no, I never forgave. And I never really repented of my unforgiving heart. *The pains in my life were too many and too deep, how could I possibly forgive?* I needed to be awakened that no one was more wronged than Christ, and yet He forgave. I needed to be reminded that each of my sins was a rejection of God, and yet, if I repent, God will forgive. *But how is it that I still couldn't forgive others?* I needed divine intervention to break through this rotten, unforgiving heart.

One by one, by God's grace, I was able to recall, through the Holy Spirit, not the sins that were committed against me, but all those that I had sinned against. What I did to them. When I wronged them. How I hurt them. God had given me an amazing gift of memory – a gift to remember names, dates, and events in my life. Even the most mundane incident many years ago can still be recalled with clarity. Every semester, in all my 38 years of teaching, I would memorize the names of my students (sometimes, up to 50) on the first day of class. That both impressed – and intimidated – my students. But I had perverted this gift by using it to keep a running list of all those who had wronged me. And now God was using this gift to rebuke me for all those that I had wronged.

Awakened to the wrongs that I had done to others, I was also awakened to God's forgiveness. The Holy Spirit enabled me to recall what Jesus said: "For if you forgive others their trespasses, your heavenly Father will also forgive you, but if you do not forgive others their trespasses, neither will your Father forgive your trespasses" (Matt. 6:14-15, ESV). As I held on to the fallen tree stump, this word shook me so traumatically that all of my pent-up anger, grudges, bitterness, and wounds were at once expelled out of my system by the Holy Spirit. I surrendered to Jesus Christ and His word. I was set free from the bondage of unforgiveness.

Dear, Lord, please forgive me for all the sins I have committed against you, my wife and children, my relatives, church leaders and fellow members, and my friends. I broke your heart and the hearts of many, especially my wife. Dear Lord, I repent of all these wicked sins with a broken and contrite heart. What can I say? I deserve to die. I deserve to be blotted out. I forgive all those who had wronged to me. I truly do. Please forgive me! Please forgive me for not forgiving others. Please wash away all the stains of my poor soul with your blood. Please have mercy on me!

Repentance, Not Just Confession

In response, God spoke to me. "Uproot them all!"

It was a command not just to verbally confess and acknowledge my sins, but to uproot them entirely. Repentance is pulling out sin by its roots. *Oh, how many times had I confessed my sin and immediately turned around to commit the same sin again and again?* God then showed me an image of a beautiful lawn. The grass was so green. Pristine. But I started seeing some weeds sprouting. Eventually, the weeds spread throughout the lawn. Then, I saw a worker mowing the grass and the lawn was beautiful again because everything was cut evenly – you couldn't tell there were weeds anymore. But soon the weeds would sprout again, and this time, they grew and spread faster. They covered the grass. Suffocated it. And now the grass was dying. It was a dreadful scene.

The Holy Spirit convicted me. *Unless the weeds are pulled out by their roots, not only will the weeds spread faster and grow stronger, but they will eventually kill the good grass. In the same way, sin will kill the soul unless it is pulled out by its roots. Every single sin, big or small, must be yanked out by its roots. Confession is only mowing the lawn. Repentance is uprooting and killing the weeds.*

I realized that up until that moment in my life, I only superficially confessed my sins, but never repented. I would commit the same sins over and over again because there was only confession, not repentance. True repentance involves pain, heartache, mourning, weeping, and brokenness, as our sins are nakedly exposed before the presence of a holy God. *How could I have become so sinful? How could I be so bad, so filthy?* The pain and mourning for me came from realizing how arrogant, prideful, lustful, and selfish I was. I had to cut off what had to be cut off and throw away what must be thrown away. *Please grant me your favor and the fullness of your mercy and forgive my sins!* I cried profusely. My body was spent. I had no strength left. My eyes were swollen from the tears. But by the power of the Holy Spirit, I repented one sin after another after another through the night. Never had I experienced anything like this. I was desperate. I was bold. I had nothing to lose. I was frail. I was heaving. I kept going. I kept repenting.

As the night wore on, I gained confidence knowing that my sins were being washed away by the blood of Jesus Christ. The Holy Spirit continued to assure me that my sins were being forgiven as I repented of them. The pain and mourning started to subside. I started to feel free. Free from the bondage of my sins. "In my anguish I cried to the LORD, and he answered by setting me free" (Ps. 118:5).

God's Forgiveness

I then earnestly pled to God to heal me. *Dear Jesus, I believe that you are my Savior and Lord. I know that even if I die right at this moment, you will accept me in your Kingdom. I know that whether I live or die, it is completely in your sovereign hands. I believe that you do all things for my good. I want to live a different life! For you! Please give me one more chance to live in this world for your glory. I wasted my life in living for me – give me a chance to live my life for you and you only. I resolve with all my heart that whatever you ask me to do, I will do it. Please heal my body. Please heal this wretched man. I want to live a life marked by loving you with all my heart and with all my soul and with all my strength. I resolve to commit my life to you and serve you wholeheartedly. Whatever you ask. Whatever you want. Please give me another chance to live.*

As I continued to pray, plead, and repent for hours, God challenged me in three ways. First, I took my health for granted. I realized that no matter how many goals and aspirations one has, none are attainable if you are physically ill. I did not serve the Lord faithfully and wholeheartedly when I was young and energetic. I assumed that I was going to have a long and healthy life. That I would have plenty of time to serve Him. Later. After I achieved all that I wanted to achieve. Now at the age of 37, I could barely drink water. I could hardly sleep. I had less than a year to live. *What a waste. What a shame.*

Dear God, please heal and restore my body so that I may serve you with all my strength and with all my heart and with all my mind. I am so sorry that I took my health for granted. I am so sorry that I did not take care of my body, the temple of God. Your temple. I'm so sorry that I used my body for my own glory, and not yours.

Second, I took my life for granted. Instead of treating my life on earth as precious, I had wasted it by complaining and arguing about received (mostly perceived) slights and injustices from society, from school, from the church, from my wife's family, from my own family. Instead of using the gifts that God had given me for His Kingdom, I wasted them with grumbling and conflict. I didn't value others. Only if it served my purposes, if it saved my and my family's face, if it relieved (temporarily) a "han," and if it was used to right an injustice. Outside of that, I disregarded others. Edifying them did not matter to me. Encouraging them did not matter to me. That God had sent His Son to die for them did not matter to me. That they were citizens of heaven did not matter to me. What mattered to me was me. The Lord was chastising me for this.

Dear Lord, please grant me one more chance to live so that I may live a life worthy of your calling and extend your gifts that you have given me to others to the fullest extent for your glory.

Third, I took Jesus for granted. God spoke this to me. "You are so precious to me that I freely gave up my most precious Son, Jesus Christ, to die on the cross to save you from eternal death and to give you eternal life. But up until now, what have you done for me? Where is the fruit of your faith? For all that you've done, for all that you've accomplished, name one person who willingly died for you? I wanted so much to adopt you as my child into my Kingdom that I sent my one and only Son, Jesus Christ, who was without sin, to be tortured and crucified so that you may live. You met me in 1955 when you received my Son as your Savior and Lord. Today is June 24, 1977. For whom have you lived for these past 22 years? For what have you lived for these past 22 years?"

I was, at that moment, broken into a thousand pieces. I was speechless. I could say nothing in my defense. I felt completely crushed and emptied. Like my past life had no longer existed. And then this peace that I had never experience before began to come over me. As if being smashed was freeing. Freed from my old life. And its sins. Like being able to start all over again. From scratch. I had to be broken into bits for me to truly become a new creation (Rom. 12:2; 2 Cor. 5:17).

Dear Father, please grant me another chance. Please heal my illness. I know that I have been cleansed by the blood of Jesus Christ and I am now whiter than snow. I know that I have been set free by your Truth. I will never be able to pay you back for the incredible love and grace that you have poured upon this wretched man. But please allow me to live the life that I should have lived - according to your will, Lord. Heavenly Father, please grant me one more chance.

I kept pleading to God in this way. Clutching that fallen tree stump as if I were Jacob at the Jabbok River, stubbornly wrestling with God. Determined for an answer from Him. *Father, I resolve not to leave this mountain until you show me a distinct sign that you are going to give me another life to live in this world – even if I die here on this mountain!*

It was now dawn.

Then a vision came to me in my prayer. A grand Being clothed with bright, shining white linen with a long train pulled me into His chest and embraced me. He gently patted me on my back. Three times. With each pat He said, "I forgive you, I forgive you, and I forgive you." Even though I could not see this majestic Man's face, I knew I had been forgiven – and healed. With all the strength I could muster, I burst out with joy and thanksgiving, *This is it! I shall live again! My Heavenly Father will give me another life! Thank you, Father!*

This vision was the defining moment of my life. It was not a fantasy. I was not delusional. It was vivid. It was real. It was supernatural. It was God. It cannot be explained any other way. This was His way of answering my prayer. This was his way of assuring me that I would be healed. This was the sign that I asked Him for. This was the grace of God.

With Repentance, Comes Revival

Exhausted, but encouraged, I leaned on the fallen tree to gather myself up. I saw the sun starting to rise over the mountains in the east. It was glorious. Magnificent. I took several deep breaths and raised my hands toward the rising sun, worshipping the Lord. A new day. A new beginning. A new life. As I headed back slowly to my cabin, I began singing the hymn, "Where Jesus Is, Tis Heaven":

> Since Christ my soul from sin set free,
> This world has been a Heav'n to me;
> And 'mid earth's sorrows and its woe,
> 'Tis Heav'n my Jesus here to know.
>
> [Chorus] O hallelujah, yes, 'tis Heav'n,
> 'Tis Heav'n to know my sins forgiv'n,
> On land or sea, what matters where?
> Where Jesus is, 'tis Heaven there.
>
> Once Heaven seemed a far off place,
> Till Jesus showed His smiling face;
> Now it's begun within my soul,
> 'Twill last while endless ages roll.
>
> What matters where on earth we dwell?
> On mountain top, or in the dell,
> In cottage, or a mansion fair,
> Where Jesus is, 'tis Heaven there.[35]

This was a familiar hymn to me – but familiar in the way where you know about something, but you don't think much about it, so it doesn't mean much to you. Now, as I arrived at the door of my cabin, tears were streaming down my face as each phrase and every word of the song moved me like never before. Sorrows. Woe. Mountaintop. Sin. Forgiven. Set free. Smiling face. Jesus. Hallelujah. This was my song of worship to Him. This was my song of praise. And it became the song of my life. One that I, to this day, sing over and over again in remembrance of my time on Big Bear Mountain, "where Jesus" was with me.

My chains were broken. My soul was restored. My heart was

revived. My mind was renewed. My life was transformed. I was free (John 8:31-36). I was born again. I was a new creation. I had experienced the immeasurable love of Christ (Eph. 3:17-19). I had encountered the unfathomable grace of God. From my awakening and my repentance came my revival. This personal revival – this supernatural transformation – we cannot know, we cannot learn, we cannot understand unless we encounter and experience it for ourselves. Unless it is all God.

After some rest in the cabin, I walked to a public pay phone to call my wife. She had not heard from me for seven days. I could only imagine how worried and anxious she was. She picked up the phone. She was crying.

She asked, "How are you?"

I recited to her Psalm 118:17, "I will not die but live, and will proclaim what the Lord has done." "Yeobo! God will give me a new life to live. I am a going to live!" I briefly explained to her my encounter with God at the fallen tree.

I then asked her to pick me up as soon as possible.

Chapter 9

THE ROAD TO RECONCILIATION

With Forgiveness, Comes Reconciliation

My wife arrived at the cabin about three hours later. Our exchange was deeply emotional. We embraced. We held on. We cried. Many of Sung's tears were from anxiety and fear. She was still worried. She had been discussing funeral arrangements with our pastor only weeks ago. She mentioned that I looked skinnier, if that was even possible.

As we made our way down the mountain's winding roads in our car, I told my wife all that had happened, how I wrestled with God, the vision, the embrace, how he forgave me, the sun, the hymn, everything. I then asked my wife to pull the car over to the side. Looking out the window, I noticed the splendor of the flowers, trees, and mountains that lined the road. None of these were noticed in the drive the week before. I held Sung's hands and asked her to forgive me for all the pain and suffering I had caused her. I apologized for all the heartache she endured because of my pride, inferiority complex, ego, and selfishness. I said sorry for being so difficult and so stubborn.

Before I encountered God on Big Bear Mountain, my old self acted like most Korean men as far as not knowing how to ask my wife to forgive me when I did something wrong. Apologies can be a foreign concept to us. Especially if you have an inferiority complex. To do so would be seen as audacious, out of character and worse, displaying weakness. It was not in my nature to concede anything. Even if I knew I was wrong. But as Christians, we are called to be different. We are called to seek forgiveness. Without forgiving and seeking forgiveness, there can be no reconciliation. Wounds will never heal and relationships can never be restored unless there is forgiveness.

In the car, I shared with her one sin in particular that God had awakened me to at Big Bear. One that completely broke me. Crushed me. One that, when it was revealed, I could not bear to see it. My work load in graduate school was daunting. On top of my regular graduate coursework, I had to take a slew of prerequisites (having had no background in American Government and history), and complete weekly writing assignments and summaries for my Friday mentoring sessions with Dr. Lammers. There always seemed to be some term paper, some written review, some written presentation or report that was due. So being able to type was crucial to my survival. But I couldn't type. I never learned how. But thankfully, my wife was an excellent typist and was well trained in English (being an English literature major herself). Except for the final version of my doctoral dissertation, she typed (and sometimes edited) every written piece of work that I submitted at USC. She was my priceless asset.

During the final weeks of a semester, it was crunch time for me, and Sung was especially busy. After bathing Sharon and putting her to bed, she would work on my papers and assignments, usually until two or three in the morning. One night, she finished typing a 30-page paper at around 2:00 a.m. and handed it to me. I noticed some typos. Sung rarely made typos. She must have been so tired and exhausted after coming home from work at 5:00 p.m., dealing with Sharon, preparing dinner, putting Sharon down, and typing for hours and hours. But her weariness was the last thing on my mind. I was the only thing on my mind. Being the best was all that I cared about. And I was not pleased. At all. Without an ounce of thankfulness, I yelled, "How can I turn in this paper to my professor later this afternoon with so many errors? I need to get an A on this paper!" She responded, "If the content of the paper is good, you will have an A. Don't worry. Just submit it."

One of the things that angered me the most was when I felt that my wife was talking back to me. I realized during my time at Big Bear

Mountain that this came from my "hans" and my own inferiority complex towards Sung and her family. I felt very insecure in light of her accomplished family and background. It didn't help that some members of her family wouldn't even call me by my own Korean name, Choon Keun, but would mockingly address me as a "spring root" (in Chinese characters, Choon means "spring" and Keun means "root"). This inferiority complex made me increasingly stubborn, refusing any financial assistance from her family. Even when we were just hanging on by a thread, I wouldn't accept anything from Sung's father. He offered. I refused. This in turn caused greater hardship and pain for Sung. "Yeobo," I would say, "I know he wants to help us, but I am not going to accept your father's money. I don't want to hear later that we were able to succeed because of your family's help. We will work harder to overcome our situation by ourselves. If you accept even a dollar from him, you may pack your bags and go back to Korea. I am sorry, I cannot accept anything from your family." I was that stubborn.

So I proceeded to take the 30-typed pages of my term paper and ripped them up to pieces and threw it in the trash. Right in front of my wife. My wife didn't say a word. She bit her bottom lip and walked over to the typewriter. She sat down in front of it for awhile, her head hanging low. She took a deep breath. She then took my original manuscript and put it on the stand. With tears streaming down her face, she started typing again.

The harsh reality that I was awakened to at Big Bear was that this despicable episode was not an isolated incident, but one of many instances where I had sinned against Sung. Although I never physically abused or hit her, I was a wicked husband. She could have easily left me and been completely justified in doing so. In fact, I later learned that Sung was seriously considering leaving home with the children several times. My behavior was too much for her to bear. She called her father and told him she wanted a divorce. Her father replied, "Choon Keun is not a bad person, and he comes from a very humble and sad background. There is a lot of bitterness. But you have been nurtured in a loving family full of joy and peace. He was not. If you could not forgive him and embrace him, who could and would? Then, he may be lost forever. My beloved daughter, Sung Mai, please have pity on him and love him and cover him with all your patience. Someday the time will come for him to change." *How prophetic my father-in-law was.* After that conversation, Sung relented from seeking a divorce, forgave me in her heart, and vowed to be patient to the very end.

My wife's steadfast love and patience was rewarded as we held hands and I begged for her forgiveness in our car on the side of the road.

"Sung, I know I have caused you much pain all these years because of my insecurity, ambition, pride, and selfishness. I am so sorry for what I have done to you. Would you please forgive me?" We cried again. It was a moment of tenderness, vulnerability, and transparency that we hadn't shared in a very long time.

Then she hugged me, "Yes, I forgive you. I almost forgot about that typing incident."

"Thank you! I earnestly pray and plea to God that from now on until the day I die, I want to be the best husband that any woman could ever wish for." This was the promise I made to her.

As soon as we arrived home, I saw Sharon and Paul waiting anxiously for me on the couch. We ran to each other and I squeezed them. Tight. Overjoyed, I put them on my lap and asked them to forgive me, to forgive their father for being too hard on them. I told them about what I had experienced at Big Bear and how God had awakened me to the sins I committed against my children – the yelling, the spankings, the anger, the impatience.

"Dad, we are sorry too."

"I pray and plea to God that from now on until I die, I want to be the best father any child could ever wish for." It felt good to be home.

After a brief nap, I called my senior pastor, Rev. Chun Il Cho, of the Korean Philadelphia Presbyterian Church in Los Angeles, where I served as an ordained deacon.

"Deacon Kim, how are you?! The whole church has been continually praying for you. Are you okay?"

"Pastor Cho, I am going to live."

"Deacon Kim, I would like to stop by and see you tonight." Pastor Cho and his wife and other members of the church came over to pray for me. I asked my pastor for his forgiveness. I shared that I had complained about the church and about him. I confessed other sins where I wronged him. I promised him that I would be a faithful and committed member and deacon, serving the Lord and him in our church. One of the members who accompanied the pastor and his wife to my home – a pastor's widow, Mrs. Anna Kim – told me that she had prayed for me for many hours earlier in the day.

"In fact," she added, "each person in our church has been assigned a specific prayer time so that you will be prayed for 24 hours a day. We've been doing this ever since you went up to the mountain."

I had the chance to see Mrs. Anna in 2010 (she's in Chicago now) and she is still the powerful prayer warrior that I had always remembered. She's over 90 years old now, but even to this day, she never misses her church's daily dawn prayer meetings. She was so happy to see me and my wife, she hugged us and planted a huge kiss on my cheek. Whenever I see former church members, usually when I'm in the Los Angeles area, it's like seeing family. The warmth and love that they have for me is so humbling. Some of the elderly members who daily prayed for my healing are now with God in His Kingdom. Tears of gratitude come easy when I think of them. But tears never came during my first ten years in America. I did not have time to cry. I was so consumed with survival and success and proving everyone wrong. It wasn't until those seven days on the mountain that I cried. And ever since then, I have often shed tears of thanksgiving whenever I think of these church members.

I asked Pastor Cho if he would graciously give me about ten minutes to share my testimony after his sermon this coming Sunday. He thought that would be a good idea. That Sunday, in front of the entire congregation, I took to the podium and said, "Words cannot express how thankful I am to all of you for your prayers for me. Many of you have prayed, every day, that I would be healed. I believe your prayers have been answered. Through my prayers and repentance, I not only received God's forgiveness, but I also received God's promise that I am going to live a new life. As it says in Psalm 118:17, 'I will not die but live, and will proclaim what the LORD has done.' I am going to live to proclaim His amazing love, grace, righteousness, power and glory to this generation and generations to come. Please keep me accountable in that regard. Please forgive me for my arrogant, selfish, complaining, grumbling, and difficult behavior that has hurt many of you. I have already asked Pastor Cho to forgive me for all my wrongdoings. Now, I am asking you to do the same. I am so sorry for what I have done to you and to the church. I will be in contact with specific brothers and sisters in Christ that I have specifically sinned against and will ask for their forgiveness. Please keep praying for a speedy recovery from my liver disease. I will live and I will be different by God's grace."

I then briefly shared my encounter with God and the vision He revealed to me. Later, I learned that some of the congregants in attendance thought I had lost my mind and was hallucinating on the mountain given my frail physical state. *That may have been a vision from God but how could he possibly survive this? How could he be so confident – just look at him. He really doesn't look well.* I could see why they thought that on that Sunday morning. I'm sure my wife had similar thoughts. Who could blame her? My appearance had not changed much – in fact, you could say

I looked worse since I still was unable to eat much. It was still difficult to sleep. It was still difficult to drink. I was still weak. I was still 120 pounds. I still resembled a pregnant woman.

Yes, I still really didn't look well. But ultimately God's gracious promise was fulfilled.

Chapter 10

THE ROAD TO RECOVERY

Spiritual Redemption and Physical Recovery

Assured that my sins were forgiven, I now put my faith in God to restore my health. He delivered. In about a week my stomach began to shrink and I was able to drink fluids without much discomfort. Without any medicine. It was astonishing. After consulting extensively with Dr. Harter, I embarked on a strict dietary regimen. Although not officially sanctioned by the American Medical Association, there were clinical studies which showed that the diet program was effective against epilepsy and certain cancers. After praying about it with Sung, we decided that this would be the way to go. We were fully committed. Sung even quit her job to devote herself completely to my new diet for a year. (Because my dean and colleagues covered my courses for me, Pepperdine was generous enough to keep me on salary and pay me every month).

The similarities between this diet and the diet of Daniel and his three friends were striking. This gave me even more hope. In Daniel 1, when Jerusalem fell, Daniel and his friends were taken to Babylon as prisoners of war. Daniel resolved not to defile himself with the royal food and wine of the Babylonian court and asked the chief official for permission not to defile himself this way: "Please test your servants for ten days: Give us nothing but vegetables to eat and water to drink. Then compare our appearance with that of the young men who eat the royal food, and treat your servants in accordance with what you see" (Dan. 1:12-13). At the end of the ten days, Daniel and his companions looked healthier and better nourished than any of the men who consumed the royal food. Daniel was truly before his time when it came to the benefits of natural, "organic" foods.

Water, vegetables, and prayer (as Daniel was a man of prayer, praying three times a day towards Jerusalem (Dan. 6:10)). That would be the theme of my recovery program. Water, vegetables, and prayer.

Dr. Harter's dietary instructions were as follows:

1. Drink a glass of juice squeezed out of five apples first thing in the morning.
2. Start drinking 12 ounces of distilled water every hour on the hour 12 times a day (if my stomach could take it; start slow).
3. Start drinking 12 ounces of freshly-squeezed lemon juice every other hour on the hour 12 times a day (if my stomach allowed).
4. 43 tablets of natural vitamin supplements, including Liverflex, three times a day.

By the grace of God, I was able to gradually increase my intake of water and lemon juice. Weeks before, I wasn't able to hold anything down. Now, I could tolerate the constant drinking. Within a month, my stomach shrank almost to its normal size, enabling me to reach the level of intake required by the diet. It was not easy. I was always using the restroom. But I was feeling better. I was sleeping better. The water helped to expel the toxins and impurities from my system and the lemon served as a cleansing agent for my blood. The vitamin supplements (all 43 of them!) were introduced because I couldn't eat solids. These vitamins were specially processed (at 60 degrees below zero Fahrenheit) and were not available in regular health stores.

I was on Dr. Harter's diet for six straight months, without skipping a day. Each week, my wife and I would visit Dr. Harter who would test my urine and blood and examine my progress. He was surprised by the speed of my improvement and suggested that I start drinking fruit smoothies (constituting three glasses of a fruit juice blended with seasonal fruits and fiber) every morning in lieu of the apple juice. For lunch, he instructed me to eat salads with spinach, green onions, beets, carrots, avocado, cucumber, radish, bean sprouts and other fresh vegetables with an olive oil and vinaigrette dressing (olive oil also serves as a cleansing agent). For dinner, but only if I could handle it, he suggested fish (such as grilled salmon) with lemon, along with some starch (usually a baked potato or sweet potatoes).

Dr. Harter's regimen required a lot of discipline (and prayer). It took a lot of patience knowing that it would take time before there was real recovery. It also took a tremendous amount of teamwork with my wife. It was Sung who was tasked to follow Dr. Harter's instructions, pouring the water and lemon juice, making all the smoothies, salads, and dinners. She would never let me stray from the diet and always kept to schedule. Remarkably, my tolerance for solids began to improve (altering the types of supplements I needed to take) and my appetite was increasing. I began to feel hungry again. I was gaining strength. I was also gaining weight. Noticeably. At the start of 1978, my body was beginning to fill out. It was unbelievable. I even had the strength to start teaching again that spring semester. Colleagues were saying it was a miracle. It was. By the summer of 1978, I had returned to my normal weight of 165 pounds. I felt like I was at full strength. Dr. Harter couldn't believe his eyes. "Dr. Kim, I think it's time for you to see your primary doctor to confirm your recovery."

I returned to Glendale Community Hospital to pay a visit to Dr. Wakelin. He ran a battery of tests for me, including X-rays, liver scans, sonograms, an ultrasound, urine and blood work. A few days later, we saw him again to discuss the results. As soon as my wife and I walked into his office, he couldn't hold it in.

"Choon, you're supposed to be dead. You are completely different from the person I saw in October of 1976. Your liver looks normal, looks healthy. This . . . this is a miracle. What happened?"

"It's a long story, Dr. Wakelin."

Whatever he felt about the brief account I then gave him of my supernatural experience at Big Bear and subsequent recovery I do not know, but Dr. Wakelin was ever the gracious and loving gentlemen and was, more than anything, elated to see that his patient was doing well. Just to be safe, he sent me to see an internationally renowned liver specialist whose practice was at St. Jude Hospital in Orange County. Dr. Lloyd Herndon had more tests for me and performed a liver biopsy. The biopsy was optional, but my wife and I opted for it to get medical closure on the entire ordeal, even though the procedure could be painful. Placed under anesthesia, Dr. Herndon made an incision just below my navel and filled my stomach with air. The doctor then removed some tissue from my liver. The procedure was not complicated, but when I awoke in the recovery room, there was excruciating pain in my belly as the air that was used to fill my stomach caused severe swelling in my abdomen muscles. It took a month before the pain went away.

A week later, we returned to Dr. Herndon's office. He had nothing but great news. "Dr. Kim, you will live a long life. Your liver is in top shape. You can do all the things you used to do before you got sick – play tennis, jog, swim, run around with your kids. I want you to know that this is, and I never ever say this, this is a miracle." My wife and I cried. Our hearts melted with thanksgiving. We hugged Dr. Herndon. We praised God.

From awakening to repentance to revival. From darkness to dawn. From despair to joy. From brokenness to healing. From mourning to dancing. From a death sentence to full physical recovery. From the impossible to the possible.

All by the grace, power, and love of Jesus Christ.

Chapter 11

A NEW LIFE

I wrote down a total of 52 pages of sins that I committed. I repented of them. And they were all forgiven by God on Big Bear Mountain. My relationship with Jesus Christ was restored. I became His child again (John 1:12). A co-heir with Christ (Rom. 8:17). To memorialize my freedom from the bondage of these sins, I later placed these 52 pages in my fireplace and lit a match. As I watched the flames, I was reminded of Christ's complete forgiveness and knew I could start anew.

The Measureless Love of Christ

At Big Bear Mountain I caught a glimpse of how wide, how long, how high, and how deep is Christ's love (Eph. 3:18). As I was meditating on the love of my Savior (Rom. 8:35-39) after returning from the cabin, I could not escape from the work of Christ on the cross. Everything that I had read, sung, or had reflected on pointed me to the cross. The cross was always on my mind. It was always on the tip of my tongue. In my quiet time, as I looked upon the tree of Calvary, I wrote this prayer:

> *Dear Jesus, thank you for your indescribable mercy and unfathomable love that was shown by shedding your blood on that cross. All the shame, all the pain, all for my sin. As the only Son of the omniscient, omnipotent, almighty, and sovereign God, you had all the power to quash Satan. Yet you willingly obeyed your Father and was slaughtered as a lamb. Dear God, just as your Son, Jesus Christ, obediently drank the cup and endured the greatest suffering to fulfill your plan of redemption, I earnestly pray for obedience to follow your word and your way even in the midst of my suffering. Please anoint and enable my obedience.*

Even though you are without sin or blemish, even though you are the Truth and all-knowing and all-powerful, you never sought to defend yourself to the Jews or the Romans, but instead asked your Father to forgive those who were torturing and killing you. Dear Lord, you died for sinners and even forgave a wretch like me! Please bless me by enabling me to love you with all my heart and mind all the days of my life, and never forget what you have done for me.

Apart from you, there can be no forgiveness, no redemption, no salvation, no life, no purpose, and no victory over death. You showed me the ultimate love on the cross. As this sinner looks upon the cross, I place my past, present, and future life on it and fall into the unending ocean of your love. I pray that you would fill my heart with love, grace, forgiveness, obedience, humility, patience and the power of the cross. Indeed, please remove my heart and in its place transplant your heart. Please restore me and lead me to live a new life with this heart.

In my meditations after Big Bear, I would often sing the hymn, The Love of God:

"The love of God is greater far, than tongue or pen can ever tell,
It goes beyond the highest star, and reaches to the lowest hell;
The guilty pair, bow down to care, God gave His Son to win;
His erring child He reconciled, and pardoned from his sin

[Refrain]:
O love of God, how rich and pure! How measureless and strong!
It shall forevermore endure, the saints' and angels' song.

"Could we with ink the ocean fill, and were the skies of parchment made,

Were every stalk on earth a quill, and every man a scribe by trade;
To write the love of God above, would drain the ocean dry;
Nor could the scroll contain the whole, tho' stretched from sky to sky.[36]

Before Big Bear Mountain, all the head knowledge that I had obtained about God's love had minimal impact on my life. "Revival" meetings, conferences, sermons, Bible studies, quiet times, and memorized verses were helpful, but they did not bring about true transformation. I simply did not love others as Jesus commanded. Yes, I could be nice, civil, cordial, and kind, but this was more of a "religious love," a forced "love" out of Christian duty and obligation. I did not love these people as I loved myself. I loved myself and what I wanted to accomplish. It was only until I encountered God at Big Bear that I was changed. From the inside out. It was the central moment of my life.

By allowing me to personally experience the breadth, depth, width, and height of God's love through His forgiveness and restoration, God enabled me to say prayers such as, *Lord, will you enlarge the borders of my heart to their fullest extent through experiencing your love every single day, so that I may be able to extend this love to any person that I come into contact with the heart of Christ and the help of the Holy Spirit.* This enlargement process is not easy. It can actually be quite painful. In my case, it took a medically terminal illness to truly experience and know His transformative love. It's also not easy to love people that don't love you back, don't get along with you, or don't care for you. But we must. Jesus enlarged His heart to the greatest extent for those who rejected Him to the point where His heart was torn and crushed on the cross. He was forsaken (Matt. 26:38). This was cosmically agonizing. This was love.

So having reconciled my vertical relationship with God, I turned my attention to restoring my horizontal relationships with others. I realized that the only way to love them with the love of

Christ was to ask the people I had wronged for their forgiveness. As difficult as this was, I was convicted by the Holy Spirit to start right away. I met with friends, colleagues, students, congregants, and church leaders to apologize and ask for their forgiveness. For those that I couldn't meet face-to-face, I telephoned or wrote letters to them. For those that had already passed away, I repented and prayed for their families. It was all pretty humbling. And at times, awkward, uncomfortable, and tense. But God gave me the courage, perseverance, and inner peace and security to seek reconciliation and enlarge the borders of my heart in this way. By His grace I was able to not only restore friendships, but build deeper relationships with many of these people.

God loved me so much that He struck me with a deadly illness, allowed me to realize that I was the worst of sinners, convicted me to repent, healed me in the deepest parts of my heart, brought me back into Him warm embrace, and enabled me to truly love others. I became a new creation (2 Cor. 5:17). Such transformation can't be brought about with just the head – there must be a supernatural, personal, and authentic encounter with God where the process of discovering, grasping and experiencing the width, depth, height, and length of His love begins to take place. It does not have to be as dramatic as Big Bear Mountain or involve a life-threatening situation, but unless the love of Christ is truly experienced and penetrates the soul, we cannot be His witnesses, we cannot testify to His grace, and we cannot demonstrate to the world the power of the Holy Spirit. My personal encounter with God – which brought a new identification as His rescued child and the assurance that He is always with me (Ps. 118:6) – made me more bold and courageous in proclaiming His love, mercy, power, holiness, magnificence, and glory. If nothing can separate me from his love (Rom. 8:35-39), how could I not be?

My Mustache Memorial

So why the mustache? It's a question I often get. After I was fully recovered from my liver disease, my wife asked, "Honey, you don't have any wrinkles on your face but your graying mustache makes you look older. Why don't you just shave it off?" Sharon and Paul overheard their mom and agreed: the mustache that I had since 1977 had to go. Plus, they said, it made my kisses too ticklish. "Too prickly too," added Sharon. At that moment, I took Sung and the children by their hands and sat them down. I apologized first for not telling them the one secret I had with God. This secret was the only thing that I ever kept from my wife.

In Luke 17:11-19, there is the account of Jesus and 10 leprous men. "Now on His way to Jerusalem, Jesus traveled along the border between Samaria and Galilee. As He was going into a village, ten men who had leprosy met Him. They stood at a distance and called out in a loud voice, 'Jesus, Master, have pity on us!' When He saw them, He said, 'Go, show yourselves to the priests', And they went, and they were cleansed." Lepers were treated as the ultimate outcasts. They were shunned. They were separated from the rest of society. Hopeless. Powerless. Helpless. Once these 10 lepers were healed by Christ's mercy, they had to show themselves to the priests for examination and confirmation that they were completely healed (to be considered "cleansed"). Upon doing so, the priests allowed the 10 men to return and be reintroduced into their villages. They could live a normal life again. But how many of them gave thanks to the Lord? "One of them, when he saw he was healed, came back, praising God in a loud voice. He threw himself at Jesus's feet and thanked Him – and he was a Samaritan. Jesus asked, 'Were not all ten cleansed? Where are the other nine? Has no one returned to give praise to God except this foreigner?' Then He said to him, 'Rise and go; your faith has made you well.'" Ten lepers cried out, ten lepers were healed, ten men were no longer outcasts, ten men could go back to their homes. But just one came back to say thanks to the One who healed them. The other nine never looked back.

This account resonated with me, especially since I too was healed of a deadly disease by the One who healed the ten lepers. I did not want to be like those who I had seen were incredibly sick and made promises to God that if He cured them, they would commit their lives to Christ and then, after regaining their health and strength by God's grace, pushing Him back to the margins of their lives. I did not want to treat Him like some genie in a bottle or just a doctor who's on call. I did not want to say this prayer, "Lord, if you do this for me, then I will honor your name as a faithful servant, and all the glory will be returned to you," and then, upon my recovery, go back to the same old life, same old story. I did not want to be a conditional bargainer with God. All too often I have seen many who would diligently pray for God to bless their businesses, professional pursuits, earning potential, and employment prospects, and in return, they vow to wholeheartedly serve Him and His church and the expansion of His Kingdom. Yet when they become "successful" and achieve what they want, they become too busy or too tired (because of being too busy) or too distracted by the world. They forget. They forget their promises. They forget God's blessing. They forget God's grace. They forget God.

I did not want to break my Heavenly Father's heart in this way. I wanted to be like the one leper who returned to Jesus and didn't forget. I wanted to commit my life to Christ Jesus. I wanted to be different than what I was. But I knew that I could not do it by my own resolve. I knew that on my own, it would be too easy for me to fall back, too easy for me to throw away my encounter with God like a pair of well-worn shoes. No matter how hard I would try, I was still a sinner.

Dear Lord, you can do anything. You forgave me. You saved me. You healed me. *You gave me a new life. And Lord, I don't ever want to forget these truths. Please fill me with your Holy Spirit so I won't forget. Please let this Spirit reign in me. Please let this Spirit empower me to live every day for you. Please let me not go back to how I was.* As I was praying this prayer, an idea dawned on me. I began to wonder whether there was something that would constantly remind me of God's love that was poured out on me at Big Bear Mountain, that would enable me to always remember God giving me another life to live. *What about my mustache?* When I was suffering from my liver disease, I was so weak that I couldn't muster the strength to shave. When my mustache and beard grew too long, I would ask my wife to shave me. I decided to keep my mustache as a memorial to God, as a symbolic reminder for what He did for me. I felt that God was pleased with my decision.

I'm sure there are only a handful of people who don't look in the mirror while they are getting ready to head off to work. I'm not one of them. Every morning I take a shower and look in the mirror to prepare for the day. Whether I'm brushing my teeth, combing my hair, or shaving my beard area, I'm looking in the mirror. And every morning when I see my mustache in my reflection, I am always reminded of what God has done for me, especially on that day, June 24, 1977, and I recite the following out loud to Him: *Thank you, Lord for assuring your salvation for my life. Thank you, Lord for giving me another life in this world. Thank you, Lord for giving me today to live! Therefore, let it be productive, multiplying 30, 60, or 100 times in every aspect of my life today and forever, by your exceedingly abundant grace, love, power, and wisdom for your Kingdom and glory!*

When my wife and children heard this, they hugged me. My wife was misty-eyed. Everyone agreed: the mustache was staying. Ever since then, the only other time I did not have a mustache was when I had lost all my body hair in 2004 due to the effects of chemotherapy (but after being miraculously healed from cancer, my mustache made its return at the end of that year and is still going strong, although now it is mostly white).

After my full recovery, God began to work through this unworthy servant. He replaced my desire for worldly success with a commitment to see Christ glorified. He enabled me to bear and bring much fruit for and through my family, church, profession, and many new endeavors that He appointed me to do. He specifically called me to offer my body as a living sacrifice, holy and pleasing to Him, to the younger generations, challenging them not to waste their lives as I did before June 1977, and raising them to be leaders and Christ's ambassadors to further God's Kingdom. I did not know what this would look like, but I simply obeyed my Lord.

With a love for teaching already established, God gave me an immense passion for the next generations and began to open doors for me to proclaim His love. He sent me to share my testimony with hundreds of U.S. college and university campuses, thousands of churches around the world, and 56 nations. In the past 30 years I've traveled more than 3.2 million miles to awaken the hearts of His people, challenge the younger generations, and reach lost souls. God has done amazing work. I never had the slightest idea that God would have such plans for my new life. That He would allow me to be a part of something like this. It is indescribable just thinking that He would use this simple professor who was on the brink of death in this way. It is beyond comprehension. It cannot be humanly explained. And that means it is all God. *Hallelujah!*

However, sometimes we forget that it is all Him. We are, after all, human and sinful. When I was praised for my accomplishments, or for my sermons and messages, or the lives that have been changed, it was tempting to take some share of the credit. The ego feels stroked. The pride factor goes up. But when I look in the mirror, and see my mustache, there is God's gentle voice reminding me, "Beloved John, I healed you. I granted you eternal salvation. I gave you a new life to live for my glory and expand My Kingdom. You are my child and my Son's ambassador. I have poured out my Spirit and power to enable you to proclaim my word, my love, my grace, my righteousness, my glory, my Son, His cross, my power, and my salvation to this generation and the generations to come. You and your family have been abundantly and exceedingly blessed in every way. Have you forgotten my grace? Have you forgotten that it is I who is doing these things through you?" I then immediately kneel down and ask for His forgiveness. I repent. I thank God for His forgiveness, for awakening me to my sins, and for renewing our relationship again. I then recite out loud my daily "mustache" prayer.

Who knew that such an insignificant thing as a mustache can be of such help to me in keeping my relationship pure before God and reminding me of His unfailing love? God did.

PART 2
GOD'S BLESSINGS

Chapter 12

TRUE FREEDOM

Freedom in Christ

I was now an eagle set free from its cage. Soaring in the air on two powerful wings (Isa. 40:31). It was freedom that I had never experienced before. It was joy and hope that I had never known before. Freedom from the chains of idolatry and sin. New-found freedom in Christ.

> "So Jesus said to the Jews who had believed in him, 'If you abide in my word, you are truly my disciples, and you will know the truth, and the truth will set you free.' They answered Him, we are offspring of Abraham and have never been enslaved to anyone. How is it that you say, 'You will become free'? Jesus answered them, 'Truly, truly, I say to you, everyone who practices sin is a slave to sin. The slave does not remain in the house forever; the son remains forever. So if the Son sets you free, you will be free indeed.'" (John 8:31-36, ESV).

> "Jesus said to him, 'I am the way, and the truth, and the life. No one comes to the Father except through me!'" (John 14:6, ESV).

I prayerfully resolved to live life each day in the Truth, that is Christ Jesus. This freedom in the Truth cannot ever be taken away. It is not granted by any man or given by any man-made institution, but it is from God through Jesus Christ. This freedom is not to be confused with the freedom that humanity and nations have justly sought, fought for, earned, and enjoyed throughout civilization. That freedom – of the political or democratic type – can, because of sin, eventual lead to corruption and a morally bankrupt cultural system, where doing whatever makes you "feel good" regardless of the consequences is an acceptable, if not lauded, lifestyle. This is not freedom in the Truth.

Our nation's Declaration of Independence poignantly states, "... that all men are created equal, that they are endowed by their Creator with certain unalienable Rights, that among these are Life, Liberty and the pursuit of Happiness..." and the U.S. Constitution guarantees our civil liberties and freedom. Many lives have been lost and resources spent to protect this freedom. World War II. The Civil War. Freedom in this sense was, and is, not free. Dear prices have been paid to secure this freedom we enjoy in America. It is a freedom that I cherish and celebrate and, I believe, to be emulated around the world. And rightfully so. But it too has become corrupted by sin. Renowned Christian thinker and author, Dr. Os Guinness asked, "Can America keep its freedom?" He stated that the liberty of the American republic is not self-sustaining and needs a safeguard beyond that of the Constitution and the separation of powers. He offers the "golden triangle" of freedom: "freedom requires virtue, which in turn requires faith of some sort, which in turn requires freedom. Only so can a free people hope to remain 'free always.'"[37]

Some years ago, I read an editorial in a national journal (not a Christian publication by any means) titled, *"Where are the So-Called 60 Million Born-Again Adult American Christians?"* The piece was a secular challenge to the influence of Christianity in America and went something along the lines of:

> *"Aren't you supposed to be the salt of the earth and the light of the world? Why then is the Christian influence on our society so little? Crimes and social ills continue to increase and are spreading like an infectious disease in our society. Teen pregnancy, drug abuse, alcohol addiction, child abuse, juvenile delinquency, divorces, and rapes are on the rise across the nation. Pornography is rampant. Where are the*

so-called 60 million adult American Christians? Where are you?"

As I was reading this editorial, my heart ached. I cried out to God for His forgiveness on our country. On our ungodliness. On our wicked ways. Even though we as a nation have experienced liberty for over 225 years, and fought vigorously to secure it, our country has a spiritual crisis. It is a vast understatement to say that the Puritan faith and Judeo-Christian values that was (at least partially) the foundation for this country are in decline. No one can deny that. In government. On campuses. In our homes. In the media and the arts. Even in the pews and on the pulpit. There is perversion. There is corruption. There is idolatry. Without freedom in Christ Jesus, we are only left with a freedom that can be corrupted by sin.

A dear price also had to be paid for this freedom in the Truth. Because the "wages of sin is death" (Rom. 6:23), there had to be a sacrifice so I could be set free from that fate. The highest sacrifice. Death. Jesus came and was slaughtered for me. That was the price He paid for my sins, for my freedom. Jesus laid down His life and was nailed to a tree so that we could enjoy total freedom in Him. We didn't have to do a thing. God removed our death sentences and placed them on His Son, who was our substitute without sin. Because of grace. Because of mercy. Because He loved us. And in turn, we simply receive Him as our Savior and Lord by repenting of our sins and being cleansed by His blood, so that we can proclaim, "I have been crucified, and I no longer live, but Christ lives in me..." (Gal. 2:20, ESV). It was His blood and forgiveness that gave me an unspeakable inner freedom.

Freedom From "Han"

My freedom in Christ inevitably led to freedom from the particular chains that had bound me. I was set free from my "hans" and my inferiority complex, which in turn freed me from the sins of pride and arrogance, defensiveness, jealousy, bitterness, anger, and a fear of failure and rejection. The entrenchment of "han" in Korean culture is deep. It's been a powerful driving force in Korean society. Yes, it can bring achievement, accolades, and worldly success, but "han" is a deadly poison that inevitably leads to ruin. I was no exception. But God, in His mercy, freed me from it.

It breaks my heart to see that "han" and its sin-offspring are still prevalent in Korean churches. To my dismay, some Korean Christian leaders have even proclaimed that "han" is a good thing, because it can be harnessed into an effective engine for personal (and worldly) advancement. *But worldly success and achievement aside, where do they find their identities? What about their souls?*

Freedom From My "Minority Complex"

I had been very conscious about my status as a minority – in the racial and ethnic sense – when I immigrated to America. This self-imposed "minority complex" had confined me. In my own mindset, it defined me, personally and professionally. I, in essence, marginalized myself. I felt inferior. I doubted. I was depressed. Defeated. At times, without hope. *What could I possibly accomplish in this competitive, white-dominated society?* I was so preoccupied by my minority status and seeking the approval from the majority (and blaming them as well), that it limited my ability to use my God-given gifts to the fullest extent. No matter how hard I tried, I felt, consciously or subconsciously, that there would inevitably be a roadblock that could not be overcome – the color of my skin.

My wife and I had encountered racial discrimination from the day we arrived in Los Angeles 46 years ago. Since that time, and as a result of the Civil Rights Movement, our country has made tremendous strides to reduce discrimination, perhaps more so than any other nation. Yet there is still racial prejudice that exists in our society. Laws, regulations, and ordinances are necessary, but they can only do so much. Yes, they can accomplish external compliance and impose equality on the surface. Education is vital too. But there must be transformation. Of the mind. Of our consciousness. Of the heart. Of both the "majorities" and the "minorities." No law or course of study would have ever been able to truly free me from my minority complex prison. It had to be God.

As long as this minority consciousness – believing that I am a minority and inferior to others – infects and controls my mind, I become a slave to it. And I was a slave to it. This view of myself had shaped my mindset, which in turn controlled my thinking, which dictated my attitude, which influenced my behavior, which formed habits, that eventually molded my character. I realized through the Holy Spirit that I must be freed from this complex that bound me. I asked the Holy Spirit to rid me of it, to put my minority mindset on the cross and no longer be a slave to it. The Holy Spirit assured me that I was God's child through Jesus Christ (John 1:12). And not only was I His child, but also a co-heir with Christ (Rom. 8:17), Christ's ambassador (2 Cor. 5:20), and a royal priest (1 Pet. 2:9). *If that was the case (and it was!), how could I ever consider myself to be a minority in any sense of the word?!* The Holy Spirit came through. I was miraculously liberated. When Jesus sets us free, we are free indeed!

Once I was freed from my minority complex, I no longer concerned myself about what my race had to do with anything. It no longer influenced my thinking. It no longer affected how I carried myself, how I felt about myself, and how I viewed others. Not to say that there is no longer discrimination and prejudice in America (we still face it today), but it's no longer a part of my own consciousness and identity. So since then, whenever I've been discriminated against (it still happens occasionally), I would tell myself, *I know that I am God's precious child. He died for me so He could be with me. So He could adopt me. It doesn't bother me that I'm being discriminated against. I know my identity is in Him. I'm co-heirs with His Son. Your prejudices are your problem pal, not mine.* This was my way of tossing the ball back to the other person's lap (and then I'd lift up a prayer that God would change the person as He did me). "The Lord is on my side; I will not fear. What can man do to me?" (Ps. 118:6, ESV).

Today, I see the same self-imposed minority complex in second-generation Korean-Americans. This troubles me. These are Americans of Korean descent who in every way are "American" – they were born in this country, speak English fluently without any accent, they understand the cultural nuances of this country that I never knew when I stepped off the plane at LAX in 1967, and many have achieved educational and vocational success. And yet because of the influence of their first generation parents who had the same complex I struggled with, they too adhere to the minority construct, thereby self-marginalizing themselves. This, I believe, explains (at least in part) why many second-generation Korean-Americans, though highly-skilled and educated in comparison to non-Asians, are not advancing in mainstream America as influential leaders and cultural pacesetters. Many of them are content to be bystanders because that's the only way they view themselves. They can't imagine being anywhere but on the sidelines. On the margins. This mindset consciously or subconsciously has severely limited them from using their giftings from God to the fullest extent for His glory. There can be no boldness or risk-taking for Him when there is fundamentally no identity in Him.

God also freed me from my own prejudices and stereotypes towards others. Discrimination was not new to me when I came to this country. In fact, you could even say that the discrimination I received in Korea due to historical class/regional-based prejudices was worse than in America. In that sense, growing up in such a society where everything was about where you were from or what class your family was in, it was hard for me – as much as I hated that about Korean society – not to form my own prejudices towards others. Victims of discrimination are not immune from discriminating. Not in the least. But God changed me. The Holy Spirit awakened me to the truths that all have sinned, all have fallen short of the glory of God, and God's people are called to love, and to love all. This freed me from discriminating against others. He enlarged my heart to the point where I was able to embrace any person in my heart as an equal, as a person loved by, and created in the image of, God. *As a child of God and a brother to Christ Jesus, how could I discriminate against His creation? Against those He loves?*

Freedom To . . .

This freedom in Christ gave me unexplainable peace and joy. And that energized me like never before. It allowed me to experience a supernaturally dynamic life that I could have never thought possible. Freedom from my sinful chains gave me a freedom to do more than I could have ever imagined. Without being bogged down by any complex or insecurity or bitterness or fear or anxiety or self-doubt, I was abundantly more productive (in a spiritual sense), having more time to spend with God in getting on the same page with Him, communing with Him, and drawing power from Him. I didn't dwell on my limitations and weaknesses or waste time pointing out how I had been mistreated, but focused on Him and what He would have me do with what I could offer. And He took those things and used me in a way I never even dreamed (which I'll get to later). In other words, because of this freedom in the Truth, I began to live supernaturally.

This gave me a freedom to wholeheartedly serve the Lord with all my heart, with all my mind, and with all my strength in the local church. The church is the bride and body of Christ, purchased by His blood. It is not just another religious organization. Christianity is not a religion, it is life! It is a relationship with a Person! Would God send His own Son to this world and let Him die on the cross to create just another religion? Run by just another organization? Yet many of us so easily compartmentalize our lives and treat Sundays the same way. Unsurprisingly, the late Dr. D. Martin Lloyd-Jones criticized the church as being power-less, hope-less, love-less, and help-less. Did not Christ give us a new life and a new freedom? Are not His body collective called to live out this new life? A dynamic, powerful, energetic, and passionate life. A life that is loving, gracious, giving, serving, inspiring, and motivating. A life that dreams, transforms, grows, multiplies, reproduces, and bears much fruit. A life marked by courage and conviction. Are these the hallmarks of our churches? Oh, let us be free men and women in Christ and catalysts for our churches so that they become the center of love, the center of hope, the center of power, and the center of help for the world.

My freedom in Christ also gave me the freedom to be bolder. It gave me more courage to proclaim the gospel of Jesus Christ and witness to others. More willingness to share what God had done for me without fear of what others had thought. To co-workers and colleagues. To the stranger sitting next to me on an airplane. To foreign dignitaries. To local and state government officials. Soon, I was able to experience the great privilege of sharing the Good News and my testimony to hundreds of thousands of college and graduate students and young adults on campuses, at conferences, and churches across the U.S. and in more than 50 nations. With boldness. Without compromise. Without a "complex" to hold me back. I would have never dreamed that God would use me in this way.

Finally, but most importantly, this freedom gave me greater

insight into God's vision and plans for my personal life, my family, the local church and my community, for the next generations, for this nation, and for the world. Unencumbered, unhindered, unimpeded, unobstructed, and unbound by any identity issues or man's applause or acceptance, He poured out His heart, His purposes, and His desires into my heart.

What a change! What a Savior! What grace! All praise and glory to God who has allowed me to live in complete freedom.

Chapter 13

A RESTORED AND RENEWED MARRIAGE

Amazing things happened to me after Big Bear Mountain. I began to memorize Scripture. When hymn after hymn did not frequently come out of my mouth – sometimes in a loud singing voice (I still have a decent voice!), whistling (I am good at it) or humming – there would be prayers and intercession instead. My whole thinking process and worldview as well as behavior and attitude changed. Drastically. "Therefore if anyone is in Christ, he is a new creation. The old has passed away; behold, the new has come." (2 Cor. 5:17, ESV). By God's grace, this was true of me. *Is it true of you?* Have you experienced supernatural transformation in everything that you say, do, think, or feel? In everything that is within you? In your relationships with God, brothers and sisters in Christ, and fellow students and colleagues? In your relationship with your family?

It is essential that our families are built on the Good News. The family was the first institution that God created. Before the church. If we, as individuals, claim to truly be born-again in Christ Jesus and transformed by His grace, the first place people notice change must not only be in ourselves, but also in our relationships with our own families.

I have witnessed so many people claiming to be born-again Christians, yet their family life is far from transformed. Not to say that family life is never difficult – yes, there can be struggles as we all are sinners – but if we are truly renewed and reborn in Christ, at least the process of renewal (transparency, forgiveness, reconciliation, and the humility to desire change) should be apparent. There are countless servants of the church who hide their broken and bitter familial relationships and continue to serve and act as though everything's okay at home. They'd rather save face than seek the prayers of others. This has been so prevalent that

I believe the church has lost the authority and power to preach the true Gospel of Jesus Christ to the communities, the nation, and the world. How can we be salt and light when supposedly "Christian families" are no different from the rest of society? How can Christian marriages be a testimony of God's supernatural grace and power when there is only hardened, cold, and bitter hearts? How can we expect our children to be transformed by the Gospel when parents are ruled by worldly, external desires rather than a view of the cross and eternity? We need to be broken.

If God hadn't broken me and restored a new life in me, if there had been no Big Bear Mountain, if I had not been "born again," the result of my iniquities, bitter-rooted "han" and pride would have been a family no different from the families that are functionally operating on the outside, but are internally separated, joyless, and corroding.

My wife knows this all too well.

Because I was so consumed by achievement and success, and so driven by "han" and proving all the naysayers and discriminators wrong, there was no room for anything in the relationship with my wife other than my ego. She had a difficult life. Daily she was forced to submit her needs to an overbearing and unrelenting husband. It was hard for her. I cannot imagine how she was able to endure and put up with me all those years. But when I was broken and completely transformed by the work of the Holy Spirit and received the washing away of my sins by the blood of Christ, I was a new person. It was then that my wife became broken herself and experienced her own transformation. Once we had been filled with so much discontent for each other, focusing on the other's flaws and ignoring the other's merits, constantly being dissatisfied and easily (and irrationally) disappointed, and unable to talk and share with each other with open minds and transparent hearts. But when God changed me, she changed too.

After Big Bear Mountain, by God's grace, the relationship with my wife took on a completely different trajectory. We were able to share our fears and tears, express our feelings and hurts freely, seek forgiveness, extend forgiveness, and rediscover each other in love again. And through this incredible Spirit-filled process, we were able to ground our relationship on Christ and rebuild our married life together. I didn't realize until then that God had given me the world's best and suitable helper. One who was perfect for me. I rediscovered that she was "bone of my bones and flesh of my flesh" (Gen. 2:23). Just as God loved us so much he gave His only Son, I resolved to live in that same love (Eph. 5:25) with my wife. Totally by the grace of God and the power of the Holy Spirit, our married life has since been filled with love, affection, understanding, unity, and mutual respect and admiration. It's been filled with rejoicing in the work and Person of Christ. It's been wonderful.

One day, my wife chuckled and said, "Honey, we Korean wives are like a peach."

"What do you mean?" I asked.

"A peach looks beautiful and soft on the outside. And it also tastes delicious when you bite into a ripe one. But don't bite too deep and too hard, because you may break your teeth. There is a very tough seed inside."

Her witty fruit analogy got me thinking. Wives can appear meek and soft in appearance, but inside, I have found that many of them can be more resilient and hardy than their husbands. This is not a bad thing.

So I self-deprecatingly responded, "Oh! Then Korean husbands are like coconuts. On the outside, coconuts can look very strong and intimidating, and they are tough to break. But when they do break, there is nothing but juice inside."

Sometime later my wife told me another gem: "Honey, I acknowledge that you are the head of this household. But I want you to know that I am the neck. The head can't move unless the neck does. And unless the neck is smooth and soft and gentle, you can't move your head freely without pain. If your neck gets stiffened up, it's difficult for the head to move in different directions. You remember how hard it is for you to drive with a stiff neck, right?"

My wife's funny. But I do think there's some biblical truth behind what she said. God commands husbands to love their wives "as Christ loved the church" (Eph. 5:25). Just as Jesus is the head of the church, I am the head of my family. And just as Jesus loved the church, I am to love my wife with a Christ-like love. Therefore, I am called to love my wife and ensure that she (the neck) is treated with great care, kindness, and gentleness so that our journey together, with me as the spiritual head, will stay in whatever course Christ leads, even if that involves trials and struggles. I learned a great lesson – if you are a husband, love your wife with great care and gentleness!

Five Perspectives on the Husband-and-Wife Relationship

I prayed and petitioned to God to give me His wisdom on how to love and treat and view my wife in this way. In everyday living. I was so excited about discovering five nuggets on the relationship between husbands and wives that have been essential to the success of my marriage. After sharing them with my wife one morning, I resolved to practice them on a daily basis throughout my life.

First, my wife is like an older sister.

My real older sister, who is five years my senior, has a tremendous heart. Though I could be a rascal as a boy, she took great care of me growing up. I noticed the same thing in my daughter, Sharon, who is six years older than her brother, Paul, and was always very good about looking after him and loving him like a second mom. I'm sure that there are many cases like that. I do think there is something special in an older sister's heart for her younger brother.

There are many occasions when I acted like a spoiled child, difficult to handle and quite demanding; I bothered my sister all the time. And yet she was always patient with me and tried, ever so gently, to get me to settle down, especially when I whined or cried to get what I wanted. She didn't always let me get what I wanted and in this way she was loving, but firm and knew where to draw the line. I envisioned and prayed that my wife would be like this calm, sweet older sister. It may sound a bit strange, but I found that a husband needs an older sister-like wife. Let me explain. For me, I needed to have a wife that would patiently embrace me with a huge heart and have the affinity and ability to take care of me, even when I acted like a spoiled kid. My wife has taken on this role with the understanding of a gentle, older sister (she's also looked to me as an older, protective brother). In this mutual relationship we have found tremendous comfort, joy, and much laughter. We began to know each other's needs and see that they are cared for even in the midst of difficulties. We began to prosper in Christ.

Second, my wife is my best friend.

Jesus said, "No longer do I call you my servants . . . but I have called you friends" (John 15:15, ESV). We became friends of Jesus through the Gospel. Jesus wants to talk to us about everything and anything. That's what friends do. He wants to tell us of His love, His passions, His ways, and He always shares everything with us without holding back. Jesus wants us to talk to Him about our pain, our trials, and our struggles. He, the Creator of the universe and the One who knows how many hairs we have on our heads, wants intimacy with us!

In the same token, my wife and I resolved to talk about anything and everything, even the most difficult, sensitive, or embarrassing. We wanted honesty and transparency, leaving no secrets between us. We wanted mutual humility and, if the need arises, mutual grace-extending forgiveness. My wife and I pledged to daily share our ups and downs, our joys and our pains. When we share good news, we share in thanksgiving and praise. When there is bad news, we comfort each other and ask God for His wisdom in dealing with such things.

This practice of complete openness was not easy. Especially for me. My wife was born in the northern part of Korea where people were relatively straightforward and direct. She was also raised in a very open and communicative Christian family. I, on the other hand, was born in the Southwest where people were much less straightforward and more diplomatic. I was raised in a more "face saving" (*chae myun*) society. If you were too honest, that often meant trouble or ridicule. That practice still holds to a certain extent, even in most Korean-American churches where transparency is wanting. Therefore, it was a much bigger challenge for me to be honest than my wife.

When I was growing up, I never saw mutually transparent, mutually edifying and confessing husband-wife relationships. They are still hard to find. However, my wife and I were fortunate to have found a number of co-laborers around America and the world who have in fact lived and are living in such relationships. They have become our role models. Before Big Bear Mountain, when my wife asked me how my day was at school or whatever I did, my attitude was basically, *You don't need to know. It's none of your business.* Since Big Bear Mountain, and in emulating our "role model" couples, anything and everything that happens on a day, whether good or bad, is her business and my business.

If we truly want to grow in Christ and walk with Him as a family unit, the relationship between husband and wife is foremost. In addition to Jesus, who else can you turn to and share about your day and pray together in thanksgiving, intercession, and repentance? Shouldn't that be your spouse? Who should be the person closest to you to share your daily highs and your daily lows? Shouldn't that be your wife or husband? The closest person to you who praises God in your times of joy and who comforts you in your times of sorrow? If we only share the "good things in life" with our spouse, but not our struggles – no matter how shameful or painful – then you're not close friends with your spouse. You are not one flesh. I believe that a husband and wife should be each other's closest confidante to work together in persevering through such hard times. When this is put into practice, couples learn to rely on each other as they are relying on God, thereby strengthening the bonds of marriage. Acting as true friends. As Jesus called us His friends. It becomes habitual.

Although my wife and I are mostly together (at home or when traveling), whenever I happen to be on the road away from her, I call her at least twice a day. With my morning call, I let her know the day's schedule and tell her my specific prayer requests, and at the end of the day, before I go to bed, I share how my day went in detail. She shares with me how her day went. And then before hanging up the phone I say, "Good night, I love you very much" and she responds by saying "I love you too." God is truly amazing!

While we were living in Anchorage, Alaska, I had to go to the former Soviet Union in July 1990 with Ambassador Ed Wolf and my assistant to organize the North Pacific Fisheries Cooperation Conference. We initially flew to Moscow (connecting through Copenhagen) to meet with the Soviet Minister, Deputy, and Assistant Ministers of Fisheries, and then flew to Vladivostok for a meeting with the governors and fisheries leaders in the Russian Far East region. Although we were able to successfully reach an agreement with Moscow in holding the conference in October

1991 in Vladivostok, I had access to a phone just once during the entire two-week trip. It drove me crazy that I could only talk to my wife just one time. When we returned to Copenhagen, our hotel had a phone so I was able to catch up with my wife on all that had happened during my absence. But I was short more than $300 as I failed to read the hotel's fine print for international calls. Ouch! Long distance, especially international calls, were very expensive back then before pre-paid calling cards, Skype and Google Chat. But compared to hearing the voice of my best friend, the cost was nothing to me.

Third, my wife is like a loving mother.

A sound and healthy physical and emotional relationship between husband and wife is crucial. A little child couldn't be more content than when he is in his mom's arms. In the same way, I, even though I'm a grown man, find much comfort in my wife's arms. In her embrace. It is emotionally and physically therapeutic. It gives me tremendous peace and tranquility. This kind of calming-of-the-soul is important for a husband to experience, given the many demands on his time and resources. I found that these kinds of interactions create a deeper connection between husband and wife that is profoundly important in sustaining the sturdiness and strength of the husband-wife relationship. Problems in marriage can arise when these simple moments of a lingering embrace are taken over with the busyness of life. Let it not be so. I thank God for being able to find this rest and security in the loving arms of my wife.

Fourth, my wife is my lover.

My wife wasn't just my lover when we were dating or when we were "madly in love" during the "honeymoon stage." She is my lover every day of my life. After Big Bear Mountain, I petitioned God to enable me to love my wife with all my heart and with all my mind and with all my soul as my lover. Although us married couples vowed in holy matrimony to love our spouses under any circumstances, how many of us continue to live as true lovers with them? I realized I had treated my wife as just a wife (or a partner or helper), not my lover. I sinned against God and my wife.

Since God transformed the both of us, our perspectives on our relationship have profoundly changed. Honestly, by God's grace, my wife and I have loved each other more and more with each passing day. We have cultivated a loving relationship – physically, emotionally, psychologically, and spiritually – in seeking to emulate the love between Christ and His church. Whenever possible, we declare our love to each other. We are very expressive of this love. Direct communication is one of our "love languages." Every morning, I greet my wife with a "Good morning, and I love you," accompanied by a big hug. On her birthday, our wedding anniversary, Easter, Mother's Day, Father's Day, Valentine's Day, Thanksgiving and Christmas, or any occasion, we not only exchange gifts, but also a heartfelt card expressing our deep love and appreciation for each other.

When I was on a trip, I always wrote a two-to-three-page letter to my wife (postcards weren't big enough) telling her about my travels and how much she means to me. Now when I'm away, we communicate through telephone on a daily basis and also email. People may wonder how I could have so much to say to my wife after 46 years of marriage, but just as Christ's steadfast love for us always abounds and never runs dry, my love for my wife always will. Each time the plane touches the runway after a trip, my heart is filled with joy, excitement, and anticipation in seeing my wife at the baggage claim area. She always greets me with a big and bright smile and we throw our arms around our necks and kiss each other. It's like we are newlyweds. I just love these moments. They never get old.

We have also traveled together to so many different places in America and around the world. When we travel together, it's like a honeymoon for us. We do our best on these trips to take good care of each other and I try to serve my wife wholeheartedly to show that she, not the trip (or the speaking engagement), is the most important thing to me.

Annually since 1979, I have made it my practice to set aside five to seven days in late December or early January to pray (and sometimes fast) and spend time alone with God. My own personal retreat with Him. I have been immensely blessed with this annual practice. I usually spend the first few days reading the Bible and reflecting on the entire year in writing. When reflecting on the great things that have happened in my relationships with God, my wife, my children, my colleagues, my pastor, friends, and brothers and sisters in Christ, with my profession, and my work for the cause of Christ and furthering His Kingdom, I give all praise, thanksgiving, and glory to God. When I reflect on my sins and mistakes from the year, I earnestly confess and repent, seeking God for His mercy and forgiveness. As the Holy Spirit assures me that my transgressions are washed away by the blood of Jesus Christ, and forgiven, then, through further prayer and reading of and meditating on God's word, I begin to plan the coming year with God. I want to be sure we are on the same page.

During my winter break, at the end of 1997, I spent five days alone with God asking Him what He would have me do for my summer vacation in 1998. God convicted me to spend that entire break by embarking on a prayer tour around America for this nation's revival and spiritual awakening. This was the second time God convicted to go on such a cross-country prayer tour. The first time was in the summer of 1994 when I, along with my wife and son, Paul, drove 12,000 miles across America in 42 days to pray for this country. When I shared God's conviction for a second national prayer tour with my wife, she joyfully exclaimed that she was on board. She said that my vision in seeing America repent and experience true revival was her vision as well. That God brought us together to awaken America in this way. She was passionate about this. She had ownership. I was so encouraged.

By the grace of God, Pastor Chris Woon Young Kang joined my wife and me on the tour, which started on May 29, 1998 and ended on August 17. During that time, I had delivered more than 120 messages on awakening, repentance, and revival, and held prayer rallies in 58 cities. We drove more than 20,000 miles. The tour was physically grueling, so the care my wife and I had for each other was a tremendous blessing. For every message I delivered and for every prayer rally I led, my wife was always sitting in the front row, attentively listening, her eyes wide (and sometimes with tears), as if she was hearing the message for the first time (even though it was more like the 100th). The driving days were tough on her (and her back). Some days we'd drive for more than 13 hours. Yet every time I stood at the podium, no matter how exhausted I was, I was energized by her active listening. Her emotional engagement. Her nods. Her "amens." Her love and support. It was unwavering. It was amazing to see. It was uplifting. She was a "lovely deer" and a "graceful doe" to me in those moments; I was "intoxicated . . . in her love" (Prov. 5:19, ESV).

If a husband has the mentality that his wife is just his wife (a helper, domestic partner, or a home maker, taking care of the husband's needs and raising the children) and not his lover, then the husband may seek to fill that void in his heart with another person (or with the anonymous Internet). When a husband is not madly engaged in a constant love affair with his own wedded wife or when a wife cannot fill her husband's heart with her love, he may look elsewhere for this "unfulfilled lover's void." Marriages could end up broken. I know this kind of "lovers" relationship doesn't happen overnight and there will be days when life's worries have married couples doing more work (at the office or at home) and less loving, but we must be intentional about finding ways to grow in intimacy, love, and affection for our spouses. If my wife is my true lover who fulfills my heart, then would I be enticed by another woman? *Would I even be tempted?* In the same way, if a wife sees her husband as just a traditional husband (protector, provider, domestic partner, home improvement guy), then the wife may seek another man to fill the lover's void in her heart. This is dangerous.

The divorce rate for Christian couples is just as high as for non-Christians, maybe even higher since the marriage rate among non-Christians has been decreasing. Pastors – even younger ones who've only been married several years – are committing adultery. Many couples are falling apart because they are not lovers and seek to find lovers outside the marriage. This should not be. Yes, nobody is perfect and no one is without sin, but if we are indeed children of the most holy God, then we must keep our marriages pure and grace-filled. Without purity, we cannot truly love God or each other as husband and wife. We must build and edify our spouses, respecting their strengths, accepting their weaknesses, showing grace when they make mistakes, seeking forgiveness when we fall, and serve them with all our hearts as lovers, walking together with them in obeying God's commands. I thank God that my wife is my lover!

Fifth, my wife is a lifelong companion and cheerleader.

"For better or for worse, for richer, for poorer, in sickness and in health, to love and to cherish; from this day forward until death do us part, I promise to be by your side under any circumstance."

This was the vow that my wife and I made to each other on our wedding day in front of our family and friends, as well as in front of God. Since Big Bear Mountain, my wife has been my biggest cheerleader. Yes, she keeps me accountable and has no problem telling me if I made a mistake or that I sinned in a certain way (she is from the North you know!), but she is my most avid supporter. I don't know how many thousands of times she's heard my testimony and my supernatural encounter with God at Big Bear Mountain, but each and every time she does, she sheds tears.

As companions and lifelong partners, we share everything. Our thoughts, our prayers, our time, and our money. There shouldn't be any secret between husband and wife in any matter, including finances. I have never hid from my wife a single dollar. In fact, I asked my wife to be in charge of all the family's finances in 1978, and put my entire trust in her. I was strongly convicted by the Holy Spirit that I should be completely free from all monetary matters of the home. I am still free, and it's wonderful. After all, she studied accounting and economics in America and was working as an accountant at the University of California, Irvine and Orange County Hospital.

I never ask my wife how much she spends when she goes grocery, home, or personal shopping (she tells me anyways). I have neither questioned her spending nor questioned her financial management. Her default is always to give more to the church, which I love. She's free to manage the family's finances and I'm free from those concerns to focus on work and ministry. It works harmoniously. Yet we still share with each other everything and anything to do with how we are using our God-given resources, whether we are giving enough to our church's building fund or overseas missions or our ministry (Jesus Awakening Movement for America (JAMA)) or family members in need. No secrets. Total trust. Complete transparency. Mutual accountability. Because of that, there's never been a time when we argued over how we managed and spent our money! Totally by the grace of God!

We have witnessed so many marriages torn apart because of

money. One statistic showed that over 50 percent of divorces in America are due to monetary problems. We have only one bank account and my wife manages our credit cards. We have always put both our names on all our accounts. I don't think it's necessary (from a non-small-business standpoint) or desirable for a couple to have separate accounts. My wife and I are supposed to be one flesh. Our finances must be one as well.[38]

My wife and I were once invited to a lunch by one of our church's deaconesses. She was someone that my wife and I deeply cared for – we had led her and her family to Christ. She explained that her husband needed $5,000 for his business and wanted to borrow that amount from her. She was worried that if she lent him the money, he wouldn't pay her back. "So instead of giving my husband the money directly, can I give you the money, and then you lend it to him?" she asked. "That way, I know he will eventually pay you back and then you can give the money back to me. Because we have separate bank accounts, he wouldn't know that the money originally came from me. Could you do this for me?"

I gently rebuked her. I told her I didn't think this situation exemplified a Christian marriage based on trust, understanding, and love. I told her that the notions of lending, loans, and paying back don't arise in a marriage where husband and wife are one flesh. I explained to her how my wife and I handled our finances, that her money and my money were one in the same. She was deeply convicted of what I had to say and repented. And apologized for asking me to play the middle man. She said that she was going to give her husband the $5,000. With no strings attached.

As lifelong companions, not only do husband and wife share everything, they are there for each other in every circumstance. But there are many in this world, even Christians, who have spouses like Job's wife. When a husband faces hardship or has miserably failed, it's important to have a wife who can give him encouragement, perspective, grace, and support, rather than criticism and scoff. It's hard enough for a man to face failure, but if a husband faces additional criticism from his own wife, where or from whom can he find comfort or encouragement? But when a wife stands beside her husband and says, "No matter what, I am always with you, so do not worry, we will deal with it. Let's pray to God and ask for wisdom, strength, and peace to get through it." How soul-enriching and heart-uplifting to hear such words when you are down!

In March 2004, I was diagnosed with cancer. Lymphoma. In my lower spine. The tumor had been growing for about 8-10 years and became so big that my spinal cord was about to break. This was causing pain that I had never experienced before. It was indescribable. My nervous system was getting crushed by this growing tumor. My oncologist, Dr. John Hausdorff, told me that what I had was known as one of the most painful of all cancers. On the way from the Monterey Oncology Center, after being told of the cancer, my wife said, "You are not going to die. Simply what must come has come. God may be planning something greater. We will fight this thing together and we shall be victorious!" Here was my cheerleader. Here was my one-woman support group. We were not afraid. We were together. As a team. Under a sovereign God.

March was spent testing before the actual treatment. MRIs, biopsies, a bone marrow biopsy, and a lumbar puncture (LP) which tested the fluids going around my brain, neck, and upper spine. The LP is about as bad as it gets as far as pain. The needle is big and long. The process of the puncture and the extraction of the fluids takes about 15 minutes. The longest 15 minutes imaginable. I have to catch my breath just thinking about it now. I had to do it five times.

During this most trying time, my wife was with me every step of the way. Testing after testing, procedure after procedure, then the chemotherapy and radiation treatment and the LPs. She dedicated those difficult months to love and take care of me as my companion and cheerleader.

I had an unusual amount of side effects from the chemo. Dr. Hausdorff said he had not seen anyone who had suffered as many side effects as I had. Every time there was a side effect, like a red rash over my entire body, my wife had to call Dr. Hausdorff to order a prescription for me. I lost count with how many times my wife had to go to the pharmacy, at all hours of the day and night, in between chemo sessions. All the while, she never showed any dismay or impatience. She never complained. She never even looked tired or fatigued. She was there for me with nothing but an upbeat demeanor, wide smile, and energetic spirit. She was my 24/7 companion and cheerleader.

After my first chemotherapy session (they last for about six to seven hours), I had absolutely no strength. But I couldn't just lie down and wait until the next session. That was not me. I didn't think that would be good in beating this cancer. So I asked my wife to take me outside and help me walk a trail in our neighborhood. While she didn't say, "Are you crazy?!," she did look very surprised at my request and probably thought I was out of my mind. "Honey, you have no strength. How can you walk?"

But she saw the resolve in my eyes. She knew this fight would not be one you could win lying down. She took me outside. That day we walked a half hour, by God's grace and strength. She held me up as much as she could. The half-hour walks were very hard in the beginning and there were days when I wanted to stop and give up. But she was there right with me. And we overcame those moments. Together. Soon a half-hour became an hour. Then we went from the trail in our neighborhood to Del Monte Beach, which was nearby. We walked for one hour on the beach at least five days a week. During our walks, we prayed together and lifted hymns of praise to God. It was also a time for me to daily declare war against my cancer, "You, you little cancer! However big your tumor may be, you are smaller than me! You are infinitely smaller than God! Do you know who I am? Do you know I am God's child and co-heirs with His son, you little rascal? You dare challenge me? I am going to find you, I am going find every cancer cell! And I am going to destroy you!" This would crack up my wife. Laughing, she would say that the cancer was so afraid of me that it might run away. We were fighting this battle as a team.

Not only was I weakened from the chemo, but the stomachaches were excruciating. It was so bad that when my stomach started acting up, my whole body was drenched in sweat. Prescriptions were hit or miss (mostly miss). And my appetite was completely gone. Plus, my mouth felt like it was filled with sand. This is why most cancer patients lose a lot of weight because it's so hard to put anything down during chemotherapy due to the severe side effects. Indeed, a number of cancer patients die not necessarily from the cancer, but because of the loss of appetite and failing to eat enough to sustain body strength.

No matter how painful it was, I resolved to eat three meals a day. Each time I sat up to eat, sweat dripped down my head and eventually covered my entire body. But there was no giving up, by God's grace. Not one meal was missed, even on the day I had a chemo session. Like a pregnant lady, I was picky with what I wanted to eat (I had a particular craving for Dungeness crab, tons of which are caught in the Monterey Bay area). But whatever it was, my wife cheerfully went out to get it and cooked it for me. As a result, I did not lose weight and my body continued to gain strength, which in turn, strengthen my emotional, psychological, and spiritual well-being.

In 2004, my wife took me to the Monterey Oncology Center (now Pacific Cancer Care Center), Community Hospital of Monterey Peninsula (CHOMP), and Imaging Center for treatments, scans, and tests more than 80 times. She was my companion and cheerleader each time. Totally by the mercy and power of God, who heard the prayers of many interceding for my healing, my wife and I, my dream team, were able to overcome this cancer. My wife's unwavering dedication, loving kindness, and support, reminds me of Proverbs 31:29 (ESV): "Many women have done excellently, but you surpass them all." Indeed, in my book, my wife, through her remarkable companionship and cheerleading, has surpassed them all.

Although each one of us is different and thus each marriage is not necessarily the same, I hope and pray that you find these five perspectives of the husband-wife relationship worthy of contemplation and even practice. Oh, wouldn't it be great to see couples caring for each other, loving each other, supporting each other, liking each other, confessing to one another, forgiving each other, praying with one another, sharing everything, and enjoying deep and transparent fellowship together?! *Oh, Lord, may it be so!*

Chapter 14

CHILDREN, A HERITAGE FROM THE LORD

After Big Bear Mountain, not only did I ask God to give me wisdom and knowledge as to how to be a "born-again" husband, but also to be a "born-again" parent to my children, Sharon and Paul. Scripture tells us that, "Behold, children are a heritage from the LORD, the fruit of the womb a reward" (Ps. 127:3, ESV); "Fathers, do not provoke your children to anger, but bring them up in the discipline and instructions of the Lord" (Eph. 6:4, ESV); and, "A new command I give you: Love one another. As I have loved you, so you must love one another. By this everyone will know that you are my disciples, if you love one another" (John 13:34-35). Through fervent prayers, reading, meditating, God's transforming Spirit, and a little trial-and-error, here is how God enabled me to raise my children:

With fervent, unselfish, and God-exalting prayers

My wife and I really sought God's heart – and not our own personal desires – for Sharon and Paul. And in turn, we began to pray selfless prayers for our children. As part of my dietary regimen when I was sick, I had to drink lots of water and lemon juice. After I recovered from my liver illness, I continued drinking an average of one and a half gallons of water every day. It's no surprise that I visited the restroom a lot during the day and at least twice during the night. Each time when I woke in the middle of the night to go to the bathroom, I went into Sharon's room, knelt down on my knees, and placed my hands on her head and her chest and prayed for her as she slept:

> *Heavenly Father, you gave me this precious daughter as your inheritance and gift. Please fill her heart with the heart of Jesus Christ, and with love, grace, forgiveness, thanksgiving, patience, humility and obedience. Please*

*fill her mind with wisdom, discernment, understanding,
and the power to know "[your] good, pleasing and perfect
will," (Rom. 12:2), so that she may give you all the glory
by fulfilling your desires and your purposes for her life.
Please raise her to become a godly and faithful woman,
who loves you and loves others as herself.*

I would then go into Paul's room, again kneeling down and putting my hands on his head and his chest, and lift up a similar prayer to God and also petitioning, *Raise him to be a man of faith serving you and your people. Give him the heart of Christ with the integrity of Joseph, the courage and prayerfulness of Daniel, and the zeal of Apostle Paul to glorify your name and expand your Kingdom.*"

These were the prayers for my children every night since God had transformed me. I never prayed that they would get a certain job or attend a certain school or gain a certain interest or live a "happy life." My wife's and my perspective was, *God, they are your children, not ours. It's your will, not ours. It's their life in you, not our life in them. We may think we know what's best for them, but you truly know what's best for them. Help us as parents not to get in the way of what you have planned for them.* I never pressured them to go to this school, major in that field, play this sport, pursue this vocation, or choose this career path – they were free to choose. Yes, I was consulted and they continually sought my advice, but I made it clear to them that they would and should – after seeking God's face – make the ultimate decision. This was their life, not their mom's or dad's.

Parents can fall into the trap of praying prayers that are seemingly God-oriented and expressed in godly terminology, but are ultimately selfish, lifted up for temporary gain (for themselves or their children), and not with a view toward eternity: "Lord, help my child get into this Ivy League college, so that he could secure a high-paying job and give more to the church," or "Lord, help my child become a doctor so that he can provide for his family and give more to missions and do short-term medical mission trips." When we pray for our children, let us not be motivated with any selfish desires clothed in religiosity, but seek God's heart and will for our children.

In the fall of 1986, we flew from Anchorage to Boston and then drove to the campus of Smith College in Northampton, Massachusetts, where Sharon was going to be a freshman. Sharon decided on her own, with our counsel, and through prayer, that she wanted to attend this all-women's institution. We supported her decision, even though she would be on the other side of the country! After freshman orientation and helping her move into her dorm room, it was time to say our goodbyes. This was tough. This was our first born. This was my only daughter. We cried a lot. Afterwards, my wife and I and Paul returned to the hotel and Paul took a shower. A very long one. He was crying the whole time. He was devastated. Sharon was like a best friend and a second mother all in one. Now he was going back home without her.

When we returned to Anchorage, it was the first time in my life that I couldn't place my hand on Sharon's head and pray while she slept. So my wife and I began to go to our church's early dawn prayer service (at 5:30 a.m.) to pray for her every day. My wife was not a regular attendee at these services, but she became one after we dropped off Sharon in New England. We held on to the Lord and prayed for Sharon during this time. *Who else could we turn to? Who else would care for her, an 18 year-old, 4,000 miles away? Who else would pray for her?* All we could do was cling to the Lord with fervent prayers.

In the fall of 1992, our son enrolled in Cornell University, again more than 4,000 miles away from home. It was his decision, again with our counsel, and we supported him. Sharon joined us from Washington, D.C. (where she was working at NASDAQ at the time) to make the drive from New York City to upstate New York, to the small town of Ithaca. After helping Paul unpack, settle in and attend his orientations, we had to leave him. Here we go again. We shed tears as we hugged him in his dorm's parking lot. Sharon cried the whole way on the drive back to D.C. where we stayed with her for another week.

When we finally arrived back in Alaska, our house felt so empty. It was quiet. Too quiet. Our children were gone. It was their time to live their lives in Him. Although they weren't with us physically, my wife and I continued to do what we had been doing when we were all living under the same roof – pray for them. Daily. Even now that they are older and have their own families, my wife and I still pray for them (and our five grandchildren) three times a day. *Parents, if you don't pray for your children, who will?*

Being a role model

Family Bible studies are crucial, but I believe there is no greater way to raise our children in the Lord than to set godly examples for them to follow. To show them broken lives transformed by the Gospel. Although parents, just like everyone else, are sinners, it is their responsibility – not the Sunday school teacher or even the pastor – to reflect Christ in their lives to their children. A child's direct observation of his or her parent's spiritual life, or lack thereof, has a profound impact on the formation and establishment of that child's character. I firmly believe this. Talk is meaningless if there is no action, if there is no fruit. I have heard the complaints of many students on college campuses: "Your generation talks too much, now's the time to show us. Walk the talk."

My wife and I have sought to be role models for Sharon and Paul. To keep our promises. To practice what we teach. To walk the talk. To seek forgiveness when we have wronged them. To say "I'm sorry" to them when we've been too harsh or impatient. To show generosity to others and in our giving. To live lives of prayer. To be hospitable and welcoming. To encourage, not criticize. To care, not crush. To advise, not force. To serve and not expect to be served. It's not been easy. We weren't always at our best. But by God's grace and strength and the work of the Holy Spirit, I sincerely believe that we have demonstrated to them a life of love, faith, prayer, integrity, service, humility, and passion. All because of Him.

Our children have observed the love that my wife and I have for each other. They see how we interact, how we communicate, how we partner, how we resolve our differences, how we handle our finances, how we enjoy each other's company, how we come to decisions, how we support each other, how we are honest with each other, how we are affectionate with each other, how we respect one another, how we express our love to each other. Our children learn from these actions. It gives them security. It gives them comfort. It gives them a desire to seek the same kind of relationship. It gives them the motivation to build such a family dynamic when they are older. And more importantly, it shows them a glimpse of Christ's love for them and His people. It draws them closer to God. It plants seeds of the Gospel. It shows them the power of grace to change. On the other hand, when parents are constantly fighting and mired in joylessness, their children can feel very insecure. And it can thwart their spiritual growth as the "religion their parents believe in" or "church" is not at all compelling or transformative.

When we were still living in Alaska, my son and I were asked to lead a two-hour seminar on raising children. Paul, who was only a teenager at the time, talked about his relationship with his parents and his older sister. He shared, "I want to meet someone like my mom as my future wife. And if we have kids, I want to be a dad like my dad. I want to build our future family like ours."

When Sharon was working at NASDAQ near Washington, D.C., she was attending an English-speaking congregation of a larger Korean church in Northern Virginia. I was invited to speak at the larger Korean-speaking congregation and the smaller English ministry for three days in March 1992. Sharon was asked to introduce me when I spoke to her fellow congregants. The thought was that she would be able to share something in her introduction that people didn't know about me. She went up to the podium and said these words: "I could introduce my father with a long list of accolades that he has successfully accomplished through his life, but I do not think he wants to be introduced to you like that. If I may introduce him with one simple sentence, I believe my father is a man who really loves God through his actions." A rush of encouragement and thanksgiving filled my soul. All praise to God. All glory to Him. *What more could I ask for?* How fitting that the title of my message that evening was the "Love of God"!

In April 1995, I was invited as a keynote speaker to the Korean-American Student Conference (KASCON), which that year was held at Harvard University. Paul, a junior at Cornell, and thousands of other students (mostly from the East Coast), attended the conference. I was so glad that the two of us could spend some time together. On Sunday morning, we woke up pretty early. It was a beautiful, sunny day so we decided to take a walk along the banks of the Charles River. What we thought would be just a quick morning stroll from our hotel turned into two hours of deep conversation, sharing, vision casting, counseling, and prayer.

On our way back to the hotel, Paul suddenly stopped and turned to me. "Dad, I love you. I respect you. Through all these years, I have seen that you are a man of God. That you are a man of integrity. I am proud to be your son. I will do my best in emulating you as a man of God. I want to be a man of integrity like you." While we were hugging each other, I couldn't stop the tears. *How could I?* I would have given up anything to hear what I just heard from my son. Who cared what anyone else thought of me after hearing this. Other than God and my wife, who else had observed me both in private and in public more than my children? I was so humbled. So moved. So honored. So undeserving. I gave all praise and glory to God.

Investing time and resources without reservation

As parents, we are called to provide for our children. This involves the necessities, such as a roof over their heads, food on the table, and clothes on their backs. It could also involve committing to – if you have the means (and you continue to tithe to your church and give generously to ministries) – paying for their education, whether primary, secondary, or college. But more so than this type of "investing" of resources, parents must invest their time. A parent's investment in spending time together with his or her child is absolutely critical to their emotional and spiritual growth.

Since Sharon was in the ninth grade, I initiated an annual father-daughter dinner just before the start of the school year. Some years, we would do our "daddy dates" twice a year, before the start of each semester. I usually asked my wife to buy a new dress for Sharon for our dinner. I treated her like a little lady as I took her to a nice restaurant. She loved it. Nothing was too expensive for her to order from the menu. She loved that. By dessert time, we were both very satisfied and our conversations would gradually and naturally become more substantive and intimate. I wanted to know that she could tell me anything. That it was safe for her to open her heart. I would ask her if she had any problems with me or her mom. I told her to be honest. To feel free to express her feelings. She would complain about certain things, things that my wife and I had overlooked or neglected or overreacted to. She shared some disappointments and hurts. Times when she was angry or mad. I would sincerely apologize for my mistakes and if need be, clarify and explain her parents' perspectives to clear up any misunderstandings without being defensive. In turn, she asked me how we felt about her. I told her how proud I was about a number of things, but at the same time, I too was honest with her about my concerns. Seeing how well I took what she had to honestly say about her parents, she took my concerns very well and apologized.

Over these dinners, we also talked about improving our relationships with God, her parents, Paul, her peers and friends at school and church, and her teachers. We also talked about her study habits and grades, her aspirations, nurturing her dreams, her struggles, and growing as a godly and responsible person of Christ. I assured her of our unwavering support and unconditional love. No matter what.

A few days after our dinner she would write down all her goals and resolutions that we had shared over our meal. She would sign the bottom of the page. If I agreed, I would sign next to her signature. She would then tape the document on the wall in front of her desk, to serve as her daily reminder. This was our routine every year until she went to Smith College. Paul and I started the practice when he was much younger than Sharon. This practice has been immensely beneficial for all of us. For me and my wife, it gave us "feedback" on our parenting. It enabled us to better parent each child by understanding how they were wired individually (and differently from each other). It helped us learn how they were doing spiritually. That gave us greater insight in what to pray for for our children. For my children, it taught them personal responsibility. It taught them commitment. It taught them the benefits of transparency and openness. It taught them that relationships can grow stronger from seeking and extending forgiveness. It also deeply encouraged them that they knew they had parents who not only supported them, but wanted to know everything about them and what they were going through.

My wife and I also made a commitment to take family vacations during spring, summer, or winter breaks. To Hawaii (which was just as close as the continental U.S., but warmer!), Southern California, the East Coast, Europe, and Canada. These trips brought us closer together as a family. After Sharon had left for college, a number of times, my son and I would take a father-son trip from Alaska to Southern California to see our beloved USC Trojans play football. We would spend two to three days together, rent a car from the airport, drive around to see the popular tourist sites of Los Angeles, stay at a nearby hotel, and eat whatever food this hungry teenager wanted. On game day, Saturday, we were fired up, decked out in our USC gear, jersey, and hats. We would get so excited in anticipation of the game. On the way to the Los Angeles Memorial Coliseum, walking through a sea of cardinal and gold and seeing all the tailgaters, brought back such fond memories of going to these games with my wife when I was a graduate student and Sharon was just a baby. When the players would run out onto the field, Paul and I would go nuts. Cheering. Screaming. Singing the songs. I taught my son well. Perhaps we were the loudest in our section. Maybe even the entire stadium. We wanted to make sure that we were going to win the game. After all, we did come all the way down from Alaska!

During these father-son trips, not only did we share "the thrill of victory and the agony of defeat," but we would talk about everything: God, school, girls, church, friends, dreams and visions, and struggles. Whenever I booked a hotel, I intentionally requested a king size bed rather than two double beds. When we slept together on the bed, sometimes he would unintentionally kick me in his sleep with his feet or slap my face like we were playing a football game in the middle of the night. I loved it.

During the summer of 1994 I spent part of my sabbatical leave at my alma mater, Kyung Hee University, to help the school develop its vision and plans for the 21st century. I invited Paul, who was going to be a junior in college, to come with me to Seoul and help edit and revise all the school's international marketing and promotional materials (which were originally drafted in so-so English). We stayed together at the university's guest house for two months. We had so much fun. Just me and him. Going out to eat. Meeting up with relatives. Getting the royal treatment from my friends. Cooking kim-chee jjigae (Korean spicy stew) together. Watching the NBA Finals on AFKN. One of my best times in Korea.

When I was invited to speak to the Korean-American Christian student ministry of the University of Texas in Austin in 1999, Paul was given the opportunity to share his testimony before introducing me. I still remember the words he used before I spoke: "The next speaker is my best friend and best pal. One of my fondest memories of me growing up is feeling my father's hands on my head and my chest and hearing him pray for me. He is the same man in private as he is in public. He is a man of integrity. He is my role model and he is my dad. Here is Dr. John Kim!" By the grace of God, we still think of each other as best friends.

Spending time and resources on our children (especially time!) is an investment that will never leave parents disappointed. The returns of such an investment are more than any monetary investment could offer. The returns are clothed with eternity. The excuse of busyness may mean you lose your children to the winds of a wicked world. Parents, as much as you can, spend intimate and interactive time with your children (without the Internet or television!) while they live with you under the same roof. Before they leave your physical care. They are God's precious inheritance!

Get to know them. Talk to them. Take them to dinner. Pray with them. If those habits are solidified while you live together, they will stand the test of time and distance. Even though my children are older and have children of their own and live on the other side of the country (in Greenwich, Connecticut and Vienna, Virginia) from my wife and I (in Monterey, California), we still try to talk to each other every day, through the phone, or on Skype, or by email. I do not remember a time when Sharon or Paul have ever complained, "Mom and Dad, when I needed you, where were you?"

Allowing our children to participate in decisions – however big or small

Whether it's purchasing a home, what color to paint the living room, deciding where to go on our family vacation (and for how long and when), college majors, graduate school applications, buying a car (what make, model and color), or job searches, my wife and I always included Sharon and Paul in the decision-making process.

This involved each one of us bringing our own opinions – based on our own knowledge, biases, experiences and research – to the process as we weighed the pros and cons of the options we were considering. I usually would lead the discussion, but everyone was given equal opportunity to present their case. In most instances, we were able to reach a consensus fairly quickly, but sometimes the discussions could turn lengthy. On a few occasions, they would defer to me, and I would later make the executive decision after some prayer and further reflection. But for the most part, a final decision would not be made until all had agreed. That was the basic principle. It had to be a consensus. We have still kept to this practice with Sharon's and Paul's families when we plan entire family trips or special events, such as birthdays or anniversaries.

By involving our children in the decision-making process and allowing them to have a say, our children gained confidence in expressing their opinions without fear or rebuke. More importantly, they learned how to take ownership of the family's decisions and accept the consequences and responsibilities of those decisions. If a vacation destination wasn't as fun as they thought, for example, they had no one to blame but themselves since they were involved in the decision. The family car was truly the "family's car" as everyone was part of the decision in what we would purchase.

In December 1994, I was nominated for the candidacy of Chancellor of the University of Alaska Anchorage (UAA). The chairman of the chancellor's search committee informed me that I was nominated by a petition of a number of my fellow faculty members. I had to respond to the committee on whether I would accept that nomination and formally apply for the position. I called for an urgent family meeting. Paul was home for winter break from Cornell. Sharon was home as well, visiting us from New York for Christmas. I shared the news with them and asked whether I should accept the candidacy for UAA's chancellor. For several hours we discussed the pros and cons of applying. We prayed together, asking for wisdom and discernment from God.

At that time I immensely enjoyed what I was doing. I never thought about a high administrative position. I was too busy teaching, recently appointed by the university as a Distinguished Professor for International Business, and being the founding Executive Director of the Alaska Center for International Business, a state think tank housed on the university's campus. My passion was for teaching and research, and I was committed to mentoring my students and their learning. I was the first recipient for the Chancellor's Award for Excellence in Teaching (1984). I was also working for Alaska's governor as his advisor on Alaska's economic development and international trade and was formally commended by Alaska's state legislature for my contribution to the state's higher education. I was also deeply involved in serving the Lord at our local church as an elder as well as in the early stages of launching a spiritual awakening and revival movement called Jesus Awakening Movement for America (JAMA). JAMA was planning an unprecedented national conference in Colorado for Korean-American college students across America. Plus, the odds of being selected as the chancellor were very small because I was not trained for or experienced in university administration.

As we discussed these and other matters, Sharon asked, "Dad, what do you have to lose? Whether you get it or not, it's all God's will, right? Why don't you tell them that you'll accept the faculty nomination? We will totally support you." After we took a poll of everyone in the living room and with everyone in agreement, I submitted a letter to the chairman of the chancellor's search committee accepting the nomination.

The application required a lot of time. I had to involve my assistants to gather all the required information and documents. There were 78 other candidates across the nation who also applied. By God's grace, I made it through the first, second, and third round review stages. Through the fourth round of interviews, they told me I was one of the finalists for the job. I completed another round of interviews during which I shared my vision for the university for the 21st Century. I thought I did my best. Now, all I could do was wait.

Several weeks later, in April 1994, the chairman of the search committee informed me that I was not selected. Naturally, at that moment, I was disappointed. Not devastated, but disappointed. I thought if I became the first first-generation Korean-American to become head of a university (at a time when no Korean–American was serving as the president or chancellor of any state university system or major private universities), I would have the platform to challenge and motivate the younger generations to dream higher for their future. But alas, this was not God's will.

I called my wife at her office, and told her what happened. She felt bad for me. After the call, upon my return from class to my office, a bouquet of flowers was waiting for me on my desk with a congratulatory card. It was from my wife! I laughed. I called my wife again.

"'Congratulations'? For not getting it? That was a pretty low blow, honey!"

She laughed.

"Honey, God has already given you your appointed tasks for this time in your life – JAMA and the upcoming JAMA national conference. What would happen to His plan if you become the chancellor? You can't be used as effectively for fulfilling His vision for JAMA as a state university chancellor. God's vision is so big and so great that it can't be possibly compared with a chancellor's job. If it's God's will for you to become a chancellor one day, he will give it to you in due time."

"Sung, how did you pray for the outcome of my candidacy – for or against?"

"I prayed to God that you wouldn't be shamed as God's child. So God led you all the way as one of the finalists. You should be proud of yourself for that. I don't think anybody believed that you would make it that far due to your lack of administrative experience and skill. And also being a first-generation Korean-American. So I congratulate you!" Her conviction, honesty, godly perspective, and encouragement greatly comforted me. She is indeed the best cheerleader.

Most parents often do not allow their children to participate in the decision-making process even with decisions that directly affect them. They regard their children as either too young or immature to understand. They get brushed off too easily since parents feel that they don't have to know about "adult" or "parental" matters. So most decisions affecting the family one way or the other are made without their children's involvement. But, except for extremely sensitive, mature, or nuanced matters, we should give them a chance to weigh in. Children are smarter and more intelligent than we think. They can also be amazingly cooperative and contributing when they are allowed into the decision making process. Let's not undervalue them. Let them be involved in what restaurant to take mommy for her birthday, or where to go for spring break, or which charity to contribute to, or which movies to watch on family movie night, or which gifts to buy the grandparents for Christmas, or what extracurricular activities they wish to pursue. (At the same time, let's be careful not to overvalue our children's opinions and let them dictate, for example, which church the family should commit to. There is a difference between having them involved and participating in the process, on the one hand, and having them dictate and determine the outcome, on the other.)

If we don't involve our children in the decision-making process, how are they able to learn how to make their own decisions when they grow up? To weigh the pros and cons? To learn what it means to commit to a decision? And deal with its consequences? How would they know how to discern God's calling and His will without seeing and experiencing that spiritual search alongside their parents when they were younger? Will they learn any of these things from school (or even Sunday school)? Don't bet on it. The training of our children to make decisions in a God-honoring, God-exalting manner should come from the parents. From a young age.

Our children have learned three important things from this: first, they were able to see how my wife and I, as a couple, came to decisions that were aligned with God's will. They have seen how (and why) we put Christ as the center in all our decisions, and through those experiences, they gained the tools to make God-centered decisions on their own. Second, they learn to respect others' opinions and perspectives. Third, they learn to take ownership and responsibility to carry out the decisions that the family reaches. If I used my fatherly authority to make unilateral decisions and do what I only wanted, my family would probably follow my decision, but there would be little enjoyment for them. If my decision went well, there would be no shared sense of fulfillment or accomplishment for them since it was my decision, not theirs. There would be no sense of togetherness. And if my decision did not turn out well, then I would be the one who gets the blame. There would be no teachable moment for my children about responsibility. "It was Dad's decision, therefore it is Dad's problem, not ours." Again, there would be no sense of unity.

I have met a number of Korean-American students who were forced by their parents to go to a specific school, study a specific major, or pursue a specific vocation. Be a doctor. Be a lawyer. Be an engineer. Go into finance. Don't be a poor artist. Many of these students dutifully followed their parents' orders for their futures, but were miserable inside, despised their parents, and hated the professions they ended up in. Those who weren't as "dutiful" were miserable as well as they constantly fought with their parents; many end up being disowned. More often than not, overbearing fathers were to blame. I have counseled countless young people whose opinions, gifts, and dreams were disregarded by their parents. Whose fathers have abused their authority and ruled the lives of their children's futures.

My wife and I never forced our children to go to a certain college or major in a specific field – in fact, my preference was for them to go to the University of Alaska Anchorage so they could go for free (as they were the children of faculty) and become professors like me! They took the lead in that important decision after much discussion, consultation, prayer, and consensus-building with their parents. Although they both chose to go to the East Coast to study (one with a business degree and the other with a law degree – no Ph.Ds!), it was a decision over which they had ownership, and thus, it was a decision they were committed to. This was my and my wife's way of showing that this was their lives to live in Him, not their lives to live for us.

Not favoring one over the other

Favoritism is a sin. And it's been around. We see it in how Isaac favored Esau, how Rachel favored Jacob and how that particular sin was passed down, as Jacob favored Joseph over his brothers. The favoring of sons over daughters in particular has been, and continues to be, entrenched in Korean culture. That too is a sin. I grew up in that culture. I was favored by my mom. My older sister was not. She was treated unfairly. She was deeply hurt. I was everything to my mom simply because I was a boy. This made me that much more selfish growing up. Thankfully, my wife grew up in an exceptional (more Westernized) family where all eight kids were treated with equal dignity, respect, and fairness. When my wife and I had Paul (ironically, after my wife pleaded for another child as I was content with just Sharon!), we vowed that we would treat Sharon and Paul the same way.

By God's grace, my wife and I did not treat our children differently. We did not treat one more favorably over the other because one was the eldest, or because one was doing better in school, or because one was a boy. To us, they were both specially made, specially designed, and specially loved and cherished by our Heavenly Father and were His gifts to us. Although Sharon and Paul have their own God-given personalities and their own individual struggles and sins – to which we tailored our parenting, prayers, and advice – and Sharon, as the older child, was told to care for the younger Paul, and for Paul to respect the authority of Sharon, we never favored one over the other. This is something that we have continued to practice with respect to our five grandchildren.

Not comparing them to others

Like many parents, we used to compare our children with other children in such things as grades, work ethic, studiousness, obedience, and personalities. This was a sin that my wife and I had to repent of. We realized that whenever we compared Sharon or Paul to other kids, it caused them pain, planted seeds of inferiority, and often turned into quarrels. If left unchecked, those seeds of inferiority can lead to bitterness and envy which can lead to jealousy and hatred.

When Sharon was 10 years old, my wife compared her to a friend's daughter who was the same age and who was "gentle and always obedient."

"Sharon, why can't you be like her?"

Crying, Sharon yelled, "Mom, do you want to replace me with her?! No matter what, I am your daughter! Why don't you love me and treat me as I am!"

Through the mouth of our daughter, God awakened us at the moment to our sin. Sharon's challenge was true – she was our one and only precious daughter. A gift from God. We resolved then that we would not compare Paul and Sharon to others and that we would raise them to be the best as God meant them to be. The next day, both my wife and I apologized to Sharon and asked for her forgiveness. We also told her that we would never compare her to anyone. Ever again.

Parents can harm their children's development when they compare their children to other children not only in a negative way, but in a positive way as well. In other words, when we as parents overtly or discreetly brag and boast about our children with our peers, especially in front of our children, this could encourage pride and plant superiority complexes within them to the detriment of their characters.

Children are God's most precious gifts to parents. Let us, as parents, nurture them and raise them as unique individuals, specially and sovereignly made by our Creator. Let us love them not for what they do for us and can do for us, but for who they are. Let us cherish their thoughts and ideas and opinions. Let us harness their gifts for the Kingdom of God, not our own personal fulfillment. Let us marshal their dreams for the spreading of the Gospel, not for own personal desires. Let us pray selfless prayers for them. Let us demonstrate to them lives transformed by grace and the Holy Spirit. Let us model Christ's love to them.

For my 70th birthday in 2009, Paul gave me a fold-out picture frame. On one side there was a picture of the two of us. On the other side, there were these words printed out that, by God's grace, were written by Paul:

AS A FATHER TO A SON, YOU HAVE BEEN...
A WISE COUNSELLOR,
A CLOSE CONFIDANT,
A SELFLESS ADVISOR,
A LOVING TEACHER,
A SPIRITUAL MENTOR,
A BEST FRIEND,
A MODEL OF INTEGRITY

HAPPY 70TH BIRTHDAY, DAD

Chapter 15

OUR SILVER WEDDING ANNIVERSARY

March 11, 1992 was our 25th wedding anniversary, or "silver anniversary" as they call it. And I wanted to do something really special for my wife. I wanted to show how much she meant to me. To show her my gratitude. Back when we were living in Glendale, California, the children of our apartment owner threw their parents a surprise silver anniversary party. What an experience. To see that couple utterly astonished and surprised. Overjoyed. And the ensuing celebration. I had never seen anything like it.

That party had always stayed with me and I wanted to do something like that for Sung. The difficulty was that I wasn't really good at organizing such things. I had never really done it before. Sung did all that kind of stuff. Plus, Sharon was all the way in Washington, D.C., finishing her M.B.A. at George Washington. But I felt we had to do something. It was already early February.

The thought of a surprise party really excited Sharon and Paul. Thankfully, Sharon was a mastermind when it came to this stuff. Even though she was in Washington, D.C., she would make the calls to handle the cake and the food. She told us a list of things that Paul and I had to do immediately and we got started. Invite list. Invitation cards. Mailing them. I had to do all of that with Paul's help away from the house, at my office. My wife wondered why I needed to take Paul with me to the office on a Saturday, but thankfully she didn't suspect anything at the time. All I told her was I needed his help. The date was set for March 7. A Saturday. The guests had to arrive at our house by 6:00 p.m. Sharp.

The surprise for Sung was of course the party with friends, neighbors, and loved ones. But the bigger surprise was that Sharon would fly out for the party. So I had to come up with a way to buy her plane ticket without my wife finding out since she handled all the family's finances. I couldn't withdraw cash from my checking account. Or use a credit card. My wife would notice, especially for a larger purchase. Then I remembered that my mother, who was living with us at the time, would keep in her room a substantial amount of cash. She laughed when I asked her to lend me $800 for the ticket. I promised to pay her back. I explained to her the surprise. I begged her to keep it a secret. She laughed some more and said, "Of course!" Plane ticket purchased. Plane ticket mailed. Arrival for Sharon was set for March 6, the day before the party.

Sung still had no idea what was going on. But it came real close. Sung was a realtor and ten days before the surprise party she visited the office of the Consulate General from Korea to discuss a property matter. At one point during their conversation, he mentioned, "You must be quite busy preparing for a big party at your home next Saturday. We are honored to be invited by Dr. Kim and you. We will be there."

"Excuse me, but what party?" inquired Sung. "I didn't know about any party. You said it will be at my home? I would have known about that since I would be the one preparing for something like that. You must be confusing us with the other Dr. Kim." The "other" Dr. Kim was a medical doctor in Anchorage.

When my wife came home, she told me about her "strange" conversation with the Consul General about a party. A chill went up my spine. A cold sweat came over me. I froze.

"Honey," she asked, "why didn't Dr. Kim and his wife invite us to their house for this party?"

"Probably because we aren't that close to them. Maybe it's only for close friends."

"But the Consul General is going."

"Well, maybe they are closer to them."

Calm. Collected. Matter of fact. No hesitation. But inside, disbelief and annoyance that it was almost ruined. But relieved that it wasn't. *Thank you, Lord.* Given that the countless dinners we hosted at our home always went through her and her unmatched hosting and culinary skills, she still wasn't suspicious that anything was up. I later learned that the Consul General's secretary just looked at the date and location of the invitation, not the bottom part of the card which explained that it was a surprise party.

On March 6, Paul and I picked Sharon up from the airport and headed directly to the store to buy decorations, party plates, napkins, and plasticware, as well as fruits and vegetables and other items for the party. We then dropped off Sharon at her friend's home, where she would be staying the night. Paul and I drove separately so my wife wouldn't suspect anything. He arrived back home first. I came later, with my trunk stuffed (Paul had a pick-up truck so we had to store the items in my car). *Let's hope she doesn't need to check the car for anything.* The three of us had dinner. Just like we always did. Sung still had no clue. *Thank you, Lord.*

Paul and Sharon and our friends and my assistants needed at least six hours to get the house cleaned, decorated, and ready for the party. So the plan was to come up with an excuse to get my wife out of the house by noon. At the latest. This was the final hurdle and it wasn't going to be easy. The weather certainly wasn't on my side. Early March in Alaska is still cold, with plenty of snow still on the ground. A long drive for a day trip didn't seem feasible. And it was too random and out-of-the-ordinary for us to do at that time of the year. She would suspect something. But then again, what were we supposed to do in town for six hours?

11:30 a.m. Paul is getting anxious. He starts motioning me to get on it. His eyes are telling me to get out of the house.

"Sung, what do you think about going out to lunch? And then to a movie?"

"Why would we go to a movie during the day? Let's go out

to dinner and then to a movie."

"That may be too late for us. We have to go to church the next morning and you know that Sundays are pretty long days for us."

"That's true."

"You know what? We haven't visited the businesses of our church members recently and prayed for them that we used to do on Saturdays. And some of our members have opened new businesses that we haven't been able to see yet. They really love it when we come visit. What do you think? We can visit them after lunch and then maybe we'll stop by Nordstrom. To buy my anniversary gift to you."

"Okay. Let's do that." *Thank you, Lord.*

Almost noon. As we were about to leave, I saw that my wife was dressed in very casual clothing, underneath her everyday coat. I wouldn't have cared if we were just visiting these businesses or going shopping, but I didn't want her to be too casual for her own surprise party.

"Sung, would you mind if you put on something a little more nicer? I am visiting these businesses as their elder and I want us to look decent, presentable. Do you think you could do that for me?" Paul overheard the conversation and, not knowing where I was coming from, was visibly annoyed. Further delays. Time was of the essence.

"Okay, honey." *Thank you, Lord.* As soon as we left, Paul gave the okay for Sharon and the rest of the group who were helping us to come over.

After lunch, my wife and I were able to visit two businesses and pray for them. It was a great time of fellowship with the owners and my wife remarked that my visitation idea was a great one. When we came to the third business, it had already closed. I guess they closed early on Saturdays. This was a problem. It was only 4:30.

"Sung, I went to Nordstrom the other day after class to

look for an anniversary gift for you. I think I might've found something you'll like. Can we go check it out? If you like it, I'd like to get it for you before I leave to Washington, D.C. next week."

"Okay." *Thank you, Lord.*

I took my time driving to the Fifth Avenue Mall, where Nordstrom was. I took my time parking the car in the garage. I took my time entering the mall. I took my time entering Nordstrom. I showed her the handbag that I saw the other day. She said it was nice, but she wanted to look around some more. *Hallelujah.* We went upstairs to look at some clothes. We went back downstairs to look at more bags. And then she found one she really liked. She was very happy with the gift. I was happy too since it was 10 minutes to 6. So far, so good.

6:15 p.m. As we were about to turn left onto the street where our house was, I knew that there would be a lot of cars parked for the party. Paul had earlier handed me a scarf to blindfold my wife so she wouldn't see the cars when we returned. I stopped the car. I took out the scarf.

"Why do I have to put this on? What's going on?"

"Paul wanted to do something special for our anniversary. Especially before I leave next week. He insisted that I have you put this on before coming in the house. Maybe he wants to surprise you with something. Like a banner or sign or something."

"Really?"

"He really wants you to. Just do it for him."

She complied. Without any fuss. Just as I had imagined, there were a lot of cars. We parked in a spot that was saved for us, right across from our house. Our street was still icy so I held my wife's hand and escorted her up the driveway and to the front door. The blindfold was still secure. I rang the doorbell and Paul opened the door. I took her blindfold off. The first thing she saw to her left from the foyer was the dining table, standing alone, adorned with all kinds of food, drinks, and desserts. Her mouth kept saying, "Wow." That was the first surprise for her. Then, when she walked past the table in the dining room and into the family room, all the guests screamed.

"Surprise! Happy anniversary!"

Applause broke out. This was the second surprise. She could not believe what she was seeing. People everywhere. Her mouth was agape. Speechless. She looked at all the guests. Then she looked at me. "Oh my goodness! Oh my goodness!" I hugged and kissed her. It was the reaction I was waiting so long to see. As I saw the look on Sung's face, I thanked God for blessing us with His love and grace and for blessing me with an amazingly steadfast wife.

As laughter and joy filled the air, the phone in the kitchen was ringing. Some of the guests motioned to the kitchen, telling my wife that someone was calling. My wife picked up the phone. It was Sharon. The house got a little quieter.

"Hi, Sharon!" Mother and daughter started talking about the party and how I took her out for the day and blindfolded her so she would be surprised. Sung then put her hand over the phone and told the guests that it was her daughter on the line.

"Mom," said Sharon, "hold on one second. Someone's at the door. Let me go see who it is. Don't hang up, I'll be right back." At that moment, Sharon walked down from her old room upstairs and headed through the family room and into the kitchen.

"Hi Mom!"

My wife screamed, "Sharon!"

They hugged and cried. It was an indescribable moment between them. It was a moment of sheer bliss. Our family wasn't the only one in the room that had tears that night. It was a night that would be never be forgotten. *Thank you, Lord.*

Before the cake cutting, I shared a short testimony of God's grace towards our family and how we were able to keep the party a secret from my wife. My wife admitted that she really underestimated my ability to pull off something like this. She was impressed. Everyone laughed. I ribbed the Consul General a little too. Everyone laughed some more. I thanked everyone for coming, especially those friends, neighbors, and my assistants who helped with the party. I gave special thanks to Sharon and Paul.

The party was not the only surprise for the 25th year of our marriage. In late August, I received a call from the office of UAA's Chancellor Donald Behrend inquiring about our availability for a reception at 5:30 p.m. on September 10. Dr. Behrend's secretary specifically requested that both my wife and I be in attendance. I checked my calendar and said the both of us would be there. When we arrived at the reception, we were surprised by the huge number of attendees – the university president, the chancellor, vice chancellors, members of the University of Alaska Board of Regents, the University of Alaska Foundation trustees, deans, faculty members, local, state, and federal government officials, and even student representatives. The chairperson of the university foundation and Dr. Behrend approached us with two corsages – one for me and my wife.

"Dr. Behrend, what's this for?," I asked.

"John and Sung, this reception is for you!"

"Are you kidding me?!"

"Nope. John, this is to celebrate and honor you for receiving the Bullock award."

I couldn't believe it. Then the university president came over to congratulate me, "John, you deserve it. Your accomplishments and contributions to the university and the state are truly exceptional and exemplary. I appreciate all your hard work and dedication. I am very proud of you. Now, let's have great time!"

Although I was informed back in May by the chairperson and Dr. Behrend that I had been awarded the Edith R. Bullock Prize of Excellence, the highest honor bestowed by the university, I had no idea that there would be any reception. Sung and I were overwhelmed with thanksgiving to God by the turnout. Later that evening, I was given a heavy jade plaque commemorating my award as well as a $15,000 check. The latter would be going to my wife. Dr. Behrend also bestowed upon me the title of "Distinguished Professor." I felt so undeserving. So humbled. So honored. So joyous. This was all God's work. It was all His grace and favor. "For it is God who works in you to will and to act according to His good purposes" (Philippians 2:13, NKJ). It was an unforgettable evening.

Dr. Behrend suggested I use some of the $15,000 take Sung to a Caribbean cruise to celebrate our anniversary. Sung and I were already talking about doing such a trip since we had never done a cruise before and now we had the money to do it! God was so gracious with His timing. So the next month, in October, Sung and I took our first ever cruise on the Caribbean Sea – it was spectacular. I was also able to use some of the award money to finally buy Sung a diamond ring. When we first got married, I was only able to afford a simple, thin ring of white gold. Sung never asked for an upgrade all those years. She was always content with what we had and what we could afford. Now, after 25 years, after my liver disease, after Big Bear, after His transformation of my heart, after God's favor on me and my work at the university, I could now get her a ring with a diamond on it.

Seeing the new ring on her finger, I was reminded of Ephesians 3:20-21: "Now to Him who is able to do immeasurably more than all we ask or imagine, according to His power that is at work within us, to Him be glory in the church and in Christ Jesus throughout all generations, forever and ever." Because of God's transforming grace and power, He has immeasurably blessed me with the best wife and two precious gifts – Sharon and Paul – and darling grandchildren. All because of Jesus Christ. *What have I done to receive this grace, this love, this mercy, this favor? Lord, I give you all praise, glory, honor, and thanksgiving. You, and you alone!*

PART 3
GOD'S
CALL

Chapter 16

THE CALL TO ALASKA

"Commit your way to the LORD;
Trust in Him and He will do this:
He will make your righteousness shine like the dawn,
The justice of your cause like the noonday sun." (Ps. 37:5-6)

Decisions, decisions. Choices, choices.

While our sovereign God chose which family we were born into, what we look like, and what our gender would be, He graciously grants His children a freedom to make choices, to make decisions, to pursue paths, to pursue callings. Where to live. Where to study. What to study. What job to take. What job not to take. What man to date. What woman to marry. Whether to have children. Whether to have more children. Whether to adopt. What church to worship at. Which country to be a missionary in.

We must honor God with these decisions. We must cling to Him. Go to Him. Pray to Him. Ask for wisdom. Ask for discernment. Ask for understanding. Ask for clarity. Ask for an infusion of the Holy Spirit. Ask for faith and trust to follow. Ask for the power, strength, and ability to carry through. Ask for boldness and courage to make the hard decisions. It pleases Him when His children do this. It glorifies Him. It shows that He is not just being consulted, but that He is in charge. That He is Lord. We can never rely too much on God in making choices.

Korea vs. Alaska vs. Staying

Brigadier General Kim, a top official of the KCIA (now known as Korean's National Intelligence Service (NIS)) visited me at my office at Pepperdine University. General Kim worked out of the Los Angeles office of the Korean Consulate General. He came to campus without any advance notice. It was February 1980. We spoke for about a half hour. It was a pleasant conversation. Before he left, he abruptly mentioned that I should consider going back to Korea and serve the country as a government official. I chuckled and told him that I had no desire to go back there. I told him that I liked where I was and what I was doing.

Undeterred, a few days later, General Kim called and asked to have lunch. We went to Dong Il Jang, a restaurant on 8th Street in the growing "Korea Town" of Los Angeles. We talked about General Chun Do Hwan. He talked about his run for the Presidency in the upcoming election in May and said that General Chun was in the process of vetting potential cabinet positions (should he win the upcoming election, which he did) and top aides. In addition to policy wonks, economists, lawyers, and business leaders, he was looking for scholars and academics, of which I was on the short list. I was the second one to be contacted. This was all surprising to me. He suggested I take a trip to Korea to meet with the General and asked me to send my resumé. I told him I still wasn't interested. I said that it was deeply honoring and humbling to be asked, but I liked being just a college professor in America. He told me that he understood. "But send a resumé anyway."

Back in my office, I kept replaying the lunch conversation over and over in my head. I became intrigued at the thought of returning to Korea. In triumph. Of being a government big shot. In the new regime. To prove the naysayers wrong. I was tempted. *It's just sending a resumé. I'm not agreeing to do anything. I'm just doing this as a professional courtesy. It would be rude not to.*

My wife had other thoughts. Strong ones.

"If you want to go back to Korea, you go by yourself. I'm staying here with the kids!"

"Honey, I told him I wasn't interested."

"If you told him that, then why did you send him your

resumé?!"

"Just as a courtesy. That's all. That's it. He was very insistent."

"You still shouldn't have done that. Now, he's going to think you are interested. I'm not going back to Korea. I'm not going back."

A week later, I flew to San Francisco to present a research paper at the Political Science Association's Annual Conference. Some of the Korean-American professors in attendance were invited to a dinner reception on the first evening of the conference. Professor Park Myung Soo (former president of Joongang University), a senior of mine when I was studying at USC, and for whom I had the utmost respect, came up to me.

"Dong Saeng[39], when are you going back to Korea?"

"Hyung Nim[40], how do you know about this!?"

"I, too, was contacted. The recruitment of professors like us is already being written about in the Korean newspapers in LA. Didn't you know?"

"I had no idea until General Kim told me about it over lunch."

"If you want power, now is the time to go back. Now is the time to negotiate with General Chun and his staff for a position in his administration. Before the election, not after. By then it will be too late."

"I see."

"I know you will do greater things in Korea than in America. This seems like the best opportunity for you. If you go now and not only help with the election, but also help with forming the new government, you may land a top appointment. What do you think?"

By this time, to escape the noise, we were out in the courtyard.

"Hyung Nim, I told them I wasn't interested. I did send my resumé, but they've made no promises to me yet. Even if I go and meet General Chun, there's no guarantee what job I'm going to get. I would have to take a sabbatical or an extended, emergency leave. There's lots of risk. I need to pray more and discern God's will for me. Right now, my heart is not in that direction. What about you, Hyung Nim?"

"I have no desire to go back at this time as well. Let me know what you decide to do."

"I will. And please pray for me."

If this opportunity had presented itself prior to my liver disease and prior to my spiritual transformation, I would have probably taken the first flight out from LAX to Seoul and diligently and passionately, and with much politicking, pursued a top appointment. Driven by "han" and bitterness. Driven by my inferiority complex. Driven for success and prestige. Driven by the hatred that filled me when I left Korea. And when I would achieve such a position, I would make sure to let those people know who looked down upon me and my socio-economic (and non-Seoul University) standing that I was in power now. That I would have the last laugh. I would make them feel sorry for discriminating against me. *See, I told you so.* I would've relished that. But I was no longer that person.

The next morning, I presented my research paper at one of the energy policy panels, after which one of the participants approached me, complimenting me on my paper and presentation. He was Dr. Steve Aufrecht, a professor of Public Administration from the University of Alaska Anchorage. He asked if I had some time to talk with him. I said yes and we found some chairs in a quiet place off in the corner of the hotel lobby.

Dr. Aufrecht turned out to be a USC alumnus as well and knew a lot of the professors that I knew. They had suggested to him that we meet.

"Why meet with me?"

"Dr. Kim, you were the main reason why I came down

here from Alaska. I came here to recruit you to my school, the University of Alaska Anchorage. I've heard great things about you from my former professors and friends at Pepperdine. My dean asked me to come down to meet you. I'm actually the chairman of the faculty search committee."

"My goodness, Dr. Aufrecht. You flew all the way to San Francisco just to meet me?"

"That's right. We are looking for a person who not only teaches well, but who is well-versed in current energy and environmental issues and policies and their delicate relationship with federal, state, and local governments. We are looking for an expert in America's energy industry, of which, as you know, Alaska plays a major role, together with its native community. You come highly recommended, Dr. Kim. We want you to come to Alaska."

He handed me an application form.

"Professor Aufrecht, I am deeply honored and touched. It is very flattering. But Alaska? I have no desire to go to Alaska. I like where I am right now."

"Could you at least just fill out the application and give it back to me later today. I would be really grateful if you could do just that for me. Please. It won't take too long to fill it out."

After returning home from the conference, I got a call from Dr. Aufrecht. Apparently, he got my phone number from the application I turned in. He invited my family to his father's home in Santa Monica for a barbeque on Saturday. He was persistent. I accepted. After we finished dinner in his father's backyard, Dr. Aufrecht invited us into the house for some dessert and coffee. Then he began to show us slides of Alaska from a projector – the beautiful landscape, the majestic Mount McKinley. The sceneries were breathtaking. I never realized how beautiful Alaska was. He then began to show slides of seafood – my all-time favorite food! Alaskan king crab, Dungeness crab, snow crab, halibut, lingcod, cod, trout, and wild salmon, which was not only my all-time favorite seafood, but one that was integral to my special diet (and for which we had to pay more than $6 per pound at that time)! I was salivating. But I tried to play it cool.

I was now faced with some decisions. These were my choices. Stay. Or Go. And if I go, is it to Alaska or Korea? All of them had their pluses. And minuses too. I had no choice but to do business with my Lord and Savior. These were the five steps I took:

Renew your mind and be transformed.

"Do not conform any longer to the pattern of this world, but be transformed by the renewing of your mind. Then you will be able to test and approve what God's will is – His good, pleasing and perfect will" (Rom. 12:2).

Our minds have to be renewed if we truly desire to seek and understand God's will. This means that our hearts and our thinking and our desires must be pure in the sight of God, that they are not dictated by power, prestige, wealth, and self. We must come in repentance to God, asking Him to rid us of any improper motives or justifications, to cleanse us from within with the blood of Jesus Christ, so that nothing would be a hindrance or an obstacle in what He wants to communicate to us and ultimately, where He wants to lead us. Whether it's a small pebble or a large boulder, there are ripple effects from sin. Our conscience, through awakening, reflection and repentance, must be clear and renewed before our Almighty God when He seek His will.

Seek first His Kingdom.

"But seek first the Kingdom of God and His Righteousness, then all these things shall be added to you." (Matt. 6:33, NKJV).

A cleansed mind and heart will lead us to Scripture. After all, the Bible is not only God's gift to us, but God's will for us – in written form. Oh, how much time can be wasted when we search for "God's will" and neglect the fact that the Bible is His will?! We must rely on this word, not on our own logic, reasoning, dominant culture and worldview, or current value system. Our decisions must be dictated and aligned with His commands and teachings. Let He be the motivation. Let He be the reason. Let His word be the source. Let His word be the guide. Let His word be the justification. Let His word provide the support. We must earnestly seek His face and His Kingdom. This will further renew us. And transform us.

Don't conform to the world's standards.

"Do not conform any longer to the pattern of this world . . ." (Rom. 12:2a)

We are not of this world. But we are still called to live in it. (John 17:14-15). But not to conform to it. The pattern of this world is about power and prestige, not humility; about being served, not serving; about accumulating, not giving; about consuming, not covenanting; about personal satisfaction, not commitment; about independence, not prayerful reliance; about my needs, not my neighbor's; about what can be seen and touched, not what can't; about the here-and-now, not the eternal. In this way, we must be counter-worldly (or counter-cultural) in how we make decisions. We don't seek the approval of society, but of God. Having our hearts and minds renewed and our Bibles open before us, we must ask God to search ourselves and reveal in us the dictates of this world that influence the decision-making process. We must also ask trusted brothers and sisters in Christ, accountability partners, and our spiritual mentors and leaders to ask the hard, pointed questions of us to further probe our thinking.

Ask the Holy Spirit to come and work.

We must earnestly plead for the Holy Spirit to illuminate us. To give us wisdom and discernment. To prompt us. To give us the ears to hear His voice and the eyes to see His plans for us. This call to pray for the Holy Spirit is one we cannot take lightly. It is something we must do with great urgency and concentration. Pray for each choice that is before you and boldly ask God where He wants you to be. Pray as Jesus taught us: "Our Father in heaven, Hallowed be Your name, Your kingdom come, Your will be done, On earth as it is in heaven" (Matt. 6:9-10, NKJV). If we seek God's Kingdom first from a purified heart and renewed, counter-cultural motive, the Holy Spirit will help lead us to God's will for us on earth.

Ask God for the courage to obey His will.

If a choice seems like an easy one to make, the proverbial "slam dunk," then we don't necessarily seek God's help and guidance. We don't go to Him in prayer. We don't go to Him in the Scriptures. And when that choice turns out to be the "right" one, we get the glory. Not Him. We get puffed up, and He doesn't get magnified. I've learned that God's choice is not always the easy one; in my experience, it can be the most difficult one. It's the "narrow path." That's usually what happens when the ways of this world seem wide (and thus, more appealing to our sinful nature), but the counter-worldly way doesn't. But in the latter situations, we are left to completely rely on Him and His power. We glorify Him in this dependence. We glorify Him by asking that it's His will, not ours. We glorify Him because He gets the credit when there is fruit and blessing from our decision. The easy choice for Jesus would be not to drink the cup and go to the cross. This doesn't mean that we should always seek out those opportunities that will prove to be the hardest and most challenging for us. But when faced with alternatives (of which staying in your current situation is always one), the question is not to ask, "Which is the most challenging?" but "What would Jesus in this situation, based on the whole counsel of Scripture and the Gospel, do?" And then ask God for the courage to take that step of faith. To take that risk for Him knowing that whatever happens, we are confident that His will will be done, "on earth as it is in heaven."

Should I Stay Or Should I Go?

My wife wanted nothing to do with Alaska or Korea. My children felt the same way. Life was good for us in Orange County. My teaching. The weather. Our church. The kids loved their friends. Sharon would bring them over to our house every weekend to swim in our backyard pool. We were happy. After recovering from my illness, I thought I'd never leave Southern California. Now, I was contemplating the possibility of turning things upside down for me and my family. I went to God with my dilemma. I confessed and repented of my sins. I ask God to forgive me for being too comfortable and spiritually complacent, ever since I had been healed from my liver disease. When things go well, we have a tendency to spend less (not more) time with God and that was true of me. So I asked God to forgive me for forgetting Him at times. I asked God to search my heart and awaken me to my sins so that I may be cleansed and renewed. I ask that any worldly motive within me be exposed with His wisdom and for the courage to crush it. I asked Him to fill me with his immeasurable peace knowing that He is the Lord of all things, and directing every step.

While I was praying, the Holy Spirit reminded me of Genesis's account of Joseph (Gen. 37-50). I read through and meditated on those chapters not once, but three times. I sensed that God was convicting me to be a Joseph – in Alaska. I ignored the thought. Initially. And then I became puzzled by it. *What does becoming a "Joseph in Alaska" mean? What does that look like? How could I become one?* And then I became insecure about it. *Who am I that I could be anything like Joseph – anywhere?* And then I became intrigued by it.

At the same time, General Kim kept pestering me. He kept calling. Pepperdine was also going through some restructuring and the thought of moving to a more research-emphasis university – whether in Alaska or anywhere else – crossed my mind because I wanted to continue my research in the areas of energy resource development and international trade. I kept praying and seeking God's will and going through the five steps and preaching to myself that God was sovereign. *Maybe for some reason, I won't get an offer from Alaska. Something always can happen. That would make things a lot easier.*

I got the formal offer from UAA. From the Dean of the School of Business and Public Affairs. I was a unanimous choice by the search committee. The compensation, including benefits, was more than enough. Several days after receiving the offer, Dr. Aufrecht called to see if I had received it. He also mentioned that the duplex house they would like to rent for me and my family was only a two-minute drive from the university. "We really want you to come to the Last Frontier to build a great school together with us." I was given a month to decide. It was the beginning of May.

What Dr. Aufrecht said about the two-minute commute stayed with me. Three hours of my day were spent on the road, going to and from Pepperdine. And those were the days without traffic. *Imagine being able to have an additional three hours a day, to be more productive, to spend more time with family, to spend more time serving?* There were times when the traffic got so bad, I would be inhaling exhaust from other vehicles for two hours, giving me a severe headache before my first lecture began in the morning. When I drove back home I was spent and exhausted, physically and mentally from the day – and the traffic. As much as I loved driving, it took a toll on me. And it wasn't really driving – more like a series of starts and stops. It also didn't help that our church – which was in Los Angeles's growing Korea Town – was over an hour away.

Even as I tried to explain these and the other reasons I felt God was opening my eyes to the potential of Alaska, almost everyone discouraged me. Pepperdine's Vice President of Academic Affairs, Dr. John Nicks, summed up the thoughts of my colleagues – many of whom had the same commute that I had! – when he asked, "Why in the world, John, would you go to Alaska?! Are you crazy?!" My senior pastor and fellow elders and the deacons at my church also thought I was out of my mind. "Everything is going well for you Elder Kim, why shake things up?" Other friends and relatives either thought that staying was a no-brainer or that I had a better chance of becoming a "big shot" in Korea than the forty-ninth state. "Alaska of all places? Is there anything in Alaska?"

There was only one who supported a move to Alaska. Dr. Lammers. My former mentor at USC. America was just recovering from a major energy crisis, mainly involving oil, so it was a topic of much discussion in the classroom and in the faculty lounge. Now, with the prospect of going to Alaska, I went back and reviewed my research on energy development and came across my findings regarding the Trans-Alaska Pipeline System, a massive and unprecedented undertaking which transported crude oil from Alaska's northern Prudhoe Bay 800 miles to the state's southern Valdez Port, and then loaded onto supertankers which sailed to the refineries in the continental U.S. – or what Alaskans call the "Lower 48." I was reminded that Alaska was second to none as far as energy and natural resources. Blessed with oil and natural gas as well as minerals and seafood, far from being "Seward's Folly," Alaska was the richest state, energy-wise, resource-wise.

It was also – geographically, speaking – positioned strategically in the circumpolar region and the U.S.s closest outpost to the Russian Far East and the Asia-Pacific Rim. *Were things coming full circle?* My doctoral dissertation was on energy development and its environmental and social impacts. My research and teaching expanded on that to include international trade policy. And the man who started me on this path was the only one who was in favor of Alaska, Dr. Lammers, a brother in Christ. Perhaps, God had been preparing me for the move to Alaska all along.

"In his heart a man plans his course, but the LORD determines his steps" (Prov. 16:9).

But my family was against it. Adamantly against it. *How can I make this decision Lord if my wife and children oppose it? Even though I had sensed your call to go? If everyone's opposed to it Lord, maybe it's not your will?* I put off the decision as long as I could. I procrastinated. I was hesitant. I didn't want to think about it because it paralyzed me. I didn't want to deal with the conflict or second-guessing that would be sure to greet me if we moved to Alaska. Alaska was the hardest option that was before me. At least my wife and I grew up in Korea and had all our extended family there. In Alaska, we had nothing, and for all that my family knew, there was nothing "way up there" but snow. For my family, especially Sharon, California seemed to have everything. She excelled at Golden Elementary School in Placentia, where we lived, made a ton of friends and loved her church community. Our backyard pool was *the* meeting place for her neighborhood friends. And she was finishing up sixth grade and headed to Tuffrey Junior High School to be joined by all her friends from Golden and the neighborhood. She was the ringleader. She was 12. She was excited. Until she learned that all of that could come to an end.

Throughout the month of May, every evening when I returned

home from work, she'd ask, without fail, "Dad, are we going to Alaska?" And whatever I said to her and however I responded, she would always end our conversation with a sigh, "OK, Dad. But I don't want to go to Alaska." I dreaded coming home because of that. My heart would break each time. If we were to move, no doubt she would take it the hardest. So I kept putting off the decision. Until I was forced to on a California highway.

The Drive Home

Ever since I received the offer from UAA, I became much more sleepier behind the wheel. It didn't matter if it was in the morning with coffee in my system or in the evening when I would usually get my second wind. It was strange. I loved driving and I had never been sleepy before on my daily commutes. Now I was forced to yell at myself, sing and pray loudly, turn up the radio, slap my face a couple of times, or pinch my thighs or forearms. But that hardly helped. It got to the point where I would frequently pull off on the side of the road or an emergency shoulder and plea to God to keep me alert. I never experienced a harder time driving. I told my wife about it and hinted that maybe this means we should at least give Alaska a try for one year. She was not persuaded.

It was the last Wednesday evening in May, the 28th. I still had not made my final decision. It had been almost a month. If I didn't respond by that Friday, my offer from UAA would be forfeited. On the way home from Pepperdine, I stopped by our church for its Wednesday evening service. After service, there was an elder training session, which took an hour, and then I headed back home. It was around 10:00 p.m. I was driving in the far left lane of the freeway, known as the fast lane, when I felt sleepy again. I was going about 65 to 70 miles per hour. The next thing I remember there were loud honking sounds and I instantly slammed on the breaks. My car came to a screeching halt. My right front tire was hanging on one of the overpass rails. I had fallen asleep and apparently my car had drifted from the far left lane, across two other lanes, and to the far right lane. Had I waited just a second or two to stop my car, it would have fallen off the overpass and onto the street and the cars below.

A couple of cars stopped to see if I needed help. They turned on their hazards as they parked in front and behind my car. One rushed to bring me a blanket. Another thought that I might have had a heart attack. I'm sure others speculated that I was drunk. Slightly embarrassed, I told all of them that I was okay and I simply fell asleep. Thanking them, I told them I was fine. After they left, I drove my car slowly to a safer location off the freeway and sat there. Having almost faced death again, my eyes welled up. *Lord, please forgive me for dragging this thing out. Please forgive me for not trusting in you and your sovereignty. Please forgive me for doubting that whatever decision I ultimately make, you will redeem it for your glory. Lord, I'm not sure what just happened. I'm not sure what it means as far as staying or going, but I want to obey. Lord, I don't want to read too much into things. I want the Holy Spirit for discernment and wisdom and the faith and courage to surrender to your will.* Through that prayer, God convicted me that I was to go. "Go!" "To Alaska." It was loud and clear.

My family stayed up waiting for me to come home. I didn't know where to begin when I saw them. I asked Sharon and Paul to sit on my lap. I asked Sung to sit next to me on the couch. I told them what happened on the freeway. I told them my prayers to God throughout this month. I told them I had to make a decision by Friday. I told them what God was convicting me to do. It did not go over well, as expected. Sharon immediately burst into tears, ran upstairs, yelled at the top of her lungs, "I don't want to go!" and slammed her bedroom door. Sung and Paul followed Sharon to her room to comfort her. I, the spiritual head of the household, sat alone on the couch. My heart ached.

Not knowing anything or anybody in Alaska or what our life would be like there and now, without the support of my family, the only thing I could do was rely on Him. Completely. To trust Him. To trust in His full control. To trust that He knows what He's doing. That's what He wanted. This delighted God. God is pleased when He sees His children put their complete trust in Him and have Him work in us to fulfill His will "on earth as it is in heaven." Because then He gets all the glory. He gets all the credit. Through this, we let the world know that He is worthy of our faith. That He is worthy of our total trust. That He is worth banking everything on. That He is Lord Almighty. That He is sovereign. That whatever happens, it will be for our good (Rom. 8:28). That whatever the consequences, we are His beloved, precious children. And that whatever may come, nothing can separate us from His love (Rom. 8:38-39).

With faith, comes risk. If we knew how every decision would play out, if we were sure that every choice would turn out the way we expect or that it would be "smooth sailing" all the way, then there would be no need for God. There would be no need for faith in His promises. There would be no need to trust in His character. There would be no need for His strength to persevere. Yes, I had no idea what would happen to me or my family in moving to Alaska. Yes, I had never even visited the state. Yes, I had only seen pictures of it. Yes, the only person I knew there was Dr. Aufrecht. Yes, it was going to be really cold. Yes, there was always the possibility that it may not turn out as I expected. Yes, there were good, legitimate, and justifiable reasons for staying put. Yes, my family was already expecting the worst. Yes, Sharon had yet to crack a smile since I told her the decision. But God gave me the courage to obey and trust and follow His calling. And in that way, I was comforted by these verses from Psalm 37:

> "Delight yourself in the LORD and He will give the desires
> of your heart. Commit your way to the LORD; trust in

Him and He will do this: He will make your righteousness shine like the dawn, The justice of your cause like the noonday sun." (Ps. 37:4-6)

I had to break the news to my dean at Pepperdine and formally submit my resignation. He was stunned. None of my colleagues understood. They took it hard. My church took it harder. We all took it hard. This was our home away from home. This was our family. Their prayers and support got me and my wife through my liver disease. This is the church that trained me and elected me as an elder. There were many tears that were shed as I told the choir ministry. The students in the college ministry that I directed were shocked. They couldn't believe it. Things were going so well in that ministry and our evangelism outings to the community on Sunday afternoons were bearing much fruit. These were exciting times for them. They begged us to stay. It really hit home for us when the church had a special farewell/send-off service for us, presided by my senior pastor, Rev. Cho Chun Il. Rev. Cho initially opposed the move to Alaska, but understood we had to obey God's calling. It was a very emotional service. Sung cried a lot. It was quiet in the car on the way home. It would be the last time we did that one-hour drive from Los Angeles to our home in Placentia as members of our church.

In early August, the movers came and packed their large truck with most of our belongings. We crammed the rest of our personals and other items in our tiny Datsun hatchback, having just sold our big gas guzzler, the Ford LTD. We got up early on the morning of August 15, 1980 (35 years to the day when Korea was liberated from Japanese occupation and more than 13 years when we first arrived at LAX) and drove to our church one last time, to pray and say our final goodbyes. In the sanctuary, the four of us held hands and we prayed. Rev. Cho and others who were there prayed over us.

We got back in the hatchback and headed to San Francisco, where Sung's younger sister and her family were living at the time. After spending a few days with them, we drove further north, through the redwoods and Oregon, and then to Seattle, to visit some friends. Several days later, we dropped off the car to a ferry that would transport it to Alaska, and flew from Seattle International Airport to Anchorage by Wien Air Alaska. The look on my family's face, even though I was trying to get them to see the majestic mountains below us through the airplane's window, didn't change. It was the same it had been after I first told them my decision. Unhappy. Sad. Glum. To make them feel better, I said we might only stay in Alaska for no more than two years.

We ended up staying for 16 years.

Chapter 17

THE LAST FRONTIER

After a four-hour flight from Seattle, we arrived at the Anchorage International Airport on the afternoon of August 25, 1980. We were greeted by the new dean, Robert McMillan, and his assistant and they took us to the home we would be renting, right next to the university. Dr. Aufrecht and his family lived across the street. When he saw we arrived, his family and some of the neighbors warmly welcomed us and brought over some furniture that would hold us over until our furniture arrived from California. That evening we had dinner at Dr. Aufrecht's home and feasted on some Alaskan cuisine. It was our first time having reindeer sausage among other native delicacies. It was delicious.

A Long First Winter

It was only August, but the air was quite chilly for us. When we first landed at the airport, it was sprinkling, and it felt like it had never stopped precipitating ever since – until it turned to snow. In mid-September. Little did we know then that we were about to face one of the coldest winters in Anchorage's recorded history. What timing. The temperatures went down to almost 40-below-zero Fahrenheit three times during that winter. Our water pipes had to be fixed and there were days when we had no hot water and were forced to boil water on the stove. This was not the start that I envisioned for my family. Our strength and perseverance were already being put to the test.

Several days after our arrival, while we were eating dinner on one of the tables our neighbors had lent to us, one of the table's legs buckled. Sharon's glass of milk spilled all over the table and on her lap. She immediately stood up and yelled, "I hate Alaska and I hate you, Dad!" She stormed into her room, slammed the door shut, and started bawling. My wife and Paul went into Sharon's room and cried together with her. Tomorrow was the first day of school.

After the crying stopped, they all came out to the living room. "Dad, I do not know a single person at this school. If we were still in Placentia, I would know everyone and they would know me. I was somebody. Why did you have to bring us to Alaska and turn me into a nobody?" Sharon burst into tears. And ran back into her room.

Sharon was always daddy's little girl and we had a close relationship, especially when I was sick with my liver. Her happiness meant everything to me. And now, she resented me. She had lost interest in studying, her grades were falling, and she refused to continue learning the piano and take figure skating lessons, two of her extracurricular passions in California. She excelled as a student in Placentia. Now, she dreaded everything about junior high school – and Alaska. My wife and I were always on edge around her, just hoping she wouldn't break out in tears. I was in agony and ached over her suffering as I desperately petitioned the Lord for help.

It was hard on my wife too. Every time she spoke with Pastor Cho, the senior pastor from our old church in Los Angeles, she would cry. The Presbyterian church we were attending in Anchorage didn't sit well with us and we weren't happy with it. Thankfully, our old church would send us Pastor Cho's sermons on tape every week. Things didn't get better when our furniture arrived in early October. Almost everything got wet on the trip – the piano, paintings and pictures, chairs, books, and many other items. Sung screamed. And except for a few things, the movers were not able to bring in most of the furniture and larger pieces into the house. There just wasn't enough room in the doorways. It was a total disaster.

To top it all off, I found out that the promises that were made to me by the university – concerning compensation and benefits and faculty rank – during my recruitment were not going to be fulfilled. Sung and I were beside ourselves. We were only told that these promises may be met at some point in the future. There were no guarantees. I let the administration know how strongly disappointed I was about their broken promises and their lack of integrity. I thought about pursuing a claim with the university's grievance committee. I was reeling. But I prayed to the Lord and inquired of His heart. I was convicted that His desire was for me to let it go. Not take any action. Not do anything but do what I was hired to do, teach and research. And to demonstrate my integrity with my diligence and work ethic. I gritted my teeth, swallowed my hurt ego, and obeyed.

Although it took some time, by God's grace, we were able to persevere through and overcome these struggles that first winter in Alaska. We became close with one of my colleagues, Steve Johnson, and his family who lived very near to us. Sharon and Paul got along well with Steve's two children, Matt and Tina. Steve's wife, Vicky, helped Sharon tremendously. She spent a lot of time with Sharon and shared her own stories about her family in Alaska and how they overcame the initial hardships and came to love Alaska. Sharon's anger and resentment seemed to slowly subside as the weeks went by. She started making friends. A lot of them. Her grades shot up. She took up piano again. She also took up cross-country and downhill skiing, along with Paul. I praised God for her resiliency and that her spirits were buoyed. She started to like school – and Alaska.

It helped that we had moved to a new house. When our furniture arrived from California, an insurance assessor came and estimated the damages. We submitted pictures of the damaged items and our piled-high claim documents. We were able to use part of the money we received from the insurance company as a down payment for a new home, not as close to the university, but we liked the neighborhood. The wet furniture turned out to be a blessing in disguise.

As for my wife, she was able to find work as the comptroller of the Alaska Treatment Center, a post-operative treatment and physical therapy clinic. She had great co-workers and a wonderful staff. She enjoyed her job and was always smiling at the office. Nothing seemed to bother her and she was as fast and efficient as she was smart (I cannot keep up with her). She eventually became the financial director. As for the university's broken promises, God redeemed that as well. In His way. In His time. Dr. David Outcalt, the provost, and the Vice President of Academic Affairs, had arrived at UAA two months earlier and knew about the mistakes and broken promises that the university administration had made. Although he couldn't do anything for me at that time, he was very apologetic and took serious note of what had happened. And two years later, after he had become chancellor, he did a huge favor for me, far more than I expected. I at least was enjoying my teaching at the university and was satisfied with the school environment and my campus surroundings. God was answering our prayers about feeling a little more adjusted and settled in Anchorage.

Alaska: God's Creation, God's Showcase

Alaska is a showcase of God's awesomeness. His majesty and His beauty. It is His masterpiece of land, mountains, snow, glaciers, trees, rivers, streams, and wildlife. It is breathtaking. Indescribable. Equally grand and rugged, towering and unforgiving, vast and untamed. There is no state like it. There is no place like it. It truly is the Last Frontier.

Alaska is the largest state in America by land area, having 586,412 square miles (1,518,800 km) with a population of 722,718 residents, just a little less than one person per square mile. It is one-fifth the size of the contiguous United States. To put that in perspective, Alaska is more than twice the size of Texas and is larger than the combined area of Texas, California, and Montana, the next three largest states of the Union, and is seven times larger than the Korean Peninsula. This land was purchased from Russia on March 30, 1867, for just $7.2 million ($120 million in today's dollars) and was initially thought of as uninhabitable wasteland. It became the 49th state of the U.S. on January 3, 1959. Approximately 65% of Alaska is owned and managed by the U.S. federal government, 101 million acres are owned by the state under the Alaska Statehood Act and 44 million acres are owned by 12 regional bodies and a number of village corporations created under the Alaska Native Claims Settlement Act (ANCSA).

It is technically the northernmost, westernmost, and some say easternmost (given its proximity to the Far East) state in America. It's also probably the country's coldest and richest. Some of the highest and lowest temperatures in Alaska occur around the area of Fairbanks, which is in the central part of the state. The summers can have temperatures soaring into the 90s (Fahrenheit), while in the winter, the temperature can drop below -60 °F (-51.1 °C). The lowest official temperature on record for Fairbanks was -80 °F (-62.2 °C) on January 23, 1971. During the winter, there is no sun for three months in the northern part of the state, in the Arctic Circle region, and the temperature can go down to -100 °F, with wind chill. On the other hand, the sun does not set for three months in the Arctic Circle during the summer, amazingly just orbiting the sky.

Alaska's energy resources are virtually unmatched. Major oil and gas reserves are found in the Alaska's North Slope, Arctic National Wildlife Refuge (ANWR), Cook Inlet basins as well as the Alaskan Outer Continental Shelf (OCS). Alaska ranks second in the nation in crude oil production but was previously ranked first for two decades when Prudhoe Bay in the North Slope produced about 2 million barrels per day. Today, production is down to 400,000 barrels per day. More than 80% of the state's revenues come from petroleum production. Alaska is still incredibly endowed with crude oil reserves (proven as well as unproven) including ANWR and West Sak as well as the OCS reserves. The Alaska Permanent Fund, which is a constitutionally authorized appropriation of the state's oil revenues, has grown from its initial principal of $734,000 in 1980 to $40 billion as a result of oil royalties and capital investment programs. It is also estimated that the state's natural gas reserves are 85.4 trillion cubic feet (2,420 km3) of undiscovered, technically recoverable gas from natural gas hydrates on the Alaska slope, enough to supply Korea, Japan and Taiwan for 50 years.

Alaska also has an abundance of other natural resources such as coal, gold, precious metals, zinc and other minerals, and fisheries as well as forestry. The coal reserves (proven and unproven) are so large that, if commercially feasible, they could supply the U.S. for the next 400 years. In northwest Alaska, one of the world's largest lead and zinc reserves was found, and currently it's at the peak of its production. The Alaskan Coastline is longer than all the other states combined with more than 10,000 rivers flowing into it. During the summer, as the rivers flow out into the ocean, the number of salmon in these rivers swimming against the current are almost uncountable. The amount of Alaskan wild salmon, halibut, pollock, king crab, snow crab, Dungeness crab, cod, sea bass, herring, and flounder that are sold in U.S. markets and traded to the markets of Japan, Europe, Korea, and the rest of the world is registered at more than $2.4 billion. Alaska wild salmon is the most popular fish in Japan, and Alaska's salmon export brings the largest trade surplus to the U.S. Two of the largest forestry services in the nation, Tonggass National Forestry Service and Chugach National Forestry Service, are located in Alaska. Alaska's Sitka Spruce is the premier quality wood used for Yamaha (Japan) and Samik and Young Chang (Korea) pianos. Alaska is a country-sized state with a global business.

Alaska is a haven for wild animals such as black bears, grizzly bears, polar bears, reindeer, caribou, moose, wolf, red fox, sea lions, seals, sea otters, whales, and other species. A large number of bird watchers come to the state to see so many different kinds of hawks, eagles, and other birds every summer. Alaska has more than three million lakes, and has over half of all 100,000 glaciers in the world, one of which is larger than the size of Rhode Island. The emerald blue and aqua-green hues of these spectacular and gigantic rivers of ice, like the Columbia Glacier, College Fiords Glaciers, and Glacier Bay, are a site to behold. In the summer of 1986, Masahide Shibusawa and his wife, the same couple who had hosted us during our honeymoon in Japan, invited us to spend several days on a private, chartered boat sailing around Glacier Bay. At the time, the Shibusawas were living in Anchorage, as I invited, on behalf of UAA, Mr. Shibusawa as a Fulbright Scholar.

Paul, Sung, and I first flew from Anchorage to Juneau, the capital of Alaska, and then drove to the coast to board the "C'est Si Bon," a 10-person boat manned by a husband and wife. We sailed to 12 different glaciers that make up most of Glacier Bay. As we relaxed on the deck after dinner, in addition to whale-watching, we would see huge chunks of ice from these towering glaciers thunderously fall into the sea. On contact with the water, it sounded like a cannon. At night, in our beds, we would continue to hear the grumbling and creaking of these massive ice formations and wake up the next morning to find our boat surrounded by thousands of smaller, blue and aqua-colored icebergs, which served as a playground for sea otters. To be greeted this way in the mornings was unforgettable. As were the meals. The husband-and-wife charterers would ask what we wanted for lunch or dinner. If it was salmon or halibut, for example, they would give us a pole and a line and whatever we caught, we would eat. Fresh and delicious doesn't do justice in describing how these fish tasted. Or if we wanted Dungeness crab, we would hoist some cages over the side of the boat and later pull up our lunch or dinner, throw them in a pot, put on some bibs, and then hammer away. Literally, our meals were the catch of the day. The water. The bluest of blues. The whales. The seafood. The ocean breeze. The crashing sounds. The sunsets at midnight. The otters in the morning. It was all so perfect. It was all so Alaskan. There's no place like it.

Anchorage is in the south-central part of the state and the largest city (pop. 327,000) in Alaska. It is the hub of commerce and business and international trade (and travel) for the 49th state. The city has the largest campus in the University of Alaska System (in acreage and student population) and is a short drive from Alyeska Ski Resort, in Girdwood, a premier playground for hard-core skiers and the best the state has to offer for recreation. Anchorage is surrounded by the beautiful Chugach Mountains which turn a strawberry color during a typical clear winter day when the sun reflects on these snow-covered peaks. Absolutely beautiful.

Anchorage's temperatures are relatively mild and temperate due to its proximity to Cook Inlet and the surrounding Chugach Mountains. Nonetheless, Anchorage winters are no picnic. Snow and lots of snow (with record-breaking snowfall in January 2012). Temperatures can drop to 40 below zero Fahrenheit, as we experienced in our first Alaskan winter, but thankfully, there is really no wind chill to worry about and winters usually average in the teens. The almost-perpetual darkness is pretty tough. In the heart of winter, the sun doesn't rise until about 10:30 a.m. and then sets around 2:30 p.m. But on the flip side, during the summer, you need to close the blinds at night before bed because the sun doesn't completely set until midnight and rises in the early dawn. I don't golf, but I was told by my golfing colleagues that tee times at 9:00 p.m. are doable. Alaskans joke that there are four seasons – summer, frost, winter, and break-up (as in the snow and ice melt and "break up" when it starts getting warmer in the spring).

Mt. McKinley, the tallest mountain in the North America at 20,321 feet (and taller from its base to its peak than the base to the top of Mount Everest), attracts more than a million people for the four warmer months in the middle of the year. I've never seen anything more grand or more awe-inspiring. Its massiveness is jaw-dropping. When the first natives crossed the Bering Strait and arrived in Alaska, upon seeing the towering mountain, they exclaimed in wonder, "Denali!" meaning "The Great One"; hence the name was bestowed on the whole surrounding area, "Denali National Park and Preserve." On a clear day, Mt. McKinley can even be seen from downtown Anchorage – approximately 150 nautical miles away.

And nothing is more spectacular than the Aurora Borealis, otherwise known as the "Northern Lights." A full rainbow can't even compete. Nothing really can. On a clear winter night, blue and green ribbons of light can suddenly appear, undulating against the entire evening sky, and quickly joined in the symphony of color by yellow, red, orange, and other hues. Constant movement. Constant color. Constant amazement. These truly were pillars of light against the deep black of night. One evening, as we were making our slow descent to the Anchorage International Airport, the pilot announced that the Northern Lights were on. Through the plane's window, God's light show was on full display. From our vantage point, the colors were dancing along the tops of bushes and trees and the mountains appeared to be succumbed by incandescent brush fire as the lights raced up and down their sides. God was the conductor. The lights were His orchestra. And we were the captivated audience. I teared up. At this beauty. Which pointed to the ultimate beauty, Christ. These were the moments during my life in Alaska that not only dazzled my eyes, but nourished my soul. As if God was telling me, "You came to Alaska to follow me. Well, you've come to the right place and what you see is just a minute foretaste of my infinite splendor, magnificence, and glory."

The breathtaking scenery of Alaska and all that the state offered – fresh air, fresh water, fresh seafood – strengthened my physical health and lifted my spirits. It made me stronger. Inside and out. "And we know that in all things God works for the good of those who love Him, who have been called according to His purpose" (Rom. 8:28).

Chapter 18

A CHURCH FOR THE "LOST" FRONTIER

In November 1980, the senior pastor from our Los Angeles church, Rev. Cho, came to Alaska for a visit. He wanted to see his daughter, who was working at the Korean Consulate General's Office in Anchorage, and our family while on his way home from a trip to Scotland. He was like family to us, like a grandfather to Sharon and Paul, and we were thrilled to see him. We missed our old church a lot. Especially Sung. When he heard about our concerns that we were not spiritually clicking with the Korean-American churches in the area, and thus, were not growing, he suggested we start a new church, especially if I had no plans to leave UAA and return to Los Angeles any time soon. "I think it would be great for you to start a church here in Anchorage. We would consider it a church plant. We can provide substantial support for the first, say, three years. Until you become financially independent. What do you think?"

An Open Door

Having been in Anchorage for only about three months, we already knew a number of Koreans, both recent transplants and veteran Alaskans. The Korean students at the university would bring their parents and grandparents to meet me, curious to see a Korean professor teaching at an "American" university, as if I was some exhibit at the zoo. We also had a number of Koreans who were janitors on campus and they wanted to chat me up as well. These interactions were great opportunities for me to learn about their lives, what they thought about Alaska, and whether they were believers. Most were not Christians. There were more than 2,000 Korean-Americans who lived in Anchorage (more than any other Asian group), but very few attended church. Many were in fact Buddhists. I did have a passion for the lost, especially since my transformation, since I too was once in the same boat – lost but now found. Rev. Cho knew this. He knew of my heart to bring people to God through the local church. That's why he made the suggestion for a church plant. His suggestion threw me for a loop, so I told him I would have to pray about it. I needed to process it some more.

We realized not only from our personal experiences visiting the Korean-American churches in the area, but from hearing from other Christians – and those who had left the church – in the Korean community, that there was a need for a new church. A Christ-centered, gospel-centered, Scripture-centered church. A church that was safe for non-believers. A church that would spiritually strengthen the flock, as well as add numbers to it. It would have been easy for me to just attend an existing church and serve occasionally. I had a lot on my plate. I could come up with a lot of excuses. Adjusting to a new place. Teaching. Research. Wanting to establish myself. Raising a family. *How do I have the time to start a church?* But God was convicting me to do something. To use my zeal (and my wife's) for the lost by serving Him wholeheartedly through a Korean-speaking church that would reach out to the Koreans in Anchorage that were not saved, many of whom were from my hometown in the Cholla Province. And a church that would not only help them spiritually, but physically, emotionally, culturally, and financially as well. Indeed, in my prayers, God began to reveal that I was sent to Alaska not just to make an economic or academic difference, but a spiritual one. In January 1981, I told Rev. Cho that my wife and I were on board. He was ecstatic.

The next step was to search for a church facility. On Sundays for the next few months, my family and I visited different churches in Anchorage and finally found one we thought would work for us. After service at First Christian Church, a predominantly Caucasian congregation, my wife and I spoke with Senior Pastor Smith and told him about our situation. He seemed receptive to the idea of having us use their facilities for an afternoon service and said he would report back to us after speaking with the other leaders of the church. A week later, he asked us to come by the church to give us the good news. We would have full use of the facilities in the afternoon, starting in mid-August. At minimal rent. The church's leadership would regard our church as one of their "mission" churches. My wife could hardly contain her excitement. After giving us a tour of the church, we profusely thanked Pastor Smith, who, together with one of the elders, prayed for us and our future church before we left. Progress.

On August 2, 1981, the "Anchorage Open Door Presbyterian Church" held its first inaugural service. Because we were not yet able to use the facilities at First Christian Church, we held the service in our living room. There were 12 adults (which included me and my wife) and two children – Sharon and Paul. The service was led by Pastor Jin Koo Chung, who had just arrived from Los Angeles, after being sent upon the recommendation of Rev. Cho. Pastor Chung, who had been ordained a few months before, would stay at our home for the next 45 days until his wife and their baby son arrived. He, like us, was new to the whole starting-a-church thing.

During the fellowship time after our inaugural service, I asked everyone to provide me contact information on the Koreans they knew in Anchorage who were not believers or who no longer attended church. I added those names to a list that I was compiling from Korean last names (and businesses) I had found in the local phone book. These names were my targets and I began to sketch out an ambitious plan to visit every single one over the next couple of months. Our new church had to start somewhere and this list was it.

Two weeks later, on August 16 at 1:30 p.m., we had our first service at First Christian Church. The only adults who were there were me, Sung, and Pastor Chung. No one else. It was nerve-wracking. A bit demoralizing. People had promised they would come, but no one showed. Anxious, Sung waited outside the front door, pacing back and forth, turning her eyes to any sound and any car that drove by. No one drove up. Several agonizing minutes later, by the grace of God, a handful of people showed up and we started the service. During the prayer time, Sung and I cried. We desperately wanted more people to come. We desperately wanted our church to be a safe haven for non-believers. We desperately wanted more people to come to know the Lord.

Swallowing Them Up

So the next day, and for 45 consecutive days thereafter, I visited the Korean names and business on my list, either during the day or in the evening, depending on when I had classes, as the fall semester had started. I went to these homes and offices and shared the Gospel of Jesus Christ and invited them to our new church. I was frequently joined by Sung and Pastor Chung. On most occasions, we showed up unannounced. At the time, I was starting to become a recognized figure in the Anchorage community due to my research and teaching at the university (and being the first Korean-American faculty member there) and my involvement with Mayor Tony Knowles's administration. Having been in Alaska for just a year, I was receiving a number of requests to present and speak at various gatherings, both large and small. My name was getting out there. I was becoming known. And that helped getting us past the front door and into the living room of the homes on my list. Being a professor was also a great asset in our efforts to evangelize to the Korean community. As Korean parents are intensely committed to their children's education, having a professor come to their home and dispense advice on American education and college in their native tongue was a boon for me to establish my credibility, grab their attention and then direct them to Christ. I wanted God to "swallow up" these families!

Given that the fall semester was in full swing, it seemed that I was working two full-time jobs on little sleep. But rather than being stressed and exhausted, I was experiencing much joy – and great feedback – from my work at the university and spiritually invigorated and encouraged by the fruit we were seeing in our outreaches and visitations. More families were coming to our church and the numbers were increasing every Sunday. Soon there would be a need for a Sunday school, which Sung, with Sharon's help, ran.

One man we visited at his store, Mr. Yu, told us that he had his friend in Los Angeles "check me out" and word was that I was a "clean man." He told us that his wife would like to invite us to his home for dinner. The dinner was quite the lavish affair and my wife and I and Pastor Chung enjoyed the company at their home. During dessert, the wife shared that she grew up in a Buddhist family and that her mom, who helped prepare the dinner, was a life-long devout Buddhist.

"Please, Elder Kim, do what you can to lead my husband to church. I would be forever indebted to you. As for me, I'm obligated to follow my mother's religion. But he doesn't have to."

"We will do what we can," I replied. "We will try our best, but God is in control. It is He that can only change us. It is He that can only change your husband." *But there will be an opportune time when God will swallow up your whole family for Christ!*

Her husband, I later learned from Sung, was an addicted gambler. It was the worst-kept secret in the Korean community. It was his vice. It was something he was so immersed in, it could only take God to get him out of it. That explained his wife's request. For the next several weeks, I paid him visits at his store to get to know him, to pray for his business, and, most importantly, establish his trust in me. The humorous and joking exterior – which was a defense mechanism – eventually began to peel away and he would share more details of his life. Which was a tough one. Having come from nothing, he was consumed by making enough. For himself. For his family. All he wanted was to be a rich man. It was during these moments that I shared my testimony. How I too had come from nothing and left Korea with a big chip on my shoulder. But all that had changed, by God's grace, and I had changed. I challenged him that money (or for me, accolades and prestige), no matter how much you have, will never change you for the better. Only Christ can. Only He can truly satisfy. I then gave him a Bible and directed him to some passages for him to read and think about. I reiterated that there was no sin – whether it be excessive gambling, excessive drinking, adultery, or something else – that Christ cannot forgive.

Although he only had a fourth-grade education, he was very smart and exceptionally well self-educated. It would take more than intellectual debates to win him over; it had to be the Holy Spirit. And the Holy Spirit came through. Several weeks after I gave him the Bible, he showed up at our church and started attending consistently. It was the talk of the town. He soon received Jesus as his Lord and Savior and witnessed Him to his customers, providing their names to us so I could follow-up with them. It was a miraculous, God-orchestrated turn of events. His wife, who invited us over again to her home for dinner, was shocked. She never thought this day would come, and come so soon. She shared how hard her life had been – having to help her widowed mother raise and educate her younger brother. There was a lot of pain. There were a lot of tears. The fact that her husband had been consumed by money and gambling only added to the hurt. I asked Pastor Chung to share some verses that would speak to her. I shared my testimony and my life in Korea, my hurts, my failures, my bitterness, and my transformation. We prayed. I asked them if they would receive Jesus Christ as their Savior and Lord. Mrs. Yu and her mother, who had been a Buddhist for 60 years, by God's amazing grace, said, "Yes." That entire household would eventually all be saved – the widowed mother, Mr. and

Mrs. Yu and their children, and the younger brother and his wife and their children. The mother became my mother's best friend at our church. Mrs. Yu became the leader of our church's women's ministry. Mr. Yu and the younger brother became deacons and then, a few years after we left Alaska, elders in the church. "Believe in the Lord Jesus, and you will be saved – you and your household" (Acts 16:31). Amen to that.

And this household began to bring other non-believers to our church. One of them was Miss Han's family. Miss Han was a Vice Consul working at the Korean Consulate General's Office and was pursuing some graduate work at UAA under my supervision. She was introduced to our church by Mrs. Yu, who set up a dinner with her parents, Mr. and Mrs. Han Dong Chan, so that I could evangelize to them. Mr. and Mrs. Han were in town from Korea visiting their daughter – and they were devout Buddhists. Mr. Han was the president of the Buddhist Lay Leaders' Organization in the Korean city of Dae Jeon. The dinner with them was pleasant, without any awkwardness. They were a happy and sweet couple.

"Have you heard of Jesus Christ," I asked.

"I do not know him well," said Mr. Han, "but I think he is a great man, like other religious leaders."

I then began to share the life of Jesus Christ, who He is, who He claimed to be, and what He taught us and what He accomplished for us on the cross and the resurrection, mostly referencing the Gospel of John. They were skeptical, but actively engaged in the discussion. Never dismissive, they asked many questions and were well-versed in their Buddhist beliefs. Despite all of that, I felt that they were open-minded. I then shared my testimony through which I sensed the Holy Spirit beginning to work in their minds and hearts.

"Can I meet Jesus Christ as you met Him?" Mr. Han asked.

"Of course," I exclaimed.

"Can my sins truly be forgiven and, as you put it, 'washed

away'?"

"Yes."

"Any sin?"

"Yes, any sin."

"Can I be forgiven and saved?"

"Absolutely! Could you kneel down with me and repeat this prayer after me?"

Even though a man's tears are a sign of weakness in Korean culture, they wept over their sins. They wept from the joy of forgiveness. We all wept as we witnessed the remarkable power and work of the Holy Spirit which awakened them to their sins and their need for salvation. They then received and confessed Christ as their Lord and Savior. It was like a moment that makes your heart stop. Mr. Han was not just any nominal Buddhist, but one who was a prominent figure in the Buddhist community in his hometown. But this also was not just any moment – it was a moment brought about by the sovereign God of the universe. Mr. Han later said that evening, "I know now why we came to America. It wasn't just to visit my daughter. God sent us here to meet His Son."

Their original plan was to stay with their daughter in Anchorage for a month, but they ended up staying six months, receiving training in God's word and fellowship with other believers at our church. A few days before they were to return to Korea, they were baptized, publicly professing their new-found faith in Jesus. It was an incredibly moving service. What a Savior. Having come to Alaska as Buddhists, they were now departing the 49th state as Christ's ambassadors. A few months later, Mr. Han sent us a letter brimming with excitement and joy. Upon his return to Korea, he had led his siblings and their children as well as his and his wife's relatives to Christ. Altogether, 27 came to the Lord. What a Savior.

It was late October in 1981, and I went to visit another Korean family, the Parks, on my way home from another visitation. I wasn't planning on going to see Mr. Park, whom I had met at a reception, but I just sensed the urge to go. I knocked.

"I am so sorry to bother you Mr. Park and stop by unannounced. I hope it's not too late, but I just wanted to swing by for a visit. Do you have a few moments?"

Looking at the Bible in my hand, Mr. Park replied, "Professor Kim, it's good to see you, but now is not a good time. I'm sorry. Can we schedule this for some other time where we can have more time to talk, especially about my children's education?"

"Since I'm already here, I will only take a few minutes of your time."

If this were any other time, I would've replied differently. I would've said I understood, said my goodbyes, got in my car and drove home. But as I was about to take a step back and return to my car, the Holy Spirit was moving my heart to stand firm, get in Mr. Park's house, and not let this opportunity to witness pass.

"Professor Kim, it really isn't a good time, as I told you. Please come again some other time."

"Mr. Park, I have something important to share with you. Trust me, I did not come to waste your time. Please, would you spare a few minutes with me?

He refused.

"I beg you, Mr. Park. I wouldn't be insisting so much unless I felt it was very important. I'm a busy man too, with a class to teach tomorrow. We all have things to do. Nevertheless, I'm here right now. Please, Mr. Park. Either you kick me off your property or I'm coming in."

Apoplectic at my pushiness, he paused and then opened the door. He led me to his family room, still in an alternating state of disbelief and annoyance at my refusal to go away. I was a bit stunned as well at my aggressiveness and failure to follow protocol. It was awkward. Uneasy. Tense. Uncomfortable. A cigarette burned in the ashtray. Beer bottles were on the coffee table. The television was on. A beauty pageant was being broadcast and it was in the middle of the swimsuit program. It was obvious why he didn't want me to come in. I was interrupting his "man time."

"Dr. Kim, please have a beer."

"I don't drink alcohol."

"Beer is not really alcohol. I have seen Christians and Catholics all drink alcohol."

"No, thank you. I don't drink. Mr. Park, would you please stop smoking?"

He continued to inhale and exhale the nicotine, looking at the television screen, taking a sip from a bottle.

"Please, extinguish the cigarette."

(Sigh)

"Please, extinguish it!"

Disgusted, he put out his cigarette in the ashtray.

"Would you please remove all these beer bottles?"

"Honey, can you come in here and clear these bottles away!"

The wife said hello but hardly looked at my direction as she cleaned the table. When she headed back to the kitchen, she said loudly, "Please don't pray in this house." At that moment, I almost got up and left. *What am I doing here? Why did I put myself in this situation? Why should I go through this? It's their loss if they don't want to know about Jesus. Why should I bother?* But the Holy Spirit pressed me to persevere.

Mr. Park's eyes were glued to the television now.

"Please, turn off the T.V."

Mr. Park pretended he didn't hear me.

"Please, turn off the T.V.!"

"No. I don't want to."

"Please, just turn it off!"

"You barge into my home and now you are forcing me to turn off my own T.V.?!" Mumbling something under his breath, he got up from his seat and turned the set off.

"I sincerely apologize for showing up unannounced and forcing my way into your home. I interrupted your evening and you understandably are upset. I did not come to see you because I had nothing else to do tonight. I came here because I was compelled to share something with you." Then with my voiced raised and my heart roaring like a lion, "I did not come here tonight to ask anything of you, because there is nothing you have that I need. But I came here because you are a fellow Korean. And I could not keep to myself the precious gift of God's amazing grace and love that He has given me. So, tonight," I roared, "receive it and believe in Him!"

Immediately his frightened face responded (or, you could say, surrendered), "Yes! I will."

Despite his wife's instructions, I briefly prayed for him and his family. He was able to crack a smile as did I. I left his home with a promise of getting together soon. The next time we met was much more pleasant and more relaxed. He told me he thought his liver would explode when he heard me yell at him to believe in Christ. I don't think the method I chose in evangelizing to Mr. Park should be modeled in any way, but it just goes to show how the Holy Spirit can move us in special and bold ways in unusual circumstances. We just have to simply obey and trust. That's what I did. Mr. Park and his family eventually came to receive Christ as their Lord and Savior and were attending our church until they moved down to the continental U.S.

The name of our church, Anchorage Open Door Presbyterian Church, was taken from Revelation 3:8 (ESV): "I know your works. Behold, I have set before you an open door, which no one is able to shut. I know that you have but little power, and yet you have kept my word and have not denied my name." It was becoming the place that we had envisioned it would be – a safe place for non-believers to come to faith and be Christ's ambassadors. Our church doors would always be "open" and welcoming to those who've never attended church. Almost ninety percent of the congregation was converted through and baptized at our church. God is good. Our church was growing. We started outgrowing the facilities at First Christian Church and needed a larger place. We were eventually able to purchase a small Baptist church with 3.5 acres of land. Five years after our inaugural service, God enabled us to have our own church facility to worship God at any time without any restrictions. It was ours for Him. Hallelujah!

The Importance of the Local Church

Worship: Given that I was the only elder, our family was very involved in the church. But what I wanted to convey to my family was that yes, the local church was an integral part of our lives, but that ultimately, our lives were about worship, worshipping our Lord and Savior, Jesus Christ, whose spilt blood on the cross had purchased the church. Louie Giglio says that "the cross is where our true worship begins" and that "worship is . . . our response, both personal and corporate, to God – for who He is! And what He has done! Expressed in and by the things we say and the way we live."[41] Giglio especially challenges the church and its congregants that "the primary purpose of the church is worship."[42] In that sense, I held our Sunday worship services – from the ones in my living room to the ones in our own facilities – in the highest regard and expected my family and my fellow brothers and sisters do the same.

Every Sunday, my family would usually be the first to arrive at church. This would give me time alone in the sanctuary to kneel down and pray for the service, that the Holy Spirit would come upon us, that Rev. Chung would be anointed, that the Gospel would be preached, and for our congregation to be transformed by it. Then I would head to the nursery to pray for the little ones and their parents who would arrive and then cover the Sunday school and the teachers who were preparing their lessons with prayer. My wife and I joined the choir practice after that. Since my days in Korea, I've been in a choir for 41 years and I still love to worship Him with song!

It does not matter how big or small your church is. It is who we worship that matters. And what's more important than how we worship (through hymns verses contemporary songs, more formal and liturgical versus relaxed and personal), is our hearts when we worship. God sees and knows our heart. "I'm coming back to the heart of worship," sings Matt Redman, "It's all about you, it's all about you, Jesus."[43] Our worship is not just a Sunday service thing – it is the way we live! "Worshipping God is what we do as we respond to His mercy in our 'walking-around life.'"[44]

Discipleship and Mentoring: Because of my passion for teaching, I have always had a heart to disciple others and mentor the younger generations. I have spent considerable time in training and building up Christ-centered leaders and Spirit-filled ambassadors in small group settings, larger seminars, and personal mentoring sessions for our church. Churches often neglect training and discipling their members, choosing instead to have them just serve, serve, and serve. There needs to be balance. There seems to be an unhealthy premium for some churches, especially Korean-American ones, on work ethic and diligence and duties, rather than spiritual leadership. This should not be so. Churches desperately need servant leaders who are doctrinally-sound, Gospel-centered, open and authentic, and generous and humble – and such leaders are discovered, developed, and matured through training, discipling, and mentoring. The development of our younger generations is my greatest passion today.

Hospitality and Service: In the early years of our church, our home was the gathering place. It was where we as a church would celebrate Easter, Thanksgiving, and Christmas over meals prepared by my wife (with the help of my mother when she lived with us). It was where, after we broke bread during service, we would again "break bread" after service for lunch and fellowship. Despite feeling exhausted at times with the influx of people in our home and the constant cooking and cleaning, my wife and I were led by the actions of the early church, who "shared everything they had" with one another (Acts 4:32). Our home was their home. We found great joy in hosting and providing a safe, relaxed, and festive backdrop for our church to spur each other on in fellowship and in prayer.

Sung has an incredible knack for hospitality, is a tremendous cook, and is the most efficient person and gifted multi-tasker I know. And not only has our church been blessed by those gifts, but my colleagues at UAA (whom we would invite, along with their families to our home for annual Christmas parties), other Christian leaders and co-laborers for the Gospel, foreign dignitaries, and U.S. and local officials as well. All told, during our 16 years in Alaska, Sung has fed (and entertained with her bubbly personality) more than 12,000 guests at our dinner table. These would be opportune times – with bellies satisfied and spirits warmed – for me to non-intrusively talk with many of the non-Christian guests about Jesus Christ. Of course, who wouldn't listen to what the host had to say?! I took full advantage of "home court" for the sake of Christ.

Since we moved to Monterey, California, we have continued to open our home and our lives to many, from Silicon Valley executives, local friends and church members, campus colleagues and administrators, to more than 2,500 Christian leaders and pastors, predominantly of Korean descent, who come to what I call the "Global Leadership Forum" (GLF) and "Total Leadership Forum" (TLF). GLF and TLF are spiritual weekend getaways for pastors and lay leaders from around the country to come, usually 20-30 at a time, to Monterey to fellowship, vision-cast, brainstorm, pray, and share dreams for the furtherance of His Kingdom, the strengthening of the local church, and the renewal of our culture and the marketplace, as well as sightsee in one of the most beautiful settings in the world. These types of intimate gatherings – that encourage, convict, and edify leaders of their respective flocks – are ways in which my wife and I can serve not only them, but the churches to which they return, rested and refreshed by the Holy Spirit.

Sung also used her business savvy gifts to serve the church. After stepping down as Financial Director of the Alaska Treatment Center in 1989, Sung became a licensed realtor. No longer was she confined to an office from 8:00 a.m. to 5:00 p.m. Her schedule was now her own, giving her more flexibility for the family and our church, and more opportunities to witness Christ to people in the community. Sung led a number of her Korean-speaking clients to our church and her English-speaking clients to other local churches. Her open houses became the talk of the town as they included home-made fried rice, Korean dumplings, and Sung's effervescent charm. She certainly glorified God through her profession. I was very proud.

At the time, our church building was not large enough to hold our services any more. We had reached maximum capacity. And with the surrounding neighbors ready to protest any sort of expansion, we had to find another property that could fit us. Sung, being a realtor, was able to find a 19,000-square foot commercial building in a prime, off-a-main-highway location. After having sold our original building to a Methodist church, Sung aggressively negotiated a price for the commercial building, enabling our church to purchase it at only half the asking price. Sung also acquired property from the city for future use by our church through an auction, with the church paying only a third of the land's market value. Although Sung earned healthy commissions from these transactions, she donated all of them to the church. By God's grace, a new facility was just completed on the land that was purchased from the city auction.

Prayers: Praying is the lifeblood of a church. It's the church's acknowledgment that it is completely dependent on God. It is the church's submission and obedience to God's will. We tend to be busy in our churches with programs and events and too busy for prayer, thinking that prayer is inactivity. It is not. Prayer is action. Prayer is the engine. Prayer is the source. Prayer is power. Sadly, many churches in America today do not place an emphasis on prayer and in many ways, I believe that our culture has suffered because of it. One thing that Koreans are known to do is pray. There is even a term in evangelical circles of "Korean style" prayers – that is, praying in an expressively, passionately and openly vocal (some would say loud!) way. Most Korean churches have dawn prayer meetings, usually starting at five o'clock or five-thirty in the morning. Our church in Anchorage was no different, although 5:30 a.m. in the summer doesn't feel anything like dawn since the sun had already risen considerably, while 5:30 a.m. in the winter feels like you never slept since the sun doesn't rise until around ten-thirty in the morning. Those were tough winter mornings, especially dealing with frigid temperatures, icy roads and snowy conditions. But the prayer times were worth it. They were spiritually therapeutic and soul-nourishing and enlarged my heart towards the congregation. Unless there were particular problems or issues for myself and my family, I spent most of the time praying for the church members, submitting each person's name to the Lord. I would ask God to grant me the power to love them with the heart of Christ, and asked Him to pour out His blessings on each person's family.

Sung and I would also visit the businesses of our church members and pray for them, pray that God would be glorified in these businesses, and that God would use these businesses to serve the community and further His Kingdom. I would also visit members' homes, especially if they had children. God had giving me the ability to speak both English and Korean, allowing me to bridge language and cultural divides in many of these families and be a conduit of generational reconciliation. Often, I would bring the entire family together in the same room and share with them the word of God and have all of us hold hands as we prayed in both English and Korean. Because we are all one in Christ, I would challenge them to pray together in the same way and persevere through any cultural awkwardness and language barriers.

Character and Integrity: Apostle Paul declared to the elders who came from Ephesus for their last gathering at Miletus that he was "innocent of the blood of all men." (Acts 20:26, NASB). Are we able to proclaim the same thing? Do we have that same clear conscience that Apostle Paul had? When we serve the Lord through our local churches, are we able to declare that we are truly innocent of the blood of our fellow congregants? Of our fellow members? The importance of character and integrity and clear consciences in our service in the local church can never be stressed enough. I have seen and counseled at churches where the sins of their leadership result in strife, divisions, bitterness, conflict, stumbling, and, for some, a leaving of the faith. I've seen and heard of leaders financially manipulate wealthy widows, abuse church resources to satisfy personal interests, gossip and slander others, commit adultery, and dupe others to fund their gambling (or drug) habits or prop up failed business ventures. The list goes on and on. I've seen it all. We are killing souls, not saving them.

Recently, I asked Sung, "Honey, throughout all our years of service in L.A., Alaska, and Monterey, have we been innocent of the blood of all those people with whom we have worked together, whom we have led to Christ, and whom we have served? Have we made any person stumble or fall, or have we hurt anyone so that consequently have they lost their faith?"

Cautiously, Sung answered, "I don't remember anyone."

"By God's grace, I agree."

Indeed, all because of God's grace.

Chapter 19

MY CALLING AS A PROFESSOR

My vocational calling was to teach and by God's grace, he gave me a passion for it. I wanted to be the best teacher I could be, not for my own glory, but for God's. I loved being in the classroom and on campus. I loved instructing and mentoring students. I loved seeing them grow in knowledge and develop confidence. I loved dialoguing with them, who were so eager to learn and to whom I was so eager to teach. No profession (no matter how much the pay or the attention) would have given me the same joy and excitement that I have had for all these years. Nothing else. I've never complained about teaching. I've never grumbled about preparing for a lecture. From a "job" perspective, I've never wanted to be anywhere else than in the classroom or in my office, talking with students. With the power of the Holy Spirit and heart of Christ, I have been healthily consumed in motivating, training, mentoring, and equipping my students with knowledge and information. My Lord and my teaching can't be separated because this was His calling for me.

When I was reading through Dr. Os Guinness's book, *The Call: Finding and Fulfilling the Central Purpose of Your Life*,[45] it confirmed that God had called me to this profession to expand His Kingdom. Pastors had encouraged me to go the seminary route and become one of them. They said I'd be a great preacher and pastor. Some even misguidingly said that full-time ministry was God's higher calling. I prayed about it. Though I have the greatest respect for full-time ministers, there was no call for me to be a pastor. And it was Dr. Guinness's *The Call* which helped confirmed that I was where God wanted me to be. To be in the teaching world, but not of it.

Prayer and Memorization

Every lecture began with prayer. I would pray, before entering the classroom. I would pray over my lecture notes. I would pray over the attendance roster. I would pray for each student. I would pray that God would grant me the wisdom and teaching skills necessary to instruct these students well: *Dear Lord, let me stand before my students as your ambassador, and let me love my students and embrace them in my heart with the heart of Christ. Let me do my utmost in teaching them everything that I have prepared, so that they would fully understand what they are about to learn. Bless them with your grace and mercy, so that they may be well equipped in their hearing, understanding, and learning. Moreover, let them encounter you through my class. Let me be a conduit of blessings and grace for my students that points to you, the ultimate Teacher, the ultimate Source, the ultimate Blessing.*

As I mentioned earlier, God has also given me the gift of memorization. I would memorize the names of my students – on the first day of each semester. At the start of that first class, I would ask the students to introduce themselves and say one thing about themselves (which I would use to help me remember their names). During the subsequent roll call, and from that time forward, I would call out each student's name from memory. Sometimes, upwards of 50 students in one class! I found this to be an extremely effective tool in motivating them – instead of being nameless students, they saw the effort I took to remember their names from the very first day. It gave me a greater and more personable connection to them from the get go, made them feel that they were important to me (which they were), and, I'd like to think, enhanced their performance the rest of the semester. A little effort can go a long way. I thank God for this gift.

I would also memorize my lecture notes ahead of time and hardly look at them during the class, no matter how long the class was. Except for that first year of teaching at Pepperdine, I had my lecture notes memorized. For me, I believed it was the best way to teach my students and passionately engage them in class discussions. I think it makes a big difference to students when instead of seeing an instructor who doesn't know your name reading verbatim from their notes or an outline, they learn from a professor passionately engaging them in a controlled dialogue. The excitement from such an instructor can only rub off on the students. I think this way of teaching encouraged my students to take more of an interest in the subject matter and even enjoy their studies. Their evaluations of me have consistently said as much. Passion – in whatever setting and about whatever topic – can be contagious.

Teamwork and Storytelling

Teamwork and team building were an integral part of my classes. Seventy percent of a student's course evaluation was based on team assignments: cases, projects, in-class activities, and presentations. The exams and tests and individual work assignments consisted of the remaining 30 percent. This put a premium on teamwork, forcing the students to find ways to work effectively together. By emphasizing teamwork, I wanted to teach the students how to share (not keep to themselves) their strengths and expertise, as well as learn how to encourage, edify, and make other teammates successful in reaching a common goal: excellence. This was my way of not only teaching them group-work skills that they could use in the real world, but instilling within them the Biblical principles of giving, selflessness, community, and loving others. Teamwork is very biblical. God has always been a team – the Holy Trinity, God the Father, God the Son, and God the Holy Spirit. And we know throughout the Bible, including Jesus Christ and the disciples, as well as Apostle Paul and his fellow missionaries, God's work has been done through teamwork. And God calls us to be part of a team, His team, for

His glory! And God calls us to live in loving community with one another, to give cheerfully and generously (and not hoard), and to build up one another. Teamwork.

I've also been known by my students as a storyteller. I never took offense to that characterization because the Bible itself is about God's redemptive story. It's Jesus's story. It's His story (= History). In that way, storytelling has always been a part of my teaching. I always try to end my class with a story that's related to the instructed subject matter. This gives some real-life teeth and perspective to what was covered in the classroom and thus, enables students to better understand the material. Indeed, students can easily forget what they learn during a lecture (especially after an exam), but they seldom forget the stories, even long after their years in school. Stories motivate. Stories inspire. Stories remind. Stories excite. Stories put things in perspective. Stories get to both the mind and the heart. Just as it was for Jesus, when He spoke in parables, stories have been such an effective teaching tool for me.

Time Management

Ephesians 5:16 says, "making the most of every opportunity, because the days are evil." This verse has always been a great challenge to me. I constantly ask myself, *Have I been abundantly and exceedingly productive? Am I making the most of every opportunity?* I ask those same questions of my students each semester. The answers vary (usually they don't consider themselves that productive), but one thing I do make clear to them are these characteristics of time:

Time is opportunity: students give at least four years of their time for the opportunity to go to college and earn a degree.

Time is a resource: any and all resources, such as water,

energy, financial, human, etc., must be managed, lest they be wasted. But time is the most precious resource, because time is life.

Time is life: our life span is a confined space of time. Therefore time management is life management.

Time is a gift. Every life is a gift. So what do we do with that gift?

Time cannot be saved. We can save money, but we can't save time. No matter what we do (or don't do) each day, we only have at our disposal 24 hours a day and 168 hours a week. No more, no less.

Time is the one true equalizer. Time is the most equally and fairly distributed resource among all other resources. No one can complain that he only has 23 hours compared to someone else having 25 hours each day. The clock does not play favorites. Everyone has the same amount of time, no matter how busy – everything else, you could say, is unevenly distributed. Time is the fairest of all.

Time is the most competitive resource. We are always competing against the clock (even if we don't always realize this). Thus, the question becomes, who will make the most of each given opportunity? Who is going to make the best use of his or her life?

After introducing these concepts to my students, I would talk more practically about time multiplication, studying habits, and extracurricular activities. Each student would then be asked to develop a time management plan for the semester and I would serve as the adviser in seeing that those plans are implemented and fulfilled. The result: those who carried out what they planned performed very well, not just in my class, but in their other classes. Seeing the positive effect it had on my students, my other colleagues began to do the same with their students. Eventually, at my university in Monterey, I would conduct a special two-hour lecture for the juniors in the business program on time management.

Taking the Biblical principles of time and putting it in the classroom was never my idea. It was a challenge that God, in His mercy and wisdom, gave to me from His word. God's word is always instructive, in every work situation or setting. It always has a place of authority and guidance and counsel throughout our Monday to Friday work weeks – not just on Sunday mornings. There is no compartmentalization when it comes to Christian living. There is no Monday morning spiritual amnesia. It is about integration. It is about being one and the same, at all times, in any setting.

Mentoring

I've always believed that there can be no effective training and learning unless there's mentoring. "Mentoring" is a term that I think is a better fit for the university (and marketplace) context, even though to me it has its Biblical roots in "discipleship." Every year, I select five to seven students from different backgrounds and ethnicities (and sometimes in different grades) to be in a mentoring group. This group makes a commitment to me and to each other to meet 2 hours every week during the semester. No exceptions (except for emergencies and travel commitments). These are not my office hours, but personal time that I set aside specifically for this group. It's a big commitment. For me and for them, as I hold these sessions over the course of the entire academic year. At the first session, I share my passion for their learning. I share my desire to build leadership qualities in them. I tell them my expectations, which are high. Then, to break the ice, I have everyone introduce themselves and share their life stories and the reasons why they applied to be in the group. I not only want them to be mentored by me, but to learn from the experiences and hardships (if any) of their fellow students. The diversity of the group adds to the richness of my mentoring program.

At the end of the first session, I give them their first mentoring assignment – a vision statement that they will read aloud in the next session. So for the second session, each student takes a turn reading his or her vision statement. After hearing what everyone says, I offer feedback to each of the statements, usually along the lines of whether it needs to be more streamlined or simplified. We then engage in some more dialogue about the contents of their vision statements and why they had these visions in the first place. And then, it's off to races for the rest of the semester and the next – where we cover a broad swath of topics and current issues, engaging in debates and intense discussions (sometimes heated ones!), going over reading assignments, and academic counseling and other concerns. I do not rule over them in these sessions; instead, I try to create a safe environment where everyone buys in, and everyone participates fully in the process. As the saying goes, it is what they put into it that determines what they get out it. And I don't stand in the way.

Through these times I show them how teamwork, communication skills, critical analysis and thinking, and passion (not emotion!) can be utilized to enhance their performance. Although they know I'm a Christian, rather than force-feeding them "Christianese," I focus on the character of Jesus Christ in these sessions (without having to mention His name) to subtly build up His character traits in them. I stress the importance of integrity, humility, and honesty. I tell them that leadership is not lording over, but serving, giving, and sacrificing. I tell them that leadership is about personal responsibility and not dwelling on other's faults, but looking to themselves to see how they can improve. Never shifting blame, but taking responsibility. Over time, the group begins to care for each other and they converge into a team. It is amazing to witness this trajectory toward unity when most of these students would've never even known each other, much less been friends, if it weren't for the mentoring group. It is the same feeling I have when I see a Bible study group – made up of sinners who happen to go to church together but who may not otherwise have any other basis to relate to one another – come together in loving unity and community.

Not only that, but I share my own life experiences – the ups and downs, the failures and defeats, the mistakes, the suffering and pain, the successes and achievements. To me, mentoring is life on life. I put my life on them in hopes that they would be better prepared to face their futures. On the final day, I treat them to dinner at a local restaurant and have them share what they learned from the mentoring sessions. For many, it had been a life-changing experience. For even some, it opened their eyes to God. I would share more of my personal testimony with them, leaving Korea, studying in a foreign land, my rise at Pepperdine, and then my liver disease and how Jesus Christ had saved me. I would share that my heart beats for mentoring because Jesus was my spiritual mentor and Dr. Lammers was my academic mentor. That I wouldn't be where I was without them. And to pass on what they did for me to this mentoring group. I still keep in touch with some of my mentees and some of the mentees are still good friends with each other. It has been such a rewarding experience for me and I thank God for giving me those opportunities to not only instruct, but to minister to many students for His glory. Praise God!

Research and Teaching

Alaska is known for its frequent earthquakes. In March of 1964, on Good Friday, Alaska had an earthquake that was registered as a 9.2 on the Richter Scale. It was the biggest earthquake in U.S. and North American history (and the second largest earthquake in recorded history). The earthquake and the resulting tsunamis caused some 140 deaths. The effects were felt throughout that part of the globe, with damage even in Hawaii, California, and Japan. The federal government spent millions to investigate the earthquake. In the wake of that investigation, Washington,

D.C. developed federal earthquake policies involving mitigation, preparation, first responders (search and rescue), and short-term and long-term reconstruction. The earthquake policies, as drafted, would have immensely affected every facet of private and public life, including the construction of residential and commercial structures (including schools), the protection of existing structures, resource development, environmental protection, cultural heritage protection, transportation infrastructure, and city planning.

But according to some investigating by myself and three colleagues, these policies had not yet been implemented. It was a classic case of federal policy decisions with no federal follow-through. With that in mind, in 1981, the four of us submitted a grant proposal to the National Science Foundation regarding earthquake policies and problems with their implementation. We received $250,000 on behalf of the university. After two years of hard work, in 1983, we finished our research document and submitted it to the NSF with our proposed policy recommendations as well as implementation strategies. Our research findings and recommendations were so well received by the NSF that they submitted them to the Federal Emergency Management Administration (FEMA) for consideration. We later learned that FEMA would adopt all our recommendations.

In June 1984, to my surprise, because of our research, I was one of 33 experts and scholars that FEMA invited to come to Washington, D.C. and Emmitsburg, Maryland. First, we toured the White House and were ushered to the next building, the Executive Building, where we spent the next two days listening to presentations by FEMA and National Security officials on natural and man-made disasters. We were then taken to the Senior Executive Policy Center in Emmitsburg where we were holed up for two weeks. Each participant was given an opportunity to present their research. The group was impressive. Every one of them was a giant in his or her field, with far more research and field experience than me. We presented, commented, and debated on issues related to natural calamities (major floods, hurricanes, major fires, earthquakes, volcanoes, tornados), and man-made disasters (oil spills, gas leaks, nuclear power plant explosions, terrorist attacks, and nuclear holocaust). Each group was then assigned with specific disaster(s) scenarios to reach possible policy recommendations that would be presented to the entire assembly and then, if formally adopted, to FEMA.

During the final session at the end of those two weeks, the participants unanimously elected an Indiana University Professor, Mick Charles, and me to edit and publish a book on "Crisis Management." Dr. Charles was well known and an accomplished scholar and expert, but me? I was not. I was taken aback by their confidence in me. We were bused back to D.C. and everyone went home. As promised, the groups sent us their manuscripts, and Mick and I compiled, reviewed, and edited them. In 1989, "Crisis Management: A Casebook" (Charles C. Thomas, Publisher, Springfield, Ill.) was published. The book was the first of its kind and was widely used by federal, state, and local governments, libraries, universities and schools, and many institutions and private entities for emergency and crisis management. It also became a teaching supplement for some crisis management professors. Recently, the publisher told us that they would like to issue a second edition.

My real research passion, however, was on energy development and environmental policies, specifically the oil and gas development on the Outer Continental Shelf, and their impact on social, economic, cultural, and physical environments in coastal communities. Consequently, I presented 19 research papers to professional conferences and learned societies, including journal publications, within a year and a half. I was elected as the chairperson by my peers for three major energy and environment forums in Denver, New York, and Honolulu with experts, scholars, and top managers in relevant fields invited. As a result, I edited the "The Current Issues in Energy Policy: A Special Edition for Policy Studies Journal" (Policy Studies Organization, Urbana-Champaign, IL), which was published in 1985. Later, in 1987, along with my colleague, Dr. Rick Ender, I was able to write and publish, "Energy Resources Development: Politics and Policies" (Quorum Books, New York).

With two other colleagues, I also had an opportunity to do research on 260 "blue chip" cities, counties, and school districts, examining their tax policies and budgeting systems in relation to their respective quality of life and economic growth. Our research, "The Current Budgeting and Accounting Practices in the U.S.," which found that lower taxes and a more lean and austere budget (in other words, less government spending) improved quality of life and economic growth, was recognized as one of the best papers at the American Institute of Decision Science National Conference in 1985 (Honolulu, HI).

All of this was just the beginning of God's blessing on my work at the university.

In the fall of 1984, after four years at UAA, I submitted an application for promotion and tenure. The university's Retention, Tenure and Promotion (RTP) Committee unanimously approved my application, which was subsequently recommended to and approved by Chancellor Outcalt, who, in the spring of 1985, commended my performance in all areas in such a short period of time. While a 10% salary increase is standard for a promotion, the chancellor awarded me a 21% increase! I believe this was his way of partly restoring the broken promises that were made to me when the university first recruited me. It was also God's reminder for me that responding to wrongs and slights with grace and forgiveness and forging ahead with integrity and diligence glorifies and pleases Him.

On October 17, 1984, I received a call from Chancellor Outcalt's assistant to confirm my attendance at UAA's convocation, for all university personnel (administrators, deans, faculty, and staff) and students, which was held the next day at the school's sports arena. At the time, after confirming my attendance, I didn't think much of the call and thought these were standard courtesy calls to university faculty. Little did I know that I was in for quite a surprise. After the speeches of the new university President Don O'Dowd and Chancellor Outcalt, awards were given out recognizing years of service to the university. The provost then took the stage announcing that UAA established two new awards, the Chancellor's Award for Excellence in Teaching and for Excellence in Field Work, and introduced the chairperson of the awards committee. The awards committee, made up of 18 members across the campus, went through a painstaking process sifting through formal nominations and faculty and students evaluations, and conducting countless interviews of nominated candidates, their colleagues and others. They wanted to do everything they could to be sure that the very first recipients of these awards were truly deserving.

The chairperson continued: "I want you to know that we have kept the identities of the award recipients confidential. Up until this point. Not even the recipients know. So, let me first present the first recipient for the Chancellor's Award for Excellence in Teaching to . . . Dr. John Kim!" *What?!* My jaw dropped. I was so shocked that for a moment, I couldn't move, much less get out of my seat. *Thank you, Lord. It's all for you. It was all done by you.*

Making my way up to the stage to the sound of applause, whistles, and shouts, I could not stop thanking my Lord and tearing up. I shook the hand of the new president and hugged the chancellor, who presented me with a plaque and a white envelope. They asked me to make some remarks. I think I was in such disbelief and out-of-sorts that I wasn't nervous in addressing the crowd: "Thank you so much for this award, Chancellor Outcalt! I am deeply humbled and honored. There are a number of distinguished faculty members here who are more qualified than I am. I am shocked. I am really shocked. I will accept this award on behalf of my family, all my students, fellow faculty members, and deans, administrators, and staff without whom I couldn't possibly be here. Thank you so much for the hard work of the selection committee. I give all the thanks to God and thank you everyone. May God bless all of you!"

Now I knew why the chancellor's assistant called to make sure I would be in attendance. After the convocation, there was a reception where I was able to get more acquainted with the new university president, which set the table for God to fulfill His greater purposes for the state through me in the future.

Community Service

Professor Ender and I were also involved in helping elect Tony Knowles as Mayor of Alaska in 1982 and were part of his transition team. After he became elected, we continued to work in his administration, with Rick as his polltaker and I as his policy advisor. It was a steep learning curve for me having never worked in this capacity and being fully immersed with the issues and problems that were facing the Anchorage community. It was good for me to get away from academia – which in and of itself can be isolating – and serve my community in this way. One problem facing the mayor had to do with the increased massage parlors (which were also most likely fronts to other illegal activity), drug and alcohol abuse, and motels that were heavily used for narcotics, alcohol binging, and possible prostitution in one particular section in downtown Anchorage. We also noticed that these motels were making money illegally by abusing Alaskan natives, easy targets who struggled financially.

In a meeting with the mayor and his cabinet, various suggestions were offered as to what to do. I suggested that the city buy out the entire section, demolish the area, and build a parking structure for the mall downtown. Others thought that the idea was too bold (never really been done before), too expensive (to demolish and rebuild), and politically controversial (the owners could protest). I suggested that the city could charge a minimum parking fee for the structure to defray the cost of the project. I was convinced that people would pay to park – especially during the long, winter season when they wouldn't have to drudge through the snow and the elements to get to the mall. The police chief agreed with me and eventually, so did the mayor. The owners were fully compensated and the parking garage more than paid for itself after several years. The area soon became revitalized as seediness was replaced with development.

I was also invited to speak at Alaskan native youth meetings in various locations throughout the state. The suicide rate among this youth group is one of the highest in the U.S. You could call it an epidemic. It's heartbreaking. Many of these Alaska native boys and girls have no dreams or visions for their lives – they have no hope. Their lives wasted away with drink and drugs. There have been some outstanding Alaska native leaders, but the suicides among the young have taken a toll.

I don't know if it was because they looked a lot like Asians or because Alaska really became a home for me in my heart, but I had a tremendous affinity for them. And deep compassion. In addition to the formal speaking engagements, I would volunteer my time to reach out to them, meet with them, and share my testimony with them. I wanted to encourage them. That there was hope. That my life was an example of what God could do when the cards were stacked against you. No father, no money, no food for over three days, suicide attempts, and a grave, seemingly incurable illness. Yet, Jesus saves. Jesus transforms. Jesus redeems. I challenged them not to waste their lives. That they were ahead of the game at this point in their lives than I was. That life is the most precious thing. "Don't waste it. It's not too late. Live it out." When I saw some of the Alaska native students who left their villages and came to UAA struggling to adjust to the college workload, and campus and city life, I invested my time to help them as much as I could. With their studies. With their extracurriculars. With their lives.

My research and work at the university led to other opportunities to serve the communities and state. In 1980, President Carter signed the Alaska National Interest Lands Conservation Act (ANILCA). ANILCA covered the state's land program and resource development, production, and conservation, as well as wild life preservation, national parks and refuges, native reservations, and forestry conservation. To implement these policies, the federal government, along with Alaska's state government and local native representatives, created the Alaska Land Use Council, of which I was named advisor and vice president. Later on, I became an official advisor to the state governor, primarily focused on the promotion of trade and commerce and environmentally-friendly development, and recognized as such by many cities in Asia.

These were the opportunities provided by God as He began to unfold His dream for me to be a Joseph in Alaska.

Chapter 20

A VISION FOR MY STATE

It was a Friday afternoon in the middle of October 1983. The chief of staff to Alaska Governor Bill Sheffield was on the line. The governor, having just returned from a trip to East Asia and impressed with what he saw going on in the region, wanted to have a meeting with me. He was interested in talking about expanding Alaska's international trade opportunities in Asia.

"John, I suggest that you bring some ideas for the governor. I'll let you know the time and date of the meeting."

"You got it."

A couple of weeks later, I flew down to Juneau, the capital, to meet with the governor and his chief of staff. The three of us met in the governor's office. The governor thanked me for the honorary doctoral degree he received from my alma mater, Kyung Hee University, while he was in Seoul, which I had arranged with Kyung Hee's chancellor, Dr. Young Shik Cho. He talked some more about his trip and his impressions of East Asia. He talked about his desire to open Alaska to the Asia-Pacific region through international trade opportunities as well as educational, cultural, and student exchange programs.

"What are your thoughts on that, John?"

"I think that's a great idea, Governor."

"Then John, I need you to gather your ideas together and formally present them to me and my staff and cabinet. Can you do that?"

"Of course. I'd be happy to do that. It may take me a few months because of my teaching schedule, but I should be ready by early next year."

"Sounds good."

This would not be an easy task. I was the new kid on the block. But God had called me to Alaska with a vision of Joseph for a reason.

God used Joseph to make Egypt better and save the peoples of the world, including the Israelites. Perhaps, through this, God would use me to make Alaska's future better. If this was the case, I had to get out of the way and let God work. His way, not mine. His glory, not mine. His work, not mine.

After I returned home from Juneau, my mind was racing. I needed to settle myself before God and pray and pray some more. I repented of my pride and any fleeting thoughts that I had anything to do in arriving at this moment. I praised God that He had given me this chance to make the place He called me to better. I repented of the bitterness and lingering regret of having come to Alaska and the difficulty the initial adjustment had been for me and my family. I repented of having even questioned God's calling after I had poured myself onto many tasks (to show how competent I was), which only left me spent, feeling unappreciated, and a little more hardened. I needed to repent of my iniquities because of my desire to have this plan for Alaska be His and His alone. I needed to be wiped clean so that He would get all the glory. He reminded me of His forgiveness. He reminded me that He was always there for me. He assured me that He loves me – no matter what. Giving His Son up to die for a sinner like me was that assurance that I needed to hear again and again.

My Plan for Alaska and the University

With that "blessed assurance" and confidence, I asked the Holy Spirit to fill me with discernment, wisdom, and understanding. I asked that the Holy Spirit would fill my heart and renew my mind. To give me focus. To make me sharp. To illuminate and direct. Graciously, God's vision, not my own dream or the governor's desire and ambitions, led me to see a long term plan for Alaska's future and its role in relation to the Asia-Pacific region and to the world. God enabled me to formulate a dozen premises upon which I developed a comprehensive and strategic plan involving state and local government, industry and commerce, and the state university working together in a tripartite partnership. This plan was not only for the well-being of the state, but also for the entire North Pacific region. The first draft took me almost a month.

I invited several senior faculty members and my dean to lunch to share my plan with them and have them review and critique it. We were then set to get together again in a few days to go over it, before the spring semester began. The day after the lunch, Dean Brad Tuck, an economist, came in to my office and said, "This is fantastic, John! Let's work to get this finalized ASAP. I will call George [Geistauts], Vern [Hauk], and Rick [Ender] to my office tomorrow." These trusted colleagues helped me complete the final draft and, with the dean's endorsement, I hand delivered it myself to Chancellor Outcalt. A few days later, the chancellor invited me and Dean Tuck to his office and said he was very pleased with the proposal. The chancellor promised that he would strongly endorse the plan to university President Jay Barton, who would then submit the proposal to the chairperson of the Board of Regents of the University of Alaska in hopes of getting it on the agenda for the board's annual meeting next March.

"But John," warned the chancellor, "there's no guarantee. It looks pretty good, but there are always politics involved with the university."

"I'm planning on meeting soon with the governor and key leaders in Juneau. Just me," I emphasized. "So this is probably something that the university administrators may be a bit sensitive to. But ultimately this is not my call, but the governor's call."

I contacted Governor Sheffield's chief of staff in late December 1983 and urged him to set up a meeting with the governor and his cabinet, the budget director, and other staff. I was ready to present my plan. On the day of the meeting, I went to church for early prayer service. I prayed that God would fill me with wisdom and speak through me at the meeting. Later that dark winter morning, I flew to Juneau and was escorted to the governor's conference room, where the governor, three key staff and three cabinet members greeted me. I distributed copies of the proposed plan around the conference table and spoke for about a half hour.

My plan, in a high-level nutshell, went as follows:

> Alaska almost exclusively depended on crude oil production for its revenues. No economy can be considered robust if 85% of its revenues come from one major industry. Because of that, Alaska's economy was hostage to the price setting of OPEC (Organization of the Petroleum Exporting Countries). It was critical that Alaska's portfolio be diversified through international trade and business. The state must be a competitive player in the global market, specifically in the Asia-Pacific and circumpolar regions. Passivity and OPEC-dependency was disastrous in the long run.

> In this regard, the state must invest its petroleum revenues in new ventures and businesses to promote economic diversification and increase the state's exports. Education and training of the state's businesses are necessary, with an emphasis on the how-to of international business and negotiation. To that end, a research center should be established to provide international market data and trends, international business know-how, and shared faculty expertise from the university to usher in a new era of the state's economy. I wanted to name this center the "Alaska Center for International Business (ACIB)."

> Paramount to all of this is that government, business/ industry, and the university build a symbiotic, tripartite

partnership not only to advance the state's economy, but thereby enhance the well-being of the peoples of Alaska and the peoples of the Asia-Pacific region for generations after generations.

I concluded my presentation with an emphasis that the time to create ACIB was of the essence. The opportunity was now to be bold. To make a difference. And that I would do my best to fulfill this vision and get my university on board, mentioning that the proposed plan was now in the hands of President Barton. That because we were a state university, I told them my belief that I had a responsibility to make my university, my community, and my state better. In closing, I thanked them all for listening so attentively to a no-name professor and then asked if anyone had questions. No one did. The governor remarked that he was impressed. After instructing me to continue working with his staff, as the governor left the conference room he said, "Keep up the good work, John."

In Politics, Nothing's Guaranteed

Bad news greeted me soon after my return from Juneau. The regents were divided on my proposal and President Barton was opposed. I was naïve to think it would be easy. Discouraged by the politics, I was comforted in my prayers. I resolved not to give up, but to fight all the way. I was committed to the vision that God had given me.

My first stop was Roy Huhndorf, one of my former students who was appointed by the governor to serve on the board of regents. One of the most prominent and well-respected Alaskan native, Roy was the CEO of Cook Inlet Regional Corporation. Roy was also a close friend. After sharing my vision for the university and the state at his office, I asked for his support. He said he would do his utmost in persuading his skeptical colleagues on the board and President Barton. I knew I could trust him.

I called my friend John Sanders in Juneau, the Director of the National Forest Service and the highest ranking official of the federal government in Alaska. We had gotten to know each other through my work on the Alaska Land Use Council. He was also a fellow brother in Christ. John happened to be close with Don Avery, the chairman of the board of regents, and I asked John to persuade his close friend to support the plan. Over an earlier dinner, John was delighted in my vision. He wanted to retire in Alaska so the future of the state was something that was very important to him. Before we left the restaurant, he prayed for me and said I could count on him for his support (and he would also try to mobilize other federal directors in the state). My meetings with state legislators and business and community leaders were also very encouraging.

I arrived in Juneau on March 8, 1984, the day before the board of regents meeting on the Juneau campus of the University of Alaska. I was staying at the same hotel where all the regents and university administrators were staying. As the board and administrators were coming out of a dinner meeting at the hotel, I approached President Barton and introduced myself and asked for a few minutes of his time. He seemed a bit hesitant, but suggested we sit on one of the sofas in the lobby.

"Professor Kim, your proposal has been well received, but we're concerned about costs. It's our policy not to simply add a research center that could cost a lot of money for the university. Even if the initial money for the center comes from the state's appropriations. I myself am not so sure we need another research center for our school. I hope you understand it would be difficult to persuade the regents to support it."

"President Barton, I hear you, but our university can make great contributions to the state's economic diversification and growth and to the well-being of the people in Alaska by internationalizing our university and our economy through the work of this center. It would be a practical, action-oriented center. Not just a theoretical and academic, 'ivory tower' think-tank. Please reconsider your position. It won't cost a dime to the university."

President Barton didn't respond and walked away.

I then ran into Don Avery, the chairman, who was happy to see me and said jokingly, "So you're the one who is stirring controversy amongst us!" All kidding aside, Don gave me a glimmer of hope and said he would do his best. "We'll just have to wait and see," he said. Afterwards, I went to see the chancellor in his hotel room and told him about my encounters with President Barton and Don. He was pretty disappointed. But I put on a brave face and told him not to lose hope about tomorrow's meeting – "I believe it's not my thing or your thing, but it's a God thing."

I returned to my room. With mixed feelings. *What in the world am I doing here? I'm not the president, the chancellor, a regent, or even an administrator or official; I'm just a simple state university professor. Why should I care about this? Why should I even bother with this? With all the hard work, the ups and downs, the trips to Juneau, the constant selling, the sleepless nights? Why should I be concerned about the future of this state and the well-being of its people? Even the president of the university doesn't even care. Why should I?* From a human perspective, it was difficult to understand why I went through the trouble. It wasn't really logical. Other professors were performing their routine duties: teaching, research, and university service and I had already been recognized for my work in all three areas. *Why I am taking on this challenge and bearing this risk? I'm not even getting paid for it!* But God reminded me of His call for me to come to Alaska. At that point, I suddenly felt a stronger sense of ownership of Alaska. That I was called to embrace Alaska into my heart. That I was called to thereby serve Alaska. That I was called thereby to make it better and greater. For His glory.

I got up very early the next morning and prayed. I had done everything humanly possible. It was out of my hands. It was out of my control. *God, let your will be done.* After breakfast, I drove to the building on the Juneau campus where the board meeting was held. Because I wasn't invited to the meeting, I sat in the public gallery and watched. Thankfully, my proposal was able to make it onto the agenda. That was the first victory, to which I owed Don and Roy. Relief. The proposal was to be officially heard in the afternoon session.

I fasted lunch and kept praying as I walked around the Juneau campus. The meeting resumed and again I sat in the public gallery. The proposal was formally introduced to the board by Don. Roy then made a statement strongly endorsing the proposal. President Barton came out strong against the proposal. The debate was now on. At times it got heated. At one point I went to the bathroom and sat on the toilet and prayed for God's divine intervention.

During the ongoing deliberations, John Sanders walked up to Don and handed him a stack of letters from local leaders, business executives, and federal representatives endorsing the proposed center. As promised, John did his utmost to support the plan and get others to support it. He also handed over his own personal letter to the board and asked that Don read aloud some of these letters. As one after another endorsement letter was read to the board, a deafening silence came across the entire room. The atmosphere had changed. The momentum had shifted. The tide had turned. In favor of the plan. The debate effectively ended and the proposal was put up for a vote. And it passed. Unanimously. As applause came from the gallery, I sat in awe of God's divine intervention and welled up with thanksgiving.

Then President Barton, seeing that he was defeated, stood up and defiantly stated, "Even though the board of regents has passed the proposal for the Alaska Center for International Business,

I will not accept the state legislators' appropriation for ACIB, because ultimately the university will be forced to find additional financial resources to support this center down the road." The regents were shocked and extremely unhappy at the hearing of this. It was as if he had doused water on a beautifully lit birthday cake. This would later become known as "Barton's debacle," and the president's offensive attitude at the meeting eventually led to his forced departure a few months later.

Bewildered by what had just transpired, I immediately got into my car and drove to the state capitol building. I met with key representatives and senators and explained to them briefly what happened at the board of regents meeting. I then got their commitment to introduce a bill appropriating $680,000 for ACIB's initial funding. They said they'd be glad to introduce it. Afterwards, I flew back to Anchorage later that day and joined the Billy Graham Crusade at the Sullivan Arena to translate Dr. Graham's message into Korean for the Korean-speaking attendees. What a day!

Two days later was a Sunday and our 17th wedding anniversary, which was spent at church in the morning and then at the Billy Graham Crusade, where I had to again translate Dr. Graham's message for the Koreans in the audience. After we got home, my wife and I had to pack. We were leaving to Japan the next day.

A (Needed) Second Honeymoon

On March 12, 1984, my wife and I boarded a plane for Tokyo. This was Japan Airlines's inaugural flight for their non-stop service between Tokyo and Anchorage. The airline invited the governor, Mayor Tony Knowles, and other state, local, and business leaders to the commemorative flight. Mayor Knowles and his wife could not make the trip due to conflicts with his schedule, so he asked Sung and I to go on their behalf. We gladly accepted. It was our first time in first class. And the trip was for eight days, all expenses paid by Japan Airlines. What a wedding anniversary gift we were given!

During the flight, I asked my wife, "Remember how we spent our honeymoon in Tokyo 17 years ago? We didn't have to pay anything then either because of the Shibusawas."

"Oh, that's right!"

"Now we are headed back to Japan for our second honeymoon!"

"Amazing."

"Tell me, have I met your expectations as your husband throughout these 17 years?"

"I married you because of your sincerity and faithfulness. You have not disappointed me. You have been sincere and faithful all these years."

I held her hand tightly and gave her a kiss on the cheek. My favorite Chinese characters are loyalty, sincerity, and faithfulness. Loyalty, it has been said, is "in the center of my mind, the word is fulfilled (bears fruit)," sincerity is "when the word is fulfilled (succeeds) it will bear fruit," and faithfulness is "the man's word shall bear fruit." By God's grace and power, I have prayed that I would live a life reflecting these characteristics. I thanked my wife for her tireless dedication, loving care, and hard work for me and the children and our church and the call to Alaska. I promised that I would continue to live a sincere and faithful and loyal life to her in Christ Jesus.

Over dinner with the Shibusawas and our old Japanese friends, I proposed to Mr. Shibusawa that I would recommend him to our chancellor for an appointment as a distinguished visiting scholar for UAA and that I would do my best to get him to Anchorage. He and his wife were delighted with my proposal. Eventually, we were able to have him come as a Fulbright Scholar for the 1985-96 school year, through which we were able to work closely together for the university and Alaska.

It was an amazing eight days in Tokyo for my wife and me. But upon our return to Anchorage, a painful trial awaited.

Completely Blindsided

Upon our arrival in Anchorage, I called my office to check in. My assistant told me that the chancellor anxiously awaited my return and needed to see me immediately. As soon as we got to our home and placed our luggage inside the house, I rushed to the university. The chancellor was with the Vice Chancellor for Public Affairs. I asked them what the urgency was. The vice chancellor then explained to me what had happened:

My proposal so impressed the governor and his staff that positive word spread from the Juneau to Anchorage. Then, the board of regents' approval to establish ACIB made the Anchorage newspapers. Dr. Glenn Olds, President of Alaska Pacific University (APU), a small private university in Anchorage, learned about the plan and then contacted his personal friend, Governor Sheffield, and asked him to invite 60 state legislators, cabinet members and local leaders for a dinner banquet that would be paid by APU. The invitation went out in the governor's name, ensuring almost full attendance. After the dinner portion of the banquet was over, Dr. Olds spoke on APU's vision for the Asia-Pacific region and claimed that UAA threatened to swallow up his small private university by taking what was his original idea, ACIB, and pitching it as its own. In other words, he claimed that I had stolen his idea and presented it as my own to the governor and to the board of regents.

I felt sick to my stomach.

"John, we have to do something about this," Chancellor

Outcalt said, "He's not telling the truth. The plan originated from you and we have all the witnesses and documents to prove it.

"I know."

"Perhaps we should sue him for slander to clear your name and our university's. Or have a press conference or issue a public statement demanding a public apology since he made his claims publicly at the governor's banquet. The university community and the board of regents are anxiously awaiting our next move. They want to see what we have to say in response. They approved your proposal. They trusted you."

"I never met Dr. Olds. I never read anything he wrote, if he in fact wrote anything. The vision was not even mine, but came from God during my prayer for our university and Alaska. It was a vision that I readily shared with all of you, my colleagues, the community, and it underwent so much scrutiny to get it passed. It was an original. How could I steal it from him?"

"I know John. That's why we need to do something!"

I was shaking and numb at the same time. It was like a darkness that I never felt before. To have my integrity questioned. This was character assassination. If there were ever two words that could shame people the most, it is "liar" and "racist." With one speech, everything that I had worked to build came crashing down. In a moment, I became a liar and a cheater. A thief of ideas. A radioactive leper in the community. I asked the chancellor to allow me a few days to think and pray about what to do.

Unfair was an understatement. The shock, the hurt, the pain, the anger, the disillusionment. The nerve of him! My wife was in such utter disbelief that she could not manage to say a word for a few minutes after I told her. She had seen how much work I put into this. Day and night. For months. The all-nighters. She herself was the one who typed the final proposal for me. It pained her that her husband's honor had been destroyed by a man whom we have never met, much less knew. This was probably the most difficult trial we had encountered since my transformation. Everything we had worked for seemed to flash before our eyes – and it all seemed to us at the time to be in vain.

The next day, after my class, my colleagues who had helped me finalize the plan came to see me at my office.

"John, you must take legal action again him."

"John, it's slander. We can sue him for damages."

"John, we were your collaborators and reviewers. We can also be your witnesses."

"John, we found not one document or reference that is consistent with his claim that it was his idea. You didn't steal anything."

"John, we think that you were racially discriminated against."

"John, we have to sue him. You have to clear your name."

The Courage to Be Still and Wait

After I came home, I went straight to my study room and locked the door. Kneeling down on the floor, I petitioned my case before Almighty God. *Oh Lord! Why is this happening? My heart was pure and my mind was truthful when I worked on the proposal. There was no ulterior motive. There was no personal ambition. There was no selfish gain. Dear Lord, what am I to do now? My reputation has been destroyed. My character has been tarnished. I am hurting, Lord. How do I address this? I followed your call to Alaska and now have been wrongfully accused of stealing. How shall I be vindicated? Should I sue this man or hold a press conference or ask for his public apology through a public statement?*

God then reminded me of Joseph who was wrongly thrown into jail by an angry Captain Potiphar because of his wife's false accusation against Joseph. God wanted me to wait patiently for Him to act. For Him to restore my honor. And to do so in His way and in His time, not mine. He reminded me of His Son, Jesus Christ, who could have vigorously defended his reputation, but silently obeyed His father's will to the cross. In the same way, God's will was for me to sit tight and not do anything. To be still and obey. To "be still and know that [He is] God" (Ps. 46:10a). To be courageous by not responding. To be bold by staying silent. To trust. To let go.

After praying about it some more, I went to see the chancellor and my colleagues and told them my decision. They were very disappointed. They just couldn't understand why I chose not to do anything. Something had to be done, they kept saying. Something, anything. "Please," I pleaded, "I know how you feel. Just trust me on this. Please, I beg you. I know that one day our university will be victorious and my name will be restored. Let's wait until that time comes. We don't have to say anything or do anything or spend anything if we just wait. Now is not the time. But the time will come. I am confident." The chancellor reluctantly agreed. I thanked God for his trust in my decision. Chancellor Outcalt was also a Christian.

Even though I was innocent, water spilled on the ground can't all be put back into the jar. I limited my attendances at receptions and public functions. I didn't want to put myself in situations where I needed to defend myself. I didn't go around town as much. And it was awkward mingling with those who knew of the situation, but who didn't know my situation and my decision to keep quiet. My wife and I eventually decided to only go to those gatherings where my attendance was required. I also paid the price for not taking quick "PR" action to clear my name: my relationship with the governor and his staff and cabinet and key state legislators were strained, and the hope and dream I envisioned for the future of Alaska were put on ice (no pun intended). I was deeply saddened. I had no idea when God was going to vindicate me. And there was nothing but silence over at APU. *Wouldn't people start wondering if it was really Dr. Olds's vision if nothing's going on over there?*

God's transformation resulted in a change of my character. To be more Christ-like. In the sense that when I had been falsely accused or slandered or even mildly criticized, I did not take the matter into my own hands. I did not strike a course of defending and explaining myself to whoever would hear me. As long as my conscience confirmed that what I had done was right in the eyes of God, I resolved not to defend my decisions or actions. I learned this from Jesus Christ, who was without blame or blemish, and yet was silent before the Sanhedrin and Pontius Pilate as false accusation after false accusation was hurled at him. Even if I was misunderstood, I chose not to defend myself. I was a new creation. My identity was in Him, not what others thought about (or how clear their views were of) me. If I was unfairly characterized, God gave me the peace that whether in this life or the afterlife, that all would be cleared and my name would be exonerated in His Kingdom because of the sacrifice and righteousness of His Son. In many situations, if we feel cornered and boxed in, defending ourselves usually involves saying something negative or ungracious about the person who inflicted the criticism or injustice. That's what the old me would've done. Retaliate. Attack. Get back. Even the score. But God had changed me. Instead of an eye for an eye, I would ask God to give me patience to wait for His time. For His divine intervention. Not for my sinfulness to get involved and mess things up. His ways are always better. His time is always perfect.

Joseph waited for 13 long years after he was sold as a slave by his brothers, and waited for two-to-three years after he was thrown into jail by a false accusation. Joseph was eventually vindicated, but if vindication is not to be for us in this world, then it will be in the Kingdom of God. Indeed, I had already been truly vindicated when Jesus Christ became my Savior. I had already won – in the game that really counts – when I put my faith in Him. My name had already been cleared when God's Son became my righteous advocate.

I felt bad when I told the chancellor that I couldn't accommodate his request to do damage control for myself and in turn, the university. It's not easy saying no to the boss. Of course, my human nature wanted to control everything and have everything be resolved quickly, have my reputation instantly restored, that the center would open its doors for business and that the state would be on its way to prosperity. But God told me to wait. And I had to obey. The struggle for patient endurance and faithful perseverance had begun.

Chapter 21

A NEW ADMINISTRATION

A Brighter Outlook

With the establishment and operation of ACIB on hold, my focus and energy for the rest of 1984 was on teaching and research. I also worked diligently in organizing National Energy Symposiums in Denver, New York, and Honolulu. I was also, by the grace of God, able to lead a number of lost souls to Christ during the summer. At the time, *The Anchorage Times* ran a feature on my faith in Christ in its Religion Section, "The Other Side of John Kim." God continued to work in restoring His child's name with the Chancellor's Award for Excellence in Teaching at UAA's Annual Convocation on October 12, 1984 and in January 1985, when the state legislature passed a resolution recognizing me for my contributions to the state's higher education. The irony was that some of those senators and representatives who voted in favor of the resolution no doubt heard Dr. Olds's speech at the governor's banquet. I was deeply humbled. And in the spring of 1985, I was promoted to a full professor. God is willing and He is able!

In 1985, the new university President O'Dowd, unlike his predecessor, took special interest in ACIB. He gave me a $50,000 initial grant for starting the center. I praised God for starting to turn all of this around. I immediately hired two graduate assistants to research the fisheries industry and seafood exporting. Under my direction, they were able to analyze market data and come up with a plan for the state's seafood industry. We then gathered all the industry leaders and presented our findings and recommendations. They were impressed with our work, newspaper reports were favorable, and the center began working to increase the state's seafood exports. Happy with the results of his initial investment, President O'Dowd gave us another $50,000 grant. We used it to research the international markets of other industries in the state and were able to generate a ton of information to assist these other industries in finding export opportunities. Businesses were starting to notice. The attention was increasing. Demands for our expertise were rising. Our international business database and network were growing.

Gubernatorial Candidate Cowper

In early May of 1986, Professor Ender arranged a lunch meeting with a Democratic gubernatorial candidate, Steve Cowper, a lawyer and former state legislator whom I had never met. After Rick introduced us to each other in the UAA cafeteria, we sat down and Rick asked me to share with the candidate my vision for Alaska. It took me about an hour, at which time Mr. Cowper had to leave to another meeting. When we shook hands, Mr. Cowper asked me if I could further meet with him and his press secretary, David Ramseur, over breakfast. I said sure. A few days later, we spent three hours over breakfast discussing the vision, strategies, and action-plans that I had shared. I was very impressed by Mr. Cowper's openness, willingness to learn, straight talk, long-term thinking, and discerning leadership abilities. We were on the same page. The candidate asked whether David, his press secretary, and I would get together to distill my vision into layman's terms for public consumption on the campaign trail. He wanted to make it a part of his campaign promises. I couldn't believe it! I said I would gladly do so and reminded him of the crucial role that the university has to play in his new administration. David and I put our minds together and worked hard on framing the candidate's campaign message. Even though I was a registered Republican, I committed to help him.

Mr. Cowper was able to beat the incumbent in the Democratic primary, and was narrowly elected in November of 1986 as the new Governor of the State of Alaska. He immediately appointed me as chairperson of his economic development and international trade committee, made up of seven members. As part of his transition team, we started work on examining current government policies on economic development and international trade, and their results. We interviewed current commissioners and deputies and other officials of the various departments that were involved with these policies. We also conducted numerous interviews with industry and business leaders, mayors and local leaders and researched and collected a vast amount of documents including pertinent laws, rules, and regulations. The committee met for several weeks to discuss our work and findings with the current end goal of formulating the new gubernatorial administration's game plan for the economic development of Alaska.

On Monday, December 1, 1986, the inaugural ceremony for Alaska's new governor took place in Juneau. Unfortunately, I could not be there to celebrate his inauguration because of my teaching duties in Anchorage. Around eight o'clock in the morning the next day, the phone rang. My wife answered.

"Honey, it's Governor Cowper's assistant. She said the governor wants to speak with you now." She handed me the phone.

"Hello, this is John Kim."

"Dr. Kim, this is Governor Cowper's assistant. The governor would like to speak to you."

"Of course."

"Thank you. The first thing he asked me to do when he got in this morning is to get you on the line. Please hold on for one moment. Let me connect you to the governor."

"Hello, John?"

"Congratulations, Governor Cowper!"

"Thanks, John."

"How does your first day in office feel?"

"Feels great. John, I need you to do something for me. I need a White Paper for Alaska's economic development. I want to use it as part of my first State of the State Address in January."

"Okay."

"And I need it by Monday."

"Of next week?"

"Yes. I need you to bring the White Paper to Juneau and meet with me in my office on Monday at 2:00 p.m. I've set aside two hours for this meeting."

"Governor Cowper, that's less than six days."

"I know. I know I'm asking a huge favor of you."

"These next two weeks are the final weeks of the semester. They are the busiest. Could I at least get another week?"

"John, I hear you. But I need it by Monday. I know you can do it. You already have somewhat of a head start with all we've discussed and gone over and the work your committee has done so far."

He was not going to take "No" for an answer. "Governor, I will see you on Monday."

"Fantastic. Thanks so much, John. I really appreciate it."

As soon as I hung up the phone, I put my hands together and prayed at my desk. *Lord, you have sent me and my family here to Alaska to make it better. That time is now at hand as I have a great task before me. I cannot finish it within a week without you. It is impossible unless you do it. I do not have the requisite knowledge or experience, but you do Father. I do not have the requisite wisdom, talent, and understanding, but you do Father. Let me manifest how great and faithful you are in completing this work. May I hide behind you and your glory with this task. Please cleanse me of any passing thought that I had anything to do with this. Please rid me of any fleeting feeling that I am anything more than a sinner saved by grace. Please destroy any motive of seeking man's applause or my own glory. Please eliminate any fears of failure knowing that your love is all that really matters. Please purify me. Remind me that I am your child. Help me in my unbelief. Help me in my self-dependency and anxiety and worry. Fill me with the Holy Spirit. Fill me with strength. Help me to do my best for your name, O Lord, my God.*

Filled with peace and spiritual serenity after praying, I informed the chancellor and the dean of my conversation with Governor Cowper. I asked to be relieved of any teaching duties for the week so I could concentrate on the White Paper. They enthusiastically granted my request. I then asked my wife and Paul to cut off all outside communications for me. I needed to work without any distraction. Through the work of the Holy Spirit, I synthesized everything I had observed, studied, taught, researched, produced, and experienced up until that point. All of this crystallized around a vision of Alaska tied to her strategic, geographical position in the smaller circumpolar region and the larger Asia-Pacific Rim region. First, I identified the major forces accelerating globalization, and forecasted global trends accordingly. Second, I analyzed America's strategic role in those trends. Third, I analyzed the historical relationship between the U.S. and the Asia-Pacific region, and predicted trends of their growing relationship into the 21st Century. Fourth, I laid out the vision for Alaska in strategically positioning herself into the 21st century in light of these global and U.S.-Asia-Pacific trends. Fifth, I proposed 12 strategies to fulfill that vision for Alaska. Sixth, I developed 12 action-plans, which included ACIB, to implement those strategies.

After seventy-two hours of working non-stop, without any sleep, I finished the first draft. It was the morning of December 4, a Friday. I was spent. My body was stiff. My back ached. I took a fairly long shower and after breakfast, rested a little. By noon, I arrived at my office joyful, rejuvenated, and thankful. I handed the more than 100 handwritten pages to my assistant so she could type up the draft White Paper. It took her until early the next morning, a Saturday, to finish. She was amazing! I have always been blessed with dedicated, competent and faithful assistants all these years. Later that afternoon, as we reviewed and edited her work, she still had a smile on her face. She then took our marked-up draft home to finalize. After Sunday service the next day, I went to her home and her husband joined us in finalizing and proof reading the document. He was a tremendous help as well. My wife called and told me that the governor was changing his schedule and would be in his Anchorage office on Tuesday, postponing my meeting with him one day.

At the reception area of the governor's Anchorage office I met Tony Smith, the newly appointed Commissioner of Commerce and Economic Development, who ushered me into the governor's office. "Okay John," said the governor, "let's see what you've got for me." After about 90 minutes, I was done. The governor rolled up his sleeves and smiled. "John, this is great stuff. I like it. I like all of it."

"I'm planning on having a summit meeting at the governor's mansion in January. All my top assistants, cabinet members, and selected business leaders will be there. We will be working on the budget and the State of the State address. And John, I want to give you a half-hour to present your work and respond to questions.

"I'll be there. Just let me know when."

"We will. John, be prepared. You may face some tough questions. Maybe even some opposition."

"I'll be ready." I left the office around 4:00 p.m. It was already dark outside, but my heart was filled with joy and warmth by God's grace and favor.

The Governor's Summit Meeting

On Christmas Eve, I was informed by the governor's office that the summit meeting would take place at 2:00 p.m. on January 6, at the governor's mansion. I suggested to the governor that he invite a close friend of mine, Professor Yoon Sik Park, a professor at George Washington University. Dr. Park and I were college classmates in Korea and he was an international finance and banking expert. He also served as a senior economist for the World Bank. I thought that his knowledge and global networking would be of great assistance to Alaska's advancement. The governor agreed and sent a personal invite to my friend.

At 2:00 p.m. on January 6, all of us, including Dr. Park, assembled in Juneau. After the governor gave his introductory remarks and the agenda for the meeting, he introduced me and asked me to present my vision. I passed out copies of the executive summary of my White Paper to the attendees and presented the four-year-and-beyond development plan for the new administration. During my presentation, I emphasized the importance of the tripartite partnership, the need for funding, and the establishment of ACIB as the state's official think-tank. And to prevent being held hostage to the election cycle of the legislature, I proposed an initial $6 million endowment fund for the center as well as a $600,000 perpetual line item budget for the center's continuing operations. I thought the presentation went well. There was some applause by the attendees. Then the governor's budget director jumped in. "John, thank you for that. I enjoyed your presentation very much. But I'm sure you know that the price of crude oil dropped from $33 a barrel to $10. Our state is in a financial crisis and we are about to propose a 10% pay cut for all state employees, including the governor. Where can we possibly find that kind money to fund your plan? Your plan is great in theory, but in reality it seems impossible." Others raised similar concerns about the budget and the state's economic situation.

"It's time for us to end our complete dependency on OPEC and crude oil prices," I responded. "Unless we do something now, we will continue being OPEC's economic colony. I believe we are at a crossroads. We either continue to be passive and beholden to crude prices, or we develop alternative enterprises to be competitive in the global markets. We need diversification. We need to start investing our money into developing small and medium-sized businesses for export. We must create an environment where entrepreneurs are encouraged to innovate and develop value-added products from Alaska's other abundant natural resources. And we need all of you to develop policies so they can seamlessly enter and be competitive in the international markets. And not just to increase exports, but to reduce unemployment, which is higher than most other states. It's been reported that every billion dollar of exports creates more than 10,000 jobs. This current recession should awaken us that the future is now.

"This is where ACIB comes in. It can be the state's think tank housed on UAA's campus and a one-stop shop for international business. The center would provide global market opportunities for interested businesses with the help of the first-of-its-kind international trade database. It would host forums and conduct seminars on marketing, promotion, international negotiation, cross-cultural business ethics, and international trade management. This could be a launch pad for injecting international economic-related and cross-cultural-related courses, along with foreign language programs, on our campus and even in our statewide public schools.

"Yes, there is a cost to all of this," I continued. "But the cost is worth it. The center will be an engine driving Alaska businesses into the world's markets and in turn, a tremendous asset for Alaska's economic growth. This I believe will put us in a situation where the center would be self-funding (in part) by strategically assisting certain companies in their export volumes, so that in return, these same companies may invest in ACIB.

"I don't have to do all of this. My job is secured. I am a tenured, full professor. But I have a passionate heart for this state and a desire to transform its passive, short-sighted paradigm of 'dependency is a virtue, and independence is a vice' to a proactive mentality of 'independence as well as interdependency is a virtue, and dependency is a vice.' I don't see any other way to secure our future and enhance the well-being of all Alaskans."

"Thank you, John," replied the governor. "So, I'd like to go around the table and hear each person's response. Let's start with Professor Park."

"Governor and the staff," said Dr. Park. "Thank you for giving me the opportunity to be here. As some of you may know, Dr. Kim is a close friend of mine. But I would say what I'm about to say even if I had not met him before today. Dr. Kim is not an economist. He's not a finance expert. So I don't know how he could have formulated such an impressive vision for the new administration. But he did. And I consider this plan to be a masterpiece that all other states must adopt as their model."

The rest of the room weighed in. No one specifically opposed the White Paper or the creation of ACIB. The common refrain, however, always came back to money. Where would the money come from to implement my plan? After everyone got a chance to be heard, the governor addressed us: "Thank you all very much. After listening to what everyone had to say, it seems to me that we are all concerned about where the funds to support this plan will come from. I intend to submit two bills to the state legislature to establish ACIB – one for $6 million as an endowed fund and the other for the $600,000 annual budget for operations going forward. I want each one of you to try to come up with funds from your department. Bert, I want you to work diligently on whether you can find the funds from your shop [the Alaska Industrial Development Authority]. John, we will find the money one way or another. I promise you $6 million. So John, get together with my chief of staff, Tony Smith, and the Attorney General and work on the bills."

As we were all leaving the governor's mansion, the governor grabbed my shoulder and whispered into my ear, "John, don't worry. It will get done. You have done a great job. Thank you very much." My heart was filled with thanksgiving. I was walking on clouds, thankful for God's grace. As I drove Dr. Park back to our hotel, he turned to me and said, "Kim hyung [Korean for 'brother Kim'], you are becoming the Joseph of Alaska."

The Governor's State of the State Address

On January 21, 1987, Governor Cowper delivered his State of the State Address to the state legislature. I was not able to travel to Juneau that day due to my teaching duties, but my wife and I were able to catch the speech live on television. He was a man of his word. A lot of the White Paper was in his speech. To my surprise, he actually mentioned my name and the importance of establishing ACIB on UAA's campus to strategically position and advance Alaska in the international markets. My wife was so excited. She seemed happier than I was. "Congratulations, honey. All your work was in that speech!" She hugged me and we kissed. I was deeply humbled by all of this.

The following morning, television and newspaper reporters converged on me because of the governor's address. The governor had apparently also praised my work during the press conference after the speech. The reporters asked me a number of questions regarding the speech, the nature of my relationship with the governor, the extent of my involvement in his new administration's policy development as well as the mission and objectives of ACIB. I shared the purpose and goals of ACIB and the important role of the state university system in enhancing the well-being of all the peoples of Alaska. I declined to answer the rest of their questions and referred them to the governor's press secretary, David Ramseur. I courteously sent them away because I wanted the focus to be on the new governor, the newly elected leader of the state. I didn't want to take the attention from him that was deservedly his. "Serve wholeheartedly, as if you were serving the Lord, not men" (Eph. 6:7). This was not the time to take any credit, but to serve my governor whom God had sovereignly placed in that office of authority.

The governor's address was well received by the Democrats in both the House and the Senate and by Alaskans in general, but the battle had just begun. Republicans were rather cold to the new policy initiatives, including ACIB, mainly due to the state's economic situation. The Republicans wanted to cut spending rather than support the governor's new proposals. With the sudden and drastic drop of crude prices, reducing the state budget took on greater importance. The economic mood of the state was grim. Businesses were failing, unemployment was growing, and people were falling behind on their mortgages. Many people left Alaska for the Lower 48. We saw the effects at our church of this "Alaska Exodus" as several families had to move.

I sensed an uphill challenge ahead for the governor. And for ACIB.

Chapter 22

THE WAIT (AND WEIGHT) IS OVER

As promised, Governor Cowper submitted two bills to the state legislature for ACIB. Now, the tough sell. I met with the governor's chief of staff, the commerce commissioner, and chief legislative liaison to develop strategies to muster up enough votes in the legislature. We made a list of who was for, against, and undecided among the senators and representatives, and discussed how we would approach the ones who could get us across the finish line. The hope was that we could convince enough of the undecideds and turn a handful of the opponents – and do that with a final push from their legislative colleagues who we knew were already on board. We also worked up a tentative meeting schedule with the legislators and appearances before the relevant House and Senate committees. We agreed that I would be the front man in the hard sell and that the governor's staff would assist. They encouraged me to grow a thick skin, stay the course, and roll with the punches. Indeed, like Matthew 10:16 (ESV), I was being sent out as "sheep in the midst of wolves," so I had to be "wise as serpents and innocent as doves."

The Legislative Marathon

The process required tremendous patience and perseverance. The bills had to go through six different committees and subcommittees, several House and Senate joint committees, special committees, the House and Senate finance and budget committees, and then the final votes of both the House and Senate. This took a toll. Eighteen hour days. Presentations. Testimonies. Passionate pleas. Going back and forth between the halls of the legislature to the executive offices. Going back and forth between Anchorage and Juneau. Going back and forth between the classrooms and the airport. Going back and forth between frustration and humiliation to encouragement and confirmation. Some faculty colleagues thought I was wasting my time and that I should stick with my day job. "You're not even getting paid for this, John" was the common refrain. But God reminded me that this was part of His plan to use me to make Alaska better. He reminded me that it was Him who got me in the door. It was because of Him that I had the governor's ear. It was because of Him that the university president was backing me. It was because of Him that my reputation was being restored after Dr. Olds's speech. The power of the Holy Spirit and the love of Alaska and her people that God had given me was the well that I kept going to when my energy was spent and doubts crept in. If this was God's will, I was going to do my best to see it through. Despite the setbacks.

Though I was a registered Republican, the irony was that most of the Republicans opposed the bills to establish and fund ACIB. In the beginning of May 1987, the governor's office called to schedule a personal meeting with him in Juneau. I got on the next plane to Juneau and met with the governor, who was flanked by his chief of staff and chief legislative liaison.

"John," the governor said, "the Republicans like the bills, but they are holding them hostage right now. They have proposed their own special bill with a price tag of $100 million in spending. The deal is that they will support your bill if we support theirs. But I can't do that. I can't support their bill. And I'm not making your bill a ransom for their bill.

"I see." I was starting to feel numb. I knew what was next.

"So as it stands, we don't have a deal. John, you know how much I am committed to your vision, but they've given me no room to negotiate. I am truly sorry."

"Steve, thanks for letting me know. I know where you're coming from. I understand the position you need to take."

"John, I knew you would."

"But could you do me a favor?"

"Of course."

"Could you arrange an informal joint meeting of both the House and Senate Democratic and Republican leaders. If this is how it's going to end, I want to make one final plea to present my heart and passion for Alaska's future."

"John, you got it. I'll try to arrange a meeting." The governor then instructed his chief of staff to call the Republican leaders that the governor would not be accepting the proposed deal.

Although disheartened, I had not given up. I spent the rest of the day meeting legislators from Anchorage and the south central region of the state who strongly supported the bill and flew back to Anchorage. Obviously, it was not a good day, but I prayed to God for an opportunity to make one last plea to the leifgislative leaders. In just 10 days, the state legislature would recess for the rest of the year and the momentum would be lost. Even my strongest supporters thought I had to throw in the towel. George Geistauts, a faculty colleague who helped me with the initial proposal in 1984, said, "John, I think it's time to give it up. No one has ever brought to the university any endowed funds from the state, let alone $6 million. If you get even $10,000, I will treat you and Sung to an expensive dinner."

"George," I replied, "you better save up your money now because it will be a feast."

A few days later, the governor's chief of staff called and said that the legislative leaders of both chambers agreed to a joint meeting and that I should prepare to present for 30 minutes. *Thank you, Lord. Now take it away with your wisdom and passion.* On the day of the meeting, I flew to Juneau and stopped by the governor's offices, and was then ushered into a large meeting room by the chief of staff and Commissioner Smith. The room was packed. Legislators. Their staff. Executive branch staff. Many in the room were my cheerleaders, but the legislative leaders were the key. I gave it my all with my presentation. With passion. With gusto. I mainly drew from my remarks of January 6 at the governor's mansion. I concluded, "Is it wrong for a state university professor to commit his career to make his state better and greater and make her coming generations more prosperous? No, it is not wrong. It is right. It is why I am standing before you now. I would stake my entire reputation and integrity on the fact that I will never use ACIB for personal interest or gain. It will be a public enterprise and I will be its public entrepreneur. I beg you. See what ACIB can do for our state's university, our state's businesses and industries, and our state's people for generations after generations. Please grant me this opportunity to serve this state that I love together with you. Thank you so much for giving me this opportunity to share my heart with you this afternoon. May God bless you all."

Applause erupted. The House Majority Leader, a Republican, came forward to where I was still standing and vigorously shook my hand. And for all to hear he said, "My fellow legislative colleagues, throughout all my years as a legislator, I have never heard such a heartfelt and challenging vision. I am overwhelmed. To this day, I had opposed the twin bill but upon hearing what Professor Kim had to say, I've changed my mind. If we don't help his work now, then who will and when? The time is now. I would like to urge my colleagues from both sides of the aisle – let us unite to pass this bill."

More applause. Many of the attendees did not leave the room, but stayed behind to shake my hand and pat me on the back. After the meeting, I went straight to the governor's office with the chief legislative liaison. The tide seemed to have turned and we now had the momentum. The $100 million special bill was no longer a worry for us – the twin bill for ACIB was now alive on its own merits. We sat down to assess each legislator and concluded that there were about 19 of them that were still undecided or opposed. But rumors were circulating that the vote would happen as soon as that night. I resolved to meet with each one of them. That night. All 19.

"John," exclaimed the chief of staff, "are you crazy? How are you going to meet with every one of them in the next two hours? It's impossible."

"I have to. I can't give them any more time to possibly persuade others to vote it down. We have to."

"Something like this has never been done before."

"We can't wait, Bill. If the vote's tonight, I see no other choice for us."

The legislative offices comprised of five floors and a basement. The 19 legislators were spread throughout. At first, we traveled by elevators to meet up with the members, but that took too much time. It had to be running, not walking. And it had to be the stairs. It was at that point that I lost the chief legislative liaison and Commissioner Smith's deputy to exhaustion.

"Come on you guys! We have to get going," I yelled as sweat trickled down my temples.

"John," the chief legislative liaison gasped, "it's too much for us to chase you around this building. We're heading back to Bill to set up more meetings for you. Check in with us often. Keep us updated."

"Okay, I'll do my best."

"Best of luck to you John!"

I ran with a list of all 19 members and possible appointment times. If I visited one of the offices and a legislator was unavailable, I asked the staff for an appointment time before the night session convened. Then I moved on to the next office, then the next one. Then the next. Sometimes I would catch a legislator or his or her staff, sometimes I wouldn't get anyone. And then when it was time for an appointment, I would circle back to that office and meet with the legislator. Then move on to another office to check in on his or her availability or move to my next appointment. I hit all 19 offices and made several trips to many of the same offices. By God's grace, when I returned to Bill's office I told them that the mission was accomplished. I was able to personally meet all 19.

After we grabbed a bite to eat, we returned to Bill's office. It was getting late. The rumors were true. The twin bill was on the agenda for tonight. *Dear Father, the hour seems to be approaching. It's all in your sovereign hands. Whatever happens, I know it's your will and for my good. 'Thy will be done on earth as it is in Heaven.' I will be content with whatever may come to pass. I have no regrets. You know that I have done my best.* We still had no idea at what time the votes would be tallied. It was approaching midnight. Still no word. But several minutes later, we heard the news. Passage. Unanimously in both the House and Senate (35-0 in the House; 18-0 in the Senate). *Lord, you did it again. This was all you.* I ran to wait outside the legislative chamber to thank each of the members as they exited. All I kept saying was "thank you, thank you, thank you." One of them gave me a hug and said, "Who wouldn't have been moved by your passion and vision. I wish you all the success. And the success of our great state."

The following morning, after calling home and sharing the wonderful news with my wife and son, I went to see Governor Cowper. We hugged. He congratulated me. With tears in my eyes, I expressed my deepest appreciation for his commitment to the vision and making it come to fruition. I also went around his offices to thank his chief of staff, the chief legislative liaison, the commissioners, and other staff and assistants. It was all smiles and laughter, especially when we recounted my marathon up-and-down-and-all-around the legislative building. Before heading to the Juneau airport to catch my flight back to Anchorage, I stopped by the legislative offices to thank a dozen senators and representatives for their unwavering support from the very beginning. The passage of the twin bill made the front pages of *The Anchorage Daily News* and *The Anchorage Times*. George, my faculty colleague, ate crow as he, my wife and I and other friends dined on a lavish dinner at The Marx Bros. Café.

The twin bill signing ceremony was scheduled for June 8, 1987 at the governor's Anchorage offices. University President O'Dowd, the current and former chancellors of UAA, chairman of the board of regents, chairman of the Board of Trustees of the University of Alaska Foundation, Commissioner Smith, two industry leaders, and the governor's budget director – who never thought this day would come – attended. I was able to attend by rearranging my schedule and catching an earlier flight to Anchorage as I was in the East Coast speaking at a Christian conference for college students. We all stood around the governor and watch as he signed the two bills. It was now official.

After he signed the bills, he stood up and handed me the pen.

Overcoming Evil with Good

Seeing the successful passage of the ACIB bill, Dr. Olds surfaced again. I was informed he went to Juneau and met with the governor. He wanted substantial funds for his university too. The governor basically told him that if he wanted any money for international business projects, it would have to go through me as the Executive Director of ACIB, which "is now a state entity." I then got a call from Dr. Olds. He wanted to meet with me. I agreed. Face to face for the very first time, we briefly exchanged greetings. It was clear from the beginning that he was not there to chit-chat or have us get to know one another. He immediately asked me to share ACIB's funds with his university. There were no specifics. There were no details. There was no apology. There was no mention of his speech at the governor's banquet. No effort was there to build any sort of relationship. I told him that the $6 million cannot be touched. That it was an endowed fund from the state that will generate proceeds that will help defray the center's costs and also be partly used to match funds in hopes of bringing more outside money. The $680,000 annual appropriation is for the center's operations including overhead and staff salaries. "Dr.

Olds," I added, "if you have a specific program or project in mind that will advance this state's international trade and business, please let me know and I will do my best to help you. And by the way, we haven't received any funds yet from the state." Dr. Olds wasn't pleased with my response and left my office.

The three years since Dr. Olds's speech was no picnic for me. But in my obedience to God and His persevering strength, God granted me a larger fund that was more than 10 times my original request in 1984 and restored my name far more than I could've ever asked, imagined, or expected. Now I had the direct line and the direct ear to the university president, the chancellor of UAA, *and* the governor. In that way, instead of being angry at Dr. Olds at that moment, I was grateful to him because it was through that incident that God disciplined and humbled me and built my character and made me more like Christ. He gave me a deeper understanding of His grace in my realization that I had treated Him (each time I had sinned) in a far worse way than Dr. Olds did with me. And yet He so readily forgave and continued to love and continued to lift me up. It was His blood that washed away my anger and began to mold my character after the heart of Christ.

I proposed that the governor host a first-of-its-kind international finance and banking conference in July 1987. The purpose was to test the feasibility of opening up an international finance center in Alaska and to that end the plan was to invite many internationally renowned scholars and experts from the U.S. and other economically advanced nation-states. Because I was not a finance or banking expert, I had the governor appoint my friend Dr. Park to be the conference co-chair with the governor. Dr. Park flew to Alaska from the Washington, D.C. area and spent an entire month with us to prepare for the conference, working closely with a good friend of mine, Professor Mussa Assayat, a finance professor at UAA.

About a couple of weeks prior to the three-day conference, we were working out the details for the final night's program, the governor's dinner banquet. One of the issues was who would be delivering the keynote speech on behalf of Alaska that night. The governor suggested me. Dr. Park and everyone else in the room agreed that I was the logical choice. Dr. Park said that it has to be somebody with a passionate heart for Alaska and that somebody was me. Although I was deeply honored at the room's sentiment, suddenly God gave me the wisdom to say, "What about inviting Dr. Glenn Olds? I understand he's a great speaker." The entire room was in an uproar. "John, are you out of your mind?!" Everyone was adamantly against it; they knew the history. My staff couldn't believe their ears when I told them my suggestion.

My wife hit the roof, "Honey, I don't understand you! Why would you invite the man who called you a liar and gave you such hard time? If the governor asked you to speak at his banquet, then why don't you just do it? That's the governor's prerogative. Why do you want to ask someone else? Especially him!"

"I know how you feel, honey," I responded, "but didn't God give me 10 times more? Haven't I received far more than I expected? It's God who has done it all. In fact, I am grateful to Dr. Olds. Because of him, I have grown immensely in Christ. Why do I need to treat him as an enemy?"

The next morning, I was able to persuade the governor and Dr. Park and others to invite Dr. Olds as the keynote speaker, while I would serve as the master of ceremonies. It was decided that the governor's office would call and extend the invitation as we were not sure how he would take the invitation if I called. Dr. Olds, who was vacationing in Vermont with his family at the time the governor's office reached out to him, gladly accept the invitation.

The final evening of the conference was July 23. The ballroom of the Captain Cook Hotel was packed with invited scholars and experts from Washington D.C., New York, London, Zurich, Frankfurt, Hong Kong and Tokyo, as well as state and local government officials, industry and business leaders, and other guests and invited delegates. Dr. Olds had arrived. We shook hands and smiled. We were seated at the head table, with Dr. Olds next to Dr. Park and other distinguished guests, while the governor and state leaders along with my wife and me were on the other side of the table. During the dessert portion of the banquet, I approached the podium and commenced the evening program. After recognizing Governor Cowper and Dr. Park for their work in hosting the conference, I thanked the others who helped prepare the conference and singled out some of the many special guests who were in attendance. I then introduced Governor Cowper and thanked him for his leadership and commitment. Governor Cowper then took the podium and made brief remarks of appreciation before introducing Dr. Olds. Dr. Olds's speech was solid. He sold Alaska's future eloquently and passionately. Throughout the speech, I kept looking at my wife to catch a read on her facial expressions. She seemed to be okay with him. His speech was well received. After closing the evening program, as I was still on stage, Dr. Olds approached. He gave me a big hug.

"John, it must have been very painful because of me and what I did. I am so sorry. Please forgive me."

"Thank you, Dr. Olds." Those are all the words I could muster. At that moment. There was a flood of emotions. Closure. I hugged him back. I sensed that others who knew the history between us were curiously watching what was happening on stage.

As my wife and I and Dr. Park returned to our rooms in the hotel, Dr. Park shared with us his dinner conversation with Dr. Olds. Dr. Park had asked President Olds if he knew me well, to which he replied that he did not. When Professor Park shared my life story with Dr. Olds, he seemed moved. Professor Park also told him that I was the only one who wanted to invite him as the governor's banquet speaker. Everyone else was opposed. He told him that it was me who pushed his invitation through. Dr. Olds was quite shocked, according to Dr. Park. I learned that Dr. Olds graduated from Yale, and served as U.S. Ambassador to UNESCO as well as the President of Kent State University in Ohio. He also was a minister in the Methodist denomination. In 1977, he was asked to rebuild Alaska Methodist University in Anchorage which had been closed for two years. Under his leadership as the president, Dr. Olds worked very hard to reopen the university the next year, changing the name of the university to Alaska Pacific University. APU became a reputable private university under his leadership.

Dr. Park mentioned that because Dr. Olds was a Methodist minister, when Dr. Park shared my testimony with him and the fact that I persuaded the governor to invite him, he may have been convicted by the Holy Spirit and awakened to what he had done to me. When Dr. Park told us that Dr. Olds seemed genuinely sorry for what he did, I was reminded of Romans 12:20-21 ". . . if your enemy is hungry, feed him; if he is thirsty, give him something to drink. In doing this, you will heap burning coals on his head. Do not be overcome by evil, but overcome evil with good." I was also reminded of what Joseph said to his brothers in Genesis 50:20 (ESV), "As for you, you meant evil against me, but God meant it for good . . . ."

The next year, in 1988, Dr. Olds won the state Democratic primary for U.S. Senate, but eventually lost to Senator Frank Murkowski in the November election. While he was still serving as APU's president, the World Trade Center Alaska (WTCA) was franchised on APU's campus as an associate member. But because of a lack of local membership, it faced financial difficulties. Before his retirement from APU, Dr. Olds asked if ACIB could take over the WTCA which needed to pay off some debts. I told him I had to get the university president's and UAA's chancellor's approval to do that. I promised him that I would do my best to convince them that the WTCA would be an asset to ACIB by directly connecting sellers and buyers all over the world and promoting international trade. Despite the outstanding debts, my bosses gave me the go ahead. Dr. Olds and I signed an agreement officially transferring the WTCA to ACIB. Later, I flew to New York and met Guy Tozolli, President of the WTC Association, at the World Trade Center headquarters in downtown Manhattan. With the initiation and membership fee paid, the WTCA was formally admitted as a full member of the WTC Association.

Dr. Olds and I became really good friends. He's such a likeable person. After retiring from APU, he left Alaska for Washington, D.C. to write his book. He always told his friends who were visiting Alaska to call me and get together with me. I treated those friends well. They would tell that Dr. Olds was a huge fan of mine. That he was my cheerleader. This is the power of grace. This is the power of forgiveness. *Thank you, Lord.*

The road that God leads us on doesn't always seem to work out at all times. There are setbacks. There are obstacles. But the trials we go through on this road are His way of molding us more and more into His likeness so that we can take on His appointed tasks with more preparedness, greater strength, clearer purpose, and persevering hope. When in following His call we are met with suffering and tribulation, one of the questions we may ask is, "Lord, what greater work are you preparing me for?" In this regard, my experience over and over and over again has been this: when I have waited upon the Lord with total trust and remained perseveringly faithful to His will, at the end of each of my seasons of trial, God has always prepared something for me to do in furtherance of His Kingdom that is far greater than I could've imagined or dreamed.

Chapter 23

GOD'S GREATER PURPOSE

Since 1979, I have set aside about four to five days in January for a personal retreat with God. During this time alone with Him, I reflect on the prior year, asking God to forgive me of any sin that I had yet to repent of (or be awakened to), and praising God with thanksgiving for all He had done that previous year. I pray for my family, my church, my profession. I pray for lost souls. I pray for my pastor. I pray for friends. I pray for students and the upcoming spring semester. I pray for ever more of Him in my daily life. I would also make resolutions for the upcoming year (and take inventory on the resolutions made the year before).

In January 1985, I set aside seven days and nights to fast and pray. I rented a cabin at a Christian conference center near Wasilla, about 60 miles northeast of Anchorage. My pastor drove me to the cabin, which thankfully was well heated. This time with God, as compared to the other personal retreats, took on a different track. In addition with doing what I regular do during these alone times with Him (personal and intercessory prayers, Scripture reading and mediation, and singing hymns), I really reflected on the hurt and shame that I was experiencing after Dr. Olds's speech in March 1984, which was still fresh in many minds. In questioning why I was faced with such a difficult trial, I was moved by the Holy Spirit to desperately find God's purpose and vision for the rest of my life. Yes, I knew he had saved me, physically from my liver disease, and cosmically and eternally from my sin disease. But the question that kept coming to my unsettled mind and heart in my prayers was, *For what? Why was I saved? I'm here in Alaska because you called me here, right? So Lord, what is your will and purpose for me? Am I to just continue teaching and serving the local church? How do you want me to spend the rest of my days?* The last couple of days in the cabin I was spiritually consumed with seeking His vision for my life. I hung on to Him, praying with minimal ceasing, asking Him to reveal His further plan for my life. Then, God spoke to me. "Making America greater with Korean-American Christians by revitalizing and reviving their faith in God."

What can Korean-Americans do for America?, I asked God. *America is greater than any other country on the earth. We are a minority of minorities in this country. And Korean-American immigrants, by and large, have struggled in settling down in their newly adopted country. I was expecting something I can actually do Lord, but this . . . this is impossible.* Like Abraham's wife Sarah, I almost chuckled in disbelief. But God convicted me: "If there's something that's within your ability, intellect, and power to do, why would I even bother you with that? You wouldn't need my help in achieving it. I have given you my desire for your life, not what you think you can accomplish in your life. A vision is something you cannot do without me. It originates from me, not from you. It is my vision to you. When a vision is fulfilled, the only explanation that can be ascribed to it is that it was my work, not yours. In that way, I get the glory, not you."

If God had not disciplined me through trials such as Dr. Olds, then I probably would not have fasted and prayed as fervently as I did in seeking God's will and His purpose. He was shaping me to be more Christ-like so that I might take on His greater purposes for His Kingdom. Without that trial and resulting desperation, my Father Almighty may not have revealed His vision for America and the world to me in January 1985. But now armed with God's God-sized vision for my life, God began to use me to magnify His loving grace and expand His Kingdom with speaking engagements all around the country and the world, telling my liver-death-sentence-to-life testimony, sharing the ways I've integrated my faith with my vocation, and challenging primarily young men and women to be the Christ's ambassadors on campuses and in the marketplace. The fact that I wasn't a pastor or staff from a

Christian organization, but a business professor from a state university made me especially relatable to college students and young professionals alike. My passion for teaching, for students' learning, and the younger generations made this transition from the lecture halls in Anchorage to a Campus Crusade conference in New York, for example, seamless.

The added ministry that God had graciously blessed me beyond my local church and Alaska forced me to manage my time wisely. If I was not fulfilling my foundational callings as a husband to Sung, a father to Sharon and Paul, an elder at my local church, and a professor at UAA, then I believed all other work – even in the name of "ministry" or "vision" – is for naught. By God's grace, He enabled me to manage my time in such a way that I was able to fulfill these callings with an excellence that translated into greater credibility when my ministry took on a more national and international scope. My marriage with Sung grew stronger, forming an impenetrable partnership in life, parenting, and ministry. I never missed an important game, recital, or event, parent-teacher conference, birthday, holiday, anniversary, or special occasion with my family. And if I was traveling, I made sure to call my wife and kids every day – and with my wife, sometimes two, three times a day. Our local church continued to expand and we were able to organically raise additional elders for the church's ruling session (but I did not relinquish my role as playing Santa Claus at the annual church Christmas party!).

I ran ACIB and the WTCA with vibrancy and innovation, churning out international opportunities for local businesses and organizing first-of-its-kind conferences, like the North Pacific Fisheries Conference. During my service to the state and UAA, Alaska's exports increased 300% and the economy grew significantly. At the governor's "Export of the Year" banquet in May 1990, I was recognized as one of two individuals who made the most contributions to Alaska's economic development in the

Cowper administration (Governor Cowper did not seek a second term in 1990, to the surprise of political observers). By God's grace, I was able to bring over $23 million to the university in the form of endowments, research grants, and other contributions. I also was able to secure – with some arm-twisting of the governor – an additional $25 million to construct a new Business Education Center to house ACIB and the WTCA. All by God's grace.

And I did not forget my first love as I maintained a full course load with continued high marks in student evaluations. On September 10, 1992, Chancellor Don Behrend and the university foundation hosted a reception to celebrate my service to UAA. I was being honored as the recipient of the Edith R. Bullock Prize for Excellence, the highest honor bestowed in the University of Alaska statewide system. I was surprised to see so many guests when I arrived with my wife, my mother, and my senior pastor, Lee Dong Kyu, and his wife. Lots of smiles. Lots of hugs. Lots of joy. Lots of warmth. The festive, affectionate, heartfelt atmosphere was overwhelming. When the chancellor took the microphone at the podium, he described the award, the selection process, and a list of my achievements. He mentioned that I would now have the title of "Distinguished Professor." I was blushing. I was deeply humbled. *Lord, it is you have done all these things.* He then asked my wife and I to come to the podium. The chancellor and the president of the university foundation handed me a heavy Alaska-made jade plaque and my wife a white envelope, with $15,000 in it. I then approached the microphone:

"Thank you so much, Chancellor Behrend. First of all, I praise and thank God for this award. I am so deeply honored. Thank you to the president, the chancellor and the trustees of the university foundation for selecting me to receive this most highly-esteemed award. Thank you Mrs. Bullock for your generosity in making this award possible. I also want to thank my colleagues, university faculty members, administrators, deans, staff, my assistants, and all of you for being here to share this award with me. I couldn't have received this award without you. I'm overwhelmed. Words can't describe how encouraged my wife and I are with having all of you here.

"I know that this award is based on achievements for which I'm being recognized, but from the depths of my heart, I want to recognize God who has done all of these works. It is by His grace alone that I stand before you, not anything that I've done. Whatever the tasks and however challenging, I've put my trust in Him and let Him do His work through me. So I give Him all the credit. I also want to recognize Governors Cowper and [Walter] Hickel, state legislators and commissioners, Senators [Ted] Stevens and Murkowski.

"Finally, I want to thank my wife, Sung, and my family for their unwavering commitment, sacrifice, support, and earnest prayers which have been my inspiration, my resting place, and my driving force. I will continue to give my very best to the university and to the State of Alaska. From the bottom of my heart, I thank you. May God bless you all!"

A few days later, I received a letter in the mail. It was from one of the guests who attended the award ceremony: "I have been a Christian for as long as I can remember. I'm president of one of the largest trucking companies in Alaska. My company has been so blessed throughout all these years. But I never publicly shared God's mighty work for my company. This evening, when I returned home after the award reception, I was so convicted. I was deeply ashamed. Although it is God's grace that has been poured out on me, my family and my company, I've never publicly recognized Him as the source of my success. I thought I'd been serving the Lord well at my church. This evening my whole perspective has changed. I hope and pray that I too will now start to proclaim what God has done for my life and my company by recognizing Him in public as my Lord and Savior and my King." I called him later and we agreed to meet up for lunch. That first lunch was over three hours long and we have been dear friends and brothers in Christ ever since.

I praise God that He has used me, and continues to use me, to be a blessing to many. I am nothing, He is everything. Growing up fatherless, He has been my Father all the way through. I praise Him for His works in my life and in my family and in my church and in my work. And I praise God for the vision He gave me in January 1985, which became the foundation for JAMA, a prayer and spiritual awakening movement for the renewal and revival of America, birthed more than eight years later on November 1, 1993.

When the doctors told me I would quickly die from a liver disease in 1976, I cried out in bitter rage and anger to God, *Why me?! What I have done to deserve to die from this miserable disease at such a young age?* Now my fury has been replaced with joyful, gentle and frequent petitions and self-reminding exhortations, *Lord, why me? What I have done to deserve your immeasurable grace and endless love and enduring joy? It is all because of Jesus!*

"O love of God, how rich and pure!
How measureless and strong!
It shall forevermore endure
The saints' and angels' song."

Dear Heavenly Father, thank you that though I was fatherless since the age of six, you have been my faithful and loving Father all these years. Thank you for healing the toxins of my blood and the toxins of my heart with the innocent blood and grace-unending heart of your Son, Jesus Christ. Thank you that because your Son obediently walked up to Mount Calvary carrying the cross, my life was transformatively turned around at Big Bear Mountain.

God Almighty, thank you for blessing me with every spiritual blessing in the heavenly realms and with earthly blessings far more than I could've ever asked or imagined (Eph. 1:3, 3:20). Thank you for bringing me to this great country, America, and giving me a love for this nation and its people. That love is why you have revealed to me your vision to launch a prayer movement for the awakening and revival of America and to equip the next generations to be your catalysts of gospel-change in the mainstream of this country. Help me not to grow weary in carrying out this vision and in doing this good, knowing that in due season I will reap, if I do not give up (Gal. 6:9). Pour out your Holy Spirit upon me so that I may pursue to the very end of my days the vision that you alone have given me, with all my heart, with all my mind, with all my soul, with all my strength, and with all my abilities.

Sovereign Lord, please send another great awakening and revival to America. Oh, how I long to see in our time that such mighty deeds of yours would again be made known (Hab. 3:2)! Please help us, as your people, humble ourselves. Please help us, as your people, seek your face and turn from our wicked ways (2 Chron. 7:14). Please hear the cries of repentance from your people and forgive us. Please heal and renew our land. For your glory alone throughout all generations (Eph. 3:21). Amen!

EPILOGUE

Vision, Not Personal Ambition

I'm not a good sleeper on planes. No matter how long the flight. No matter what the time. No matter how big the seat. Even after having flown three million miles (and counting), I've never been able to sleep. So soon after takeoff I often ask God what's the best use of my time on the plane. That time's often spent on grading papers and tests, meditating on Scripture or reading a book, writing my thoughts down on pressing matters, planning a grant proposal, coming up with research topics, writing letters, and praying. I get a lot done on planes.

On August 19, 1995, I was onboard Korean Airlines departing from Kimpo International Airport outside of Seoul. I was flying back home to Anchorage. It was already twilight. After the passengers were served dinner, most of the cabin settled into their seats and covered themselves with blankets. Sleep came to many, but not me of course. So as I was petitioning the Lord for His wisdom in how to allocate the next eight hours, the Holy Spirit spoke to me and said, "Surrender, surrender." *Surrender what, Lord? I've surrendered my life to you.* "You still have a lot to surrender. I want you to surrender it all, all 13 of them."

Two years before, in the summer of 1993, I was invited to Korea to meet with some leaders to discuss my run for political office. Not for an election in Korea, but for the U.S. Senate. These Korean leaders and potential fund-raisers researched the 50 states in hopes of finding possible Korean-American gubernatorial, congressional, or senatorial candidates that they could support, and they came up with only one person. Me. Representing Alaska. I was stunned by their research. Flatly, I told them I was not interested in politics. I also told them it was illegal to receive foreign financial support for political campaigns in America.

But somehow that meeting in Korea kept residing in the back of my mind and began to seep into my heart. It didn't help that a number of Alaskans, including prominent natives, also encouraged me to run for political office. *After all, wasn't my Ph.D. in political science?* In 1994, I was nominated by senior faculty members for university chancellor. Although I made it to the finals, I didn't get to cut down the nets. Nevertheless, all of this got me thinking. *If I continue to rise through the ranks of the university, eventually becoming its chancellor and continue to increase the stature and finances of UAA, then I may have the credibility, clout, and support to run for governor, which ultimately could lead to the U.S. Senate. It could happen. Look at what I've been able to accomplish by God's grace when I put my mind and heart into it.*

"The things you are currently thinking of pursuing are not part of my vision for you. You must give them up." *But why Lord?* I asked on the plane. *If I can achieve these things as a first generation Korean-American, how much more will the next generation of Korean-Americans be encouraged to dream and pursue greater dreams for America and the world. I can be their role model and you will be honored and glorified. What am I missing here? Why do I have to surrender these dreams of mine?* "Because they are dreams of *yours*, not a vision from *me*. They are personal ambitions, not vision. Surrender them."

What is vision, Lord? What is the difference between that and personal ambition? In that moment, God convicted me that vision is a revelation of God's will and His plan and desire for His children. Vision must be biblical. And vision is not something that anyone can come up with on their own, unlike personal ambitions. In that way, a personal ambition is self-originated, self-centered, and self-motivated, and thus, when it's accomplished, it's self-glorifying. Vision, on the other hand, is God-originated, God-centered, and God-motivated, and thus when it is fulfilled, God gets all the glory. God loves to be glorified by His children.

God was asking me to surrender my personal ambitions of becoming the university's chancellor and potentially running for political office as a governor or senator. He also asked me to surrender my leadership at ACIB, the WTCA, and the new American-Russian Center. I wrote down thirteen things on a yellow pad and was asked to let them go. *Lord, what about my professorship?* "You can keep that one; you're still going to need it." God awakened me with surgical precision that these dreams of mine – which I thought had the spiritual justification and innocent motivation of "being a role model" – were tainted with personal ambition. He reminded me of my passion for teaching and for reaching the younger generations for Christ and to raise them up to be transforming ambassadors for Him. He reminded me that two years before I was called to offer my body as a living sacrifice to awaken Christians to their sins, call for repentance, and pray for America's revival and spiritual awakening.

God's Vision for JAMA

On August 19, 1993, I was returning to Alaska from New York after speaking at a Campus Crusade for Christ conference together with Don Hodel (who had served as Secretary of the Interior in the Reagan administration and later was president of Focus on the Family). During the flight home, God kept impressing on my heart the word "awakening." Over and over again. On my return, I researched the awakening and revival movements in America's history, from Jonathan Edwards and George Whitefield to Jeremiah Lanphier, the Welsh revival, and the revival in Pyongyang as well as the writings of Edwards and D. Martyn Lloyd-Jones. I was deeply convicted. My heart was filled with tremendous anguish for America and its sins. We, as a nation, were breaking his heart. We, as His church, were not without blame. We, as His people, instead of examining ourselves and being set apart, blamed "the world" on the one hand and conformed to it on the other. Reminded of my so-called

"Christian life" before Big Bear Mountain and my own repentance and "personal revival," I was moved to repent for my nation, my fellow believers, and for myself. Through this, and at a time when my energies were focused on evangelism and reaching college students (primarily, Korean-American), God also began to give me a burden for the awakening and revival of America.

I called my close friend Rev. Kang Soon Young in Los Angeles, who was the West Coast director of Korean Campus Crusade for Christ, and shared my burden for America. I asked if he could gather a few people to pray with me and seek God's wisdom and will. I then flew down to Los Angeles several weeks later. There were six of us gathered in a conference room at Arrowhead Springs Resort, the former headquarters of Campus Crusade. We fasted. We prayed. We repented. We wept. We cried out to God. We asked what we, no-named Korean-American Christians, could possibly do for America's awakening and revival. None of us were born in America. None of us considered English our native tongue. But at the end of our time together, we were all convicted to start a nationwide prayer movement: Jesus Awakening Movement for America (JAMA). It was November 1, 1993.

The prayer movement would be based on 2 Chronicles 7:14 as a call for God's people to "humble themselves, and pray and seek [His] face and turn from their wicked ways" in hopes that God would not only forgive, but bring healing and revival to America. The prayer movement would be about repentance. By repenting of our own and our nation's sins, in the same way as the prophet Nehemiah did for Israel (Neh. 1:6), we wanted God to send His sovereign wind and release His supernatural revival and healing throughout our adopted country, as He did in the Great Awakenings in the 18th and 19th centuries. The prayer movement would be about spiritual ownership of America – repenting of *our* nation's sins and praying for our nation's revival – regardless from where we came.

We had no money. We had no sponsoring church. We had no formal organization. We had no organizational partners. And we all had day jobs and families. We also faced immediate backlash and skepticism from some Korean-American Christian leaders: "We are minorities, what can we do for America? . . . This is not even our home country . . . It's not going to happen, don't kid yourself . . . Please don't bring shame to the Korean Christian community," and so on. But we had a vision. And we pressed on in obedience to God's call and with the encouragement of some pastors and leaders who were starting to buy in and take spiritual ownership of America. After sharing JAMA's birth and its burden for America with Dr. Bill Bright, the founder of Campus Crusade, he said, "John, Koreans are amazing."

With the support of that remnant, my wife and son joined me on a cross-country national prayer tour in the summer of 1994. If I truly desired to take ownership of America and embrace it into my heart of hearts, then I had to see my country and pray for its communities and churches in those actual communities and churches. After a flight from Anchorage, we rented a van at Seattle International Airport and drove over 12,000 miles in 42 days repenting and praying for each town, state, and local church we visited. The farmlands, the plains, the prairies, the southern hospitality, the smell of cattle and horses, the Grand Canyon, Mount Rushmore, the heartland, the bustling cities, the quiet mountains. This was my country. And I loved it. Because it was God's country. Because it was God who created it.

By the grace of God and the work of the Holy Spirit, about 3,000 Korean-American college students, some of whom I had met on the prayer tour, gathered at Colorado State University in Fort Collins from June 29 to July 4, 1996 to repent of our sins and the sins of America and to pray for America's awakening and revival. This was JAMA's first conference. We were blessed with messages by Dr. Bright, Josh McDowell, Nancy Leigh DeMoss, and Rev. Ha Yong Jo, the founding pastor of Onnuri Church in Seoul. We were blessed with the outpouring of the Holy Spirit when on one particular evening, a stream of hundreds of young men and women, as we were led in prayer by Ms. DeMoss, came to the stage to openly confess and repent of their sins. It lasted until 3 a.m. The sincere transparency. The humble brokenness. The Gospel-centered authenticity. I'd never seen anything like it.

Surrender, Surrender

After writing the thirteen "ambitions" on my yellow pad and continuing in prayer, the Korean Airlines flight attendant told the cabin to prepare for landing. It was now morning at Anchorage International Airport and my extended time conversing with God (almost the whole flight time!) was coming to an end. But I knew that our conversation was not finished. I was still not at peace. I had yet to confess that I would surrender everything that I wrote on the pad. I was still holding on.

On the drive home from the airport, my wife sensed something was troubling me and asked if I was okay. When we got home, I told her everything. I told her that I was convicted to immediately start fasting and praying until there would be peace in my heart. "Right now," I told her, "there's no peace." I usually turn to fasting when faced with a critical spiritual decision or conflict in order to literally empty myself of my flesh (and its desires) so that the Holy Spirit may have His full way with me. After four days of fasting and prayer, I was able to surrender the 13 to God. The struggle was now over and I was filled with tremendous peace. With great freedom. With joyful relief. With much hope.

I met UAA Chancellor Lee Gorsuch in his office and I told him that I would be stepping down from all my leadership positions except my professorship. Despite his pleas to convince me otherwise, I was adamant and recommended my deputy director as my successor. Later that afternoon, I assembled all my staff (every one of whom I had hired) in the conference room next to my executive office and told them the news. It would be effective August 31. There was a collective gasp and looks of disbelief and the room welled up with tears. It was hard and I loved them, but I was at peace. A few days later, I started the process of moving from my office to a smaller faculty office on a different floor. I was only allowed to take just one of my assistants. The rest of my staff, thankfully, were able to keep working at the centers as my deputy director later assumed my role. As word spread, my close colleagues couldn't believe their ears. They thought I was mad. It was unheard of they said. I, on the other hand, felt so much freedom.

And God was not done.

During one of my quiet times in the fall semester of 1995, I was led by the Holy Spirit to seriously consider leaving Alaska to further His work in the Lower 48. Now that my ministry with JAMA was taking on a more national scope, with the movement's headquarters solidifying in the Southern California area, I sensed that geographically I needed to be closer to the action. The long flights to and from Anchorage (almost four hours alone just to or from Seattle!) were taking a toll. Sung was also independently praying through a similar call to leave. Even so, initially, I didn't want to leave. I loved the Last Frontier and its people. I loved my school and my students. We gave our lives to help make the community, the university, and the state better. The church which started in our living room was now the largest Korean-American church in the state. The church was our home away from home.

We eventually obeyed and God provided. On August 12, 1996, over a month after JAMA's first conference, we left Alaska for Monterey, California. California State University-Monterey Bay (CSUMB), a brand new institution that was established on part of the land that had been one of the largest military bases in America (Fort Ord), offered me a senior professorship with full tenure to help build the school's business program. By God's grace, we were able to move from the breathtaking beauty of Alaska to a place that has been called "the greatest meeting of land, sea and sky." And it was only an hour flight away from Los Angeles and an hour drive to San Jose.

As we did when we first moved to Alaska, I continued to passionately teach and mentor students at CSUMB and my wife and I poured our lives into one of the local Korean-American churches. We also poured our lives into JAMA. In 1998, my wife and I, along with Rev. Chris Kang, embarked on another prayer tour for America's spiritual awakening. This time it was a lot longer (my entire summer vacation of 80 days) with more miles driven (20,000). We held 120 prayer rallies in 58 cities in 38 states, crying out to God in repentance and praying for our nation's revival. Through that tour, thousands committed to pray and fast for America, culminating with JAMA's second conference in July 1999 at San Diego State University.

Since that time, it has been an extravagantly gracious, awe-inspiring, Spirit-filled whirlwind of personal awakening for many, families reconciling, local churches becoming more unified, communities being renewed, and thousands taking spiritual ownership of the communities and countries they live in with JAMA's "New Awakening" conferences in Atlanta, Anaheim, Los Angeles, Toronto, Dallas, Washington, D.C., Philadelphia, Auckland, New Zealand, Seattle-Tacoma, Silicon Valley, and Fullerton (in November 2013). At the Pennsylvania Convention Center in Philadelphia, on July 2, 2008, just blocks from where the U.S. Declaration of Independence was signed, JAMA publicly declared and signed its own Declaration of Dependence Upon God at "New Awakening 2008" (http://jamaglobal.com/wordpress/what-is-jama/56-2/), which was then adopted by the thousands in attendance. We distributed copies of the document to the White House, all nine Supreme Court Justices, all the members of Congress, governors and state legislators, public school superintendents, university and college presidents and chancellors, Fortune 500 CEOs, military generals, and church and Christian leaders. We were later informed that the Christians at the U.S. State Department in Washington, D.C. read, adopted, and signed JAMA's Declaration of Dependence on the National Day of Prayer in May 2009.

Suffering, the Graduate School of Character

As I mentioned in Chapter 13, on March 9, 2004, at a time when things with JAMA, CSUMB, and our local church in Monterey were going well, I was diagnosed with non-Hodgkins lymphoma of the spine. There was a large malignant tumor in my lower back that had been growing for almost 10 years. Picture a large sausage inside the spine that grew along the spinal cord and the more it grew, the more it tried to force out the spinal cord, causing excruciating pain. Dr. Hausdorff said it was quite unusual. "A very strange case," he told me. I was 64.

Despite the unbearable pain of the cancer on my spinal cord *and* the treatment to kill it, I felt God's presence all the more. In my cries of anguish and desperate pleas for pain relief, God would speak to me: "Suffering is an opportunity and blessing – you must go through this. Embrace it, don't avoid it, persevere through it, and, by the power of the Holy Spirit, you will be strengthened and comforted. This will enable you to draw closer to me. And it will also enable you to comfort and encourage many others who are also suffering, bearing fruit for my glory."

Many brothers and sisters in Christ were praying for me, with some churches dedicating portions of their early dawn services to intercede for my healing. Many pastors and elders and other intercessory prayer warriors flew or drove to Monterey to pray for me. I was uplifted. I prayed through His promises in His word which encouraged me even more: "Fear not, for I am with you; be not dismayed, for I am your God; I will strengthen you, I will help you, I will uphold you with my righteous right hand" (Isa. 41:10, ESV); "So even to old age and gray hairs, O God, do not forsake me until I proclaim your might to another generation, your power to all those to come. Your righteousness, O God, reaches the high heavens. You who have done great things, O God, who is like you? You who have made me see many troubles and calamities will revive me again; from the depth of earth you will bring me up again" (Ps. 71:18-20, ESV). *O God, please do not forsake me until I proclaim your vision to reach out to, challenge, and raise up, another generation for you. O God, please do not forsake me until I proclaim your grace, your power, and your righteousness to the next generation. O God, revive me to proclaim that you are the same God who has done great things and has sovereignly brought great awakenings to this nation in the past. O God, bring me up from the depths of my cancer to proclaim the depths of this country's sins and the need for true spiritual awakening and revival. The Lord heard my prayers and graciously answered.*

By His grace, and under the exceptional care of Dr. Hausdorff, the head oncologist, and Dr. Bradley Tamler, the radiation oncologist, the tumor was remitted through chemotherapy, radiation, and lumbar punctures. The battle ended in late November 2004 when I was officially cleared and personally congratulated by Dr. Hausdorff. Sung and I hugged the doctor and all the nurses who treated me. Dr. Hausdorff and his staff were so professional, so exceptional, so understanding, and so caring. God provided the best. I have been clean and cancer-free ever since. *Why me, dear Lord? Why unto me have you been so gracious?*

I'd say that suffering is the best graduate school in building and developing Christ-like character. It was through the cancer that I became more intimate with God. Indeed, 2004, the year of my cancer, brought me closer to my heavenly Father than all the previous 49 years combined that I was a Christian. I praised God for that. I praised God that He enabled me to grow in deeper fellowship with Him. The cancer was a blessing. It was the opportunity to know Him more than at any other time in my life.

GLDI

It was through that intimacy with God that He revealed another purpose for the remaining years of my life on this earth: to coincide with JAMA's call for repentance and spiritual awakening and with my God-given passion to teach, reach, and mentor the younger generations, along with God's vision to use me to raise Christ-centered ambassadors and catalysts from those generations to impact mainstream America, and the tremendous burden I had to see the renewal and revival of the land in which my children's children and their children will live, I was to launch a sister ministry to JAMA for the training, developing, and equipping of young leaders in every field and major industry to transform America and the nations of the world for Christ.

Of course, as was my tendency, I initially resisted and doubted. *Can't you see how much I'm suffering right now? I mean, I have cancer. I am spent. I have no strength. I am weak. I am old. What can I possibly do in this condition? Isn't JAMA enough?* "Trust me," I was assured, "it is not you who are going to do anything, I am. Was there anything that I have asked you to do that was done by you? None! It was Me. You must trust Me." I had no idea where to begin, but after I fully recovered from cancer, God graciously assembled committed and competent brothers and sisters in Christ to develop a holistic curriculum with me. It would be 40 straight days of intense training, 16 hours per day, starting with mandatory morning exercises, morning devotionals, biblical exposition, general sessions, nation-building projects, community service outings, mentoring times, and family group discussions with each of the six weeks dedicated to a specific theme of spiritual maturity and leadership. The application and interview process would be rigorous, strong academic performance was crucial, references from pastors would be required, and the age group would be targeted (19-25).

With the financial help of the God-sized generosity of a beloved sister in Christ and several churches, and the use of Vanguard University of Southern California's dormitories, lecture halls, classrooms, chapel, and cafeteria, the "Global Leadership Development Institute" (GLDI) (www.jamagldi.org) officially opened its doors on June 23, 2007, with an inaugural class of over 90 participants from across the country. God came through yet again. With the tireless dedication of JAMA's staff, headed by Cathy Rabb, GLDI's Dean of Operations, and the work and wisdom of Dr. Ben Shin, the institute's Dean of Faculty, the partnership of churches, the generosity of a number individuals, and the commitment and support of renowned speakers, such as Drs. Os Guinness, Richard Blackaby, Rick Langer, and Scott Bae, pastors, theologians, professors, and marketplace professionals, GLDI has produced almost 400 alumni from the U.S. and 11 nations, two of which joined me on my third national prayer tour in 2010. In 2014, GLDI will have its first overseas program in Jeju, Korea for the countries of east and southeast Asia with further plans to extend the franchise in (and utilize the networks of overseas GLDI alums from) Brazil and New Zealand and other parts of the world.

At the age of 73, God's still not done with me. Although I stepped down from teaching at CSUMB in May 2009, it was not a "retirement" in the traditional sense – but what I'd like to call a changing of the "tires" (or "re-tiring") to more fully focus my energies and passions on JAMA and the expansion of GLDI. Although no profession in the world could have given me as much joy as teaching on a university campus and building a program from the ground up, I now find that same joy in hearing about young children adopting U.S. states into their hearts and praying for their revival, in witnessing Koreans in Guatemala together with native Guatemalans take spiritual ownership of their adopted country and praying for awakening in Guatemala, in seeing life-long friendships formed, bold commitments made, hungry hearts and minds satiated, and lives transformed at GLDI, and listening to the prayers of repentance and revival for America from first-generation Koreans *in Korean*. God is good.

What a journey of grace it has been! From $200, three bags, and a "han"-sized chip on my shoulder to now. But the journey to see and experience God-sent revival and spiritual awakening continues. We press on. We stay the course. We endure. We remember. We hope. We pray.

ACKNOWLEDGMENTS

First, I want to thank my staff at JAMA National's headquarters in Los Angeles. To Elliot Kim for his excellent research and editing assistance, to Lauren Yang for designing the book, to Jannet Kwon for her review of the manuscript and edits, and Cathy Rabb for her enthusiasm and encouragement in seeing that all the book's (and the author's) needs were met. I'd also like to thank Hannah Yoo for her helpful translations of portions of the original Korean version of *Why Me?*

Many thanks go to my colleagues on JAMA's Board and the many senior, EM, and youth pastors as well as intercessory prayer warriors who have given me much hope with their spiritual partnership and ownership of this prayer and awakening movement and GLDI.

Special thanks go to my daughter Sharon and Edward, my son Paul and Jenny and my five wonderful grandchildren, Mark and Grace, and Noelle, Lucy, and John John. You all have given me unspeakable joy and comfort. I would like to especially thank Paul, my best pal, for his invaluable insight, wisdom, and counsel in helping me craft and edit this book.

And finally, and most importantly, a heartfelt thanks goes to my wife, Sarah Sung, to whom this book is dedicated. Just as she did when I pursued my doctorate degree at USC (and for as long as we've been together), she provided everything I needed – including enhancing the comforts of our home, her fervent prayers, and her soul-nourishing companionship – to enable me to write this book. She is second to none.

NOTES

1 Moral Re-Armament (MRA) was an international Christian, moral, and spiritual movement that, in 1938, grew out of the Rev. Frank Buchman's Oxford Group.

2 Lee, Won Sul and Hyung Tae Kim. *The New Millennium, the New "Chosen People," the New Vision* (Midwest Publishing Co., 2004), 154.

3 One noted Korean historian, Dr. Lee Sun-Kun, confirmed that "the Koreans resisted interventions, interferences, and aggressions of all kinds from their powerful neighbors and they went about building their nation." Lee, Sun Kun. *The History of Overcoming Our National Crises* (Shimsan Cultural Publications, Seoul, 1995), 525.

4 Chosun means "Land of Morning Calm."

5 The opening of Korea resulted, however, in two bloody wars between rival imperialistic powers – the Sino-Japanese War (1894-95) and the Russo-Japanese War (1904-05). The Japanese won both wars.

6 Kim, Young-Sik. "A Brief History of the US-Korea Relations Prior to 1945." Web. Available: http://www.freerepublic.com/focus/f-news/943949/posts. 30 July 2013.

7 Ibid.

8 Ibid.

9 Lee, Won Sul and Hyung Tae Kim. *The New Millennium, the New "Chosen People," the New Vision* (Midwest Publishing Co., 2004), 159.

10 Ibid.

11 Ibid.

12 Ibid.

13 Blair, William N. and Bruce Hunt. *The Korean Pentecost and the Sufferings Which Followed.* (Carlisle, PA: Banner of Truth, 1977), 71.

14 Clark, Allen D. *A History of the Church in Korea* (Seoul: Christian Literature Society of Korea, 1971), 162-63.

15 Blair, William N. and Bruce Hunt. *The Korean Pentecost and the Sufferings Which Followed.* (Carlisle, PA: Banner of Truth, 1977), 75.

16 Clark, *A History of the Church in Korea*, 164.

17 Sanders, John Oswald. *Prayer Power Unlimited.* (Moody Pub, Apr 1, 1988), 169. Print.

18 Kim, "A Brief History of the US-Korea Relations Prior to 1945."

19 Ibid.

20 Kim, Andrew E. *A History of Christianity in Korea: From Its Troubled Beginning to Its Contemporary Success*. Korea Journal 35:2 (Summer 1995).

21 Ibid.

22 Ibid.

23 Ibid.

24 Ibid.

25 Lee, Hae-Young et al. The Population of Korea. (Seoul: The Population and Development Studies Center of Seoul National University, 1975), 7. Web. Available: http://www.cicred.org/Eng/Publications/pdf/c-c30.pdf. 30 July 2013.

26 Kim, "A Brief History of the US-Korea Relations Prior to 1945."

27 Nohlen, D., F. Grotz, and C. Hartmann. *Elections in Asia: A data handbook, Volume II*. (Oxford: Oxford U Press, 2001), 428.

28 Figure includes the median of all the given estimates of both Koreas' military and civilian deaths. Available: http://www.koreanwar educator.org/topics/casualties/p_casualties_korean_chinese.htm. 30 July 2013.

29 Figure includes the approximately 34,000 military personnel as well as approximately 20,000 non-combatants. Ibid.

30 Kim, Shalom Yong Chang. "Human Suffering and Divine Shalom" (Doctoral Dissertation, 1998), 3.

31 Lee and Kim, *The New Millennium, the New "Chosen People," the New Vision*, 203.

32 Ibid., 205.

33 Korea GDP per Capita. Available: http://www.indexmundi.com/facts/korea/gdp-per-capita. 30 July 2013.

34 United States. U.S. Census Bureau. "Race Reporting for the Asian Population by Selected Categories: 2010." 2010. Web. Available: http://factfinder2.census.gov/faces/tableservices/jsf/pages/productview.xhtml?pid=DEC_10_SF1_QTP8&prodType=table. 30 July 2013.

35 Charles F. Butler (lyrics), James M. Black (music), 1896.

36 Frederick M. Lehman (lyrics), 1917.

37 Guinness, Os. *A Free People's Suicide* (InterVarsity Press, Downers Grove, IL, 2012), 129.

38 Crown Financial Ministry has great training programs in Biblical financial management. My wife and I and the staff at JAMA took its three-day course and it was incredibly helpful.

39 Dong Saeng literally means "younger brother" and is used by older members of familial relationships or older friends.

40 Male "Dong Saengs" call their more senior relatives or friends "Hyung Nim," or "older brother."

41 Giglio, Louie. *The Air I Breathe: Worship as a Way of Life* (Multnomah, 2006), 45, 49.

42 Ibid., 98.

43 Redman, Matt. *The Heart of Worship* (Worship Together 1999).

44 Giglio, *The Air I Breathe*, 73.

45 Guinness, Os. *The Call: Finding and Fulfilling the Central Purpose of Your Life* (Thomas Nelson, 1998).